NETWORKS OF MEANING

NETWORKS OF MEANING

A Bridge Between Mind and Matter

CHRISTINE HARDY

Westport, Connecticut
London

Library of Congress Cataloging-in-Publication Data

Hardy, Christine.
   Networks of meaning : a bridge between mind and matter / Christine
Hardy.
      p.   cm.
   Includes bibliographical references and index.
   ISBN 0–275–96035–8 (alk. paper)
   1. Meaning (Psychology)   2. Cognition.   I. Title.
BF463.M4H37   1998
128'.2—dc21   98–14932

British Library Cataloguing in Publication Data is available.

Library of Congress Catalog Card Number: 98–14932
ISBN: 0–275–96035–8

First published in 1998

Praeger Publishers, 88 Post Road West, Westport, CT 06881
An imprint of Greenwood Publishing Group, Inc.

Printed in the United States of America

The paper used in this book complies with the
Permanent Paper Standard issued by the National
Information Standards Organization (Z39.48–1984).

10 9 8 7 6 5 4 3 2

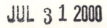

CONTENTS

PART II: MIND-IN-THE-WORLD

ILLUSTRATIONS

ACKNOWLEDGMENTS

I would first like to thank Joseph Rowe, Isabelle Stengers, Hélène Trocmé-Fabre, and Martine Winter for their encouraging support and discussions during the preliminary stages of this work.

Fred Abraham has been a continuous source of encouragement, enthusiasm, and keen feedback; he has also provided invaluable help in coaching me through the publication phase.

Many thanks to Allan Combs, Anne Dambricourt, Linda Dennard, and Louis-Marie Vincent, for their supportive comments and inspired discussions, and to the researchers of the Society for Chaos Theory in Psychology and the Life Sciences, for their enthusiasm, open-mindedness, and the rich ground of exchange they provide.

I am deeply indebted to Steve Guastello, Brian Josephson, Stanley Krippner, and Karl Pribram for reading the manuscript and providing me with insightful comments and suggestions.

Finally, my very special thanks go to Mario Varvoglis, for his constant support over the years, his in-depth vision and enlightening discussions, and his immense help on the final shaping of the text.

INTRODUCTION

The mind—the creative, evolving, mind-in-the-world—is probably the most complex system in the universe. Until recently, cognitive theories did little justice to its richness and complexity. The typical approach has been to elaborate on models inspired by simpler systems (for example, operant conditioning as shown on animals, or logical operations on data as performed by computers) and then to generalize such models to human mental processes. Invariably, this approach has led science to focus on the simplest facets of the mind—those amenable to such modeling—and to assume that more complex processes would eventually be explained through extensions and elaborations of the basic model.

Major changes are now in the air. New research directions are being explored and alternative paradigms have appeared, such as systems theory, connectionism, and chaos theory (complex dynamical systems theory). Moving beyond an analysis of structures and simple mechanisms, we are increasingly underscoring the evolutionary aspect of most natural systems and examining their transformation through the dynamical interplay of diverse forces. Contrary to the reductionistic and mechanistic outlooks prevalent over the past two centuries, contemporary science is intent on understanding systems as wholes, in their full complexity and richness.

In view of this emphasis, a truly adequate theory of the mind should account for the most unique facets of human cognition: consciousness and the sense of self; states of consciousness; nonconscious cognitive processes; the generation of meaning; and the dynamics underlying intuition and creativity. It must also address the interweaving of sensations, feelings, and abstract concepts in thought processes, as well as two-way mind-body interactions, free will and our capacity of choice. Finally, a complete theory must look beyond the individual and understand the rich exchanges of the sensory-affective-mental mind with its meaningful environment: psychosocial interactions, cultural knowledge-systems, collective consciousness, synchronicities, and "nonlocal" forms of communication. A very tall order indeed.

In many ways my approach has been the inverse of classical model building. Rather than first developing a specific formalism, and then trying to extend it to the mind, I started by focusing on the processes that needed to be explained in a systemic way and sought to develop a framework that would account for those processes. This, I felt, was the surest way to avoid constructing a theory that could not truly deal with complexity.

When I started this journey several years ago, I did not have the slightest idea that semantic fields theory would take me through so many different domains of research, each one imposing itself as an absolute necessity to the main development. Had I known what I was getting into, I would certainly have balked and given up—recognizing that I was just not up to the task.

When I began, in fact, what I had in mind was to express and formulate concepts that I had been implicitly using to make sense of my own mental processes. These concepts not only fit well with my personal experience, but they also seemed to have a life of their own, a sort of generativity: as they changed and evolved, they stimulated new inner explorations, leading to novel ideas. In retrospect, I realize I have been caught in one of those transformative, self-generative processes that make life so fascinating. I was seeking to make sense of the world and of myself by generating new sets of meaningful concepts; simultaneously, I was developing a framework in which the continuous generation of meaning is the very essence of the mind.

FIELDS AND CONSTELLATIONS

One very basic concept that came up quite early in my reflections was that of *field*—in particular, the way meaningful states and thoughts show a certain qualitative coherence. The term *semantic field* thus took on a central role; it signified, for me, the coherent organization of meaning-clusters and related processes in a dynamical, evolving network.

Over the course of several years I had traveled extensively, plunging into cultures from the Far East to Africa—something not uncommon to an anthropologist. Those travels left me with the distinct impression that in each culture my mind had become immersed in a specific semantic field. I realized that, within me, I had developed distinct constellations of meanings, behaviors, feelings, words, gestures, and mental states that reflected each specific culture—so much so that the particular constellation would be reactivated, on the spot, any time I would go back to that culture, meet with people from it, read about it, or even talk about experiences I had there.

Of course, not all of these idiosyncratic constellations of meaning expressed themselves simultaneously; indeed, few of them were activated in any specific period of my life. Yet it seemed that, deep in the psyche, they somehow continued to live and evolve. Every once in a while, one of these apparently inactive clusters would unexpectedly emerge and express itself in a rather striking manner—through a dream, music, a piece of writing, or a solution to a specific problem. This emergence indicated that the meaning-cluster had not only stayed alive deep within me, but had also matured and evolved through interaction with other meaning-clusters.

Such experiences led me to the concept of *semantic constellations* (SeCos)—self-organized, coherent clusters within a person's semantic field. I came to view SeCos as specialized and distinct networks that interact with each other continuously, and that consciousness strives to integrate into a coherent whole. These constellations, I realized, are far more than just "belief-sets" or "declarative knowledge-sets" (as classical cognitive psychology would have it). Rather, they tightly interweave a range of cognitive and psychophysical processes: ideas, concepts, and beliefs are intimately linked to specific feelings, mental states, gestures, and behaviors. For example, while describing a powerful, moving experience that I had in India, my body posture would shift to one reminiscent of the more straight and controlled posture I had developed while in India; the rhythm and tone of my speech, and of course the wording I would use, would undergo similar changes.

THE MIND'S ARCHITECTURE

Nowadays, models of the mind-brain are increasingly shifting toward a connectionist architecture, that is, a network organization of nodes (coding neurons or logical propositions) and links (weighted connections between nodes). The brain's neuronal organization is much more analogous to a network organization than to a system of rules (as in the computational paradigm). Indeed, as scientists like Gerald Edelman, Karl

Pribram, and Walter Freeman underscore, assemblies of neurons not only have a network configuration, but they also exhibit certain neural-net properties, such as distributed processes and feedback mechanisms. Also, as emphasized by a number of psychologists, neural-net learning is quite reminiscent of human learning: both processes evolve in stages and display an ability to self-organize, that is, to modify their own organization internally.

Semantic fields theory adds two features to this basic network architecture.

The first is the concept of the SeCo, a specialized network clustering and organizing related experiences. As we shall be seeing, a SeCo is often part of a larger SeCo, and may include sub-SeCos; the semantic fields model thus posits a networks-within-networks architecture.

The second added feature is the premise that SeCos link all possible types of elements, not only linguistic items or propositions, but any psychological, physiological, or brain process (such as sensation, affect, procedure, gesture, behavior, and their related neurological processes).

The introduction of this kind of architecture has some important implications. For one thing, it recasts the mind-body relation as a transversal network integration of mental and brain processes: major SeCos may reach from lower neuronal processes to higher rational ones. Another implication is the recognition that knowledge in the human mind is never strictly abstract; it is necessarily tied to numerous sensory-affective processes. A number of researchers in the cognitive sciences come to a similar conclusion. For example, Francisco Varela holds that cognition develops out of—and remains tied to—a strong coupling of sensory and motor exploratory behaviors.

The SeCos architecture also turns out to be well suited for explaining several interesting psychological phenomena. For example, the transversal architecture sheds light upon the psychological complexes described by psychoanalysis—the pathological grouping of traumatic experiences with mind-sets, behaviors, and physiological processes. Similarly, the multiple personality syndrome can be seen as resulting from SeCos that have grown pathologically autonomous—cut off from each other, and thus preventing the self from achieving a global coherence. The SeCo's organization also fits Charles Tart's description of states of consciousness as idiosyncratic patterns of sensory and mental processes, behaviors, mind-sets, knowledge-sets, and memory.

CONNECTIVE AND DYNAMICAL PROCESSES

We are coming to recognize that, while humans certainly engage in abstract reasoning, this is *not* the way our mind operates most of the time. Computational rule-bound processing, as expressed in logical or mathematical reasoning, must be seen as a high-level process—more akin to something we painfully learn and force our minds into, rather than a basic, natural working of the mind.

Semantic fields theory posits an underlying, low-level connective dynamic: the *spontaneous linkage process*. Essentially, clusters of semantic elements are attracted to, and link themselves to, other semantically related clusters. This highly generative dynamic, based on network-connections rather than algorithmic operations, is proposed to be the ground of thought. This is what creates the network of semantic constellations that operate at the semantic level and branch into neuronal networks.

Connective processes display great flexibility, plasticity, and adaptability, as well as a pronounced capacity for associating, comparing, and recombining, and consequently they have the potential for truly dynamical and creative mental processes. They may thus be a prime candidate for describing the natural elementary operations of the mind.

As I advanced in my conceptualization of semantic fields, I came to realize that *complex dynamical processes* are truly fundamental to the creative and generative aspects of the mind. Chaos theory, or the study of order underlying apparent disorder or randomness, provides very fecund ways of understanding the evolution and self-organization of a wide range of complex systems—including mental systems. Starting with the original studies of Edward Lorenz on climatic turbulences in the1960s, the study of *nonlinear systems* has progressed enormously with the work of mathematicians like Steven Smale and René Thom, physicists like David Ruelle and Mitchell Feigenbaum, and biophysicists like Ilya Prigogine. It now seems clear that nonlinearity—the ability of a system to show differentiated responses to constant environmental forces—is a feature of many natural processes. Most importantly, as shown by researchers such as Frederick Abraham, Stephen Guastello, and others, chaos theory is finding major areas of application in psychology and the social sciences.

Complex dynamical systems theory is pertinent to the present model in several ways. For one thing, my general outlook here is dynamical—emphasizing that mind processes are constantly changing, evolving in time, mutually dependent, and self-organizing. Most psychological and social systems exhibit dynamics at the edge of chaos: they display instability and show nonlinear responses to contextual forces, thus leading the system to bifurcate (i.e., to change its global organization). They also show sensitive dependence on initial conditions, chaotic behavior, and the creation of novel global orders. For example, people may live for years with constant frustration at their workplace; then, following some minor provocation, they may suddenly break into a fit of anger, quit, and radically change their professions or even their lifestyles.

Another pertinent feature of chaos theory is its focus on mutual interactions between diverse forces in a complex system. The mathematical framework of chaos theory allows us to consider a wide variety of forces as variables interacting within a system, whether biophysical, social, or psychological (such as beliefs, mind-sets, or objectives). It is through such mutual interactions that self-organization emerges.

Perhaps the most important contribution of chaos theory to the semantic fields model is the concept of *attractors*. An attractor is a mathematical structure that describes an object's motion through space; basically, an attractor traps the object in a specific region of space. In more general terms, it describes the evolution of a system over time, that is, the configuration of all states of a system and the trajectories through these states.

In the present theory, SeCos behave as attractors in the sense that, when a SeCo is reactivated by a familiar external event, the mind will tend to relive the previous states of that SeCo. Thus, SeCos typically organize similar subsequent experiences. On the other hand, a significant change in the context (or parameters) of an experience may trigger a modification of the SeCo's attractor, that is, a bifurcation. Thus we have both convergent and divergent forces, allowing for flexible, evolving processes. For example, as new clusters of meaning are created, the SeCo-system may split into two sub-SeCos that contain antagonistic and conflictual beliefs and behaviors about the same type of experience. In fact, the multiplicity and divergence of SeCos, their redundancy and competition, are precisely what gives the mind-psyche the capacity of choice and adaptive behavior.

NETWORKS OF MEANING

I truly believe the mind will not make much sense to us until we begin to study it as a system—both a semantic-neural network and a living, constantly changing, dynamical system, interacting with its social and physical environment. Many researchers share this assumption. It is no coincidence that many of the newly emergent research fields—the cognitive sciences, systems theory, chaos theory, parapsychology, and consciousness studies—are transdisciplinary in nature. In my opinion, the cross-fertilization, and possible integration, of different domains is a clear-cut sign of a paradigm-in-the-making—one that will complement the trend toward narrow focus and specialization with a novel trend toward systemic and holistic views.

Networks of meaning then, seeks to lay the foundation of a cognitive theory based on dynamical networks—a theory in which the mind is both seen as a network architecture and as a self-organizing system. Throughout, my intent has been to apply these premises to the study of mind-in-the-world—the dynamical network interactions of the mind with its physical and social environment. I have thus used real-life examples (life seldom lacks complexity!) to present the main ideas, and illustrate the ways in which the model can be conceptually useful.

The general plan of the book also follows this perspective. Part I focuses on the mind itself—SeCos, conscious experience, the mind's architecture and dynamics, learning, and broader semantic field organization. Part II addresses mind-in-the-world—its interaction with external semantic fields, or eco-fields. Here we begin with an analysis of internal and external contexts, then move on to consider interactions with external objects and events, and finally examine our exchanges with other people, and the issue of collective consciousness.

We have come a long way from the belief that any theory could express "the truth," or give an exact, eternally valid representation of its scientific object. A theory, as now understood, is a conceptual tool that permits us to describe the object under study in the most efficient and generative way. It should not only adequately account for known facts but also reveal and highlight new facets of the object under study, thereby opening new directions of research. By these criteria, at least, semantic fields theory is sufficiently developed for me to present it—even if it is still in process and evolving.

I take Karl Popper at his word, when he says that science truly advances with the posing of bold hypotheses. So here are some risky, but bold, steps toward a more global understanding of the human mind.

PART I

THE MIND

I

SEMANTIC CONSTELLATIONS

The creation of meaning is one of the most primordial characteristics of consciousness. It is also one of its most paradoxical processes: holistic yet goal directed, seemingly immediate yet complex and multidimensional, personal and internal yet based on transpersonal factors and bearing on external reality. David Bohm proposed to consider meaning as "both mental and physical in nature," adding that it could serve as a "bridge between these two sides of reality."[1] However, in contemporary cognitive science, meaning is generally conceived as an internally generated, largely epiphenomenal process. Little attention is given to its active role and its contribution to the world beyond the brain.

The basic hypothesis presented here is that the generation of meaning is, in itself, an organizing process shaping reality, while the mind is, in turn, shaped by a reality endowed with meaning. Attributing meaning is a mental act that pervades and organizes all experience. Furthermore, insofar as our relationships—with others and with the world—are also based on significations, meaning may also be considered as the pivotal point of all social and ecological dynamics. Concepts are the building blocks on which these generative semantic activities operate.[2] In the present chapter, I propose to view concepts as complex, organized semantic entities—constellations of meaning that are dynamic in nature.

CONCEPTS AS COMPLEX MEANING CONSTELLATIONS

Meaning is the essential substance of concepts, insofar as each concept—each category, quality, belief, value—essentially refers back to a signification. Even the simplest perception of an object implies recognition of its category, and categorization depends on recognizing criteria common to these objects. Indeed, these criteria themselves are grounded in significations. If this is the case at the most basic level of object perception, it is even more so at an abstract level, where concepts such as "pretty," "enthusiasm," or "honor" rely enormously on both personal and cultural meanings.

Concepts: From Definitional to Network Models

Concepts were originally equated to lexical definitions: a given definition would set the "necessary and sufficient" conditions (or features) for any item to fall into a category. It soon appeared that, when relating to a concrete concept like "table" or "tree," people would often be referring to a broader array of features, some of which extended beyond the strict boundaries of the category and thus lay outside the definition. For example, asked to give words to define the concept "forest," subjects would come up not only with "wood" and "shade," but also with "oxygen" and "the Earth's lungs."

The "definitional" model of concepts was eventually replaced by the more flexible "family resemblance" theory, which highlighted the fact that concepts are not as strictly circumscribed and distinct as earlier models had assumed. By assessing the occurrence of particular features in any given concept, this approach provided a kind of static mapping of what people generally mean by that concept.

An important advance occurred when a network architecture was added to the semantic mapping of concepts. The "propositional network" model extended the family resemblance theory while coding for the relationships between concepts. In this framework, concepts (or arguments) are nodes in a network, and relationships (between them) are specified by links. For example, in the proposition "John eats an apple," "John" and "apple" are the arguments while "eats" is the link. This approach has thus permitted neural networks to code and process simple propositions.[3]

In a neural net, units (or neurons) activate or inhibit themselves reciprocally. Learning is achieved by modifying the specific weights attributed to links: whenever a link leads to an inadequate solution, its weight is decreased. A given activation at an input node spreads through the whole network, modifying the weights of the links and rendering the processing of subsequent inputs more efficient. The network thus learns by organizing itself and memorizing the most efficient paths and organizational states.[4]

On the basis of this learning ability, propositional networks have been able to adequately simulate some experimentally established cognitive processes. For example, propositional networks have been able to duplicate priming effects. Classical priming experiments show that subjects who have been subliminally pre-exposed to a category concept will show quicker recognition of a concrete instance of this concept than those who have not been pre-exposed. Propositional networks show a similar behavior: starting network activation from a category concept leads the network to quicker recognition of a concrete concept belonging to that category. Similarly, propositional networks are able to simulate the effects of context on mental processes. In network experiments, priming effects are obtained specifically for variable or peripheral features that generally reflect context-sensitivity of a concept; no such effects are found for the more stable or central features (which are more context-independent).

Cognition as a Dynamical Process

However interesting these investigations might be (and they have led to some major achievements in artificial intelligence) we are still a long way from understanding cognition *as a living process*—involving, as Varela pointed out, cognitive subjects who are themselves changed by their cognitive acts.[5]

True, the neural network framework does emphasize links between concepts and their dynamic activation or inhibition. As in the older definitional model, however, the network framework still represents concepts as hopelessly frozen entities. It is as if each concept remains unperturbed by its interrelations with other concepts. If we take three propositions—Edith marries John, Edith lives with John, Edith divorces John—it is assumed that John and Edith each represent a fixed set of features and only the links between them change; it is presumed that Edith and John do not change through their evolving relationship. The concept, in this framework, is still seen as a stable, invariant entity that simply takes on added qualities, depending on context and links.

At the heart of the issue lies the Western intellectual tendency to overemphasize immutable categories and time-frozen descriptions as more important than dynamics and transformation—or, as Allan Combs pointed out, to emphasize structure over process.[6]

What we need, in fact, is to reintroduce the temporal dimension, as Prigogine has done in the biological and physical sciences; we need to be able to view a concept historically and dynamically, from its birth through its development.[7]

Concepts not only have fuzzy boundaries, they also are subject to modifications; they expand, merge, and split, as well as undergo distortions and drastic mutations. It is like the chair and its four legs: for a long time we considered "four legs" a necessary definitional feature of the concept "chair"—until new kinds of chairs were designed that explored an unlimited number of fancy bases and demonstrated that our understanding of "chair" can itself change radically.

We now have to move even a step further and assess the synergy of mutual transformation between concepts. To reach for a deeper understanding of the mind, we need to take into account not just the links between concepts, or the transformation of concepts themselves, but also their transformative effect upon other concepts.

In this context, the study of concept formation and evolution takes on crucial import. In her research on the interpretation of novel words by children, Linda Smith[8] used a dynamical systems framework to show that a given understanding of a word is constructed on the basis of both existing concepts and contextual features. The end product, the novel concept, amounts to a new "global order," constructed out of specific cognitive situations.

Extending this, it seems reasonable to suppose that concepts continue to evolve and shift throughout a person's lifetime. While some concrete concepts may show relative stability, as soon as we consider concepts touching on philosophical, ethical, affective, or social issues, we realize that they are constantly being "reconstructed" by our cognitive acts. For example, the concepts we have about any of the main aspects of social life (education, politics, religious institutions, health care, etc.) constantly shift with our own living experience. What we call thinking is, indeed, the process of modifying concepts: we reflect on something to reach a new understanding, and the understanding provides a set of new or modified concepts. Thus, conceptualization itself—the process of forming or refining concepts—reflects the working of the mind in its attempt to understand and express experiences.

Isabelle Stengers[9] has shown that major scientific concepts are "nomads," in the sense that efficient and highly valued concepts of a leading science may be "captured" by other scientific domains in order to establish or reinforce their own scientific ground. It seems that our internal processing reflects a similar use of "nomadic" concepts across different domains and categories of thought. The very "fuzziness" of concepts, their fluidity and context-sensitivity, is what permits us to instantiate them in a variety of ways. At an essential level, thinking is a creative act, a process by which we use certain concepts to mold or "play with" other ones.

Concepts, then, are not only shifting, changing processes but are also generative of novel processes: they are transformative and not just subject to transformation. In other words, concepts are not simply passive tools or descriptors used by the mind; being part of the meaning-generation process, concepts actively stimulate new links, realizations, associations and mental organizations. They are integrated in a dynamic thought-process that modifies them, and they are themselves dynamically generating changes in the mind's semantic network.

In summary, I have underlined several dynamical properties of concepts and meaning. Concepts evolve, they are subject to change and transformation, they have a history (in Prigogine's sense). Additionally, they are agents of mutual transformation: what we call thinking is concepts interacting with other concepts, in a self-organizing fashion. Finally, by virtue of such systemic interactions, concepts are generative, leading to the emergence of novel concepts or meanings.

The point of view I am developing here is that concepts are the building blocks with which people construct their individuality, their universe of meaning; concepts function both as landmarks (separating or linking things) and as generators of meaning. Insofar as they extend from the most basic category-recognition level to the most abstract level, the ensemble of concepts held by a person constitutes or reflects that person's idiosyncratic worldview—the significations from which one builds a sense of self, and an understanding of others and of the surrounding world. Behavior, relationships, feelings, even the structuring of the self-image—all of these translate, actualize, and are founded upon underlying significations. For example, people who have "rigid" concepts about specific social roles tend to exhibit conformity and stereotyped behaviors while those who have more "fluid" concepts like to experiment, to choose and create novel values, significations, and behaviors.

At the most global level, concept-creation instantiates an ongoing psychomental grounding and structuring process on the basis of which we construct our self and our worldview. Concepts are fundamental in organizing the psyche, and are themselves modified and complexified through the evolution of the psyche. They reflect the living consciousness and ongoing development of a sentient subject-in-the-world.

SEMANTIC CONSTELLATIONS

The meaning of any concept depends entirely upon its relations with other significations, while its link-structure is constantly subject to modification and change. In other words, the very materials with which we create, within and around us, a universe of meaning are continually being modified and put into new perspectives. They are constantly diverted, shifted and reconverted, displaced and transposed.

To express this complex link-structure, I introduce the fundamental concept of a constellation of meanings, or *semantic constellation (SeCo)*. It is the simplest semantic object, a dynamical and self-organizing system that constitutes the "unit," so to speak, of our mental life.

The semantic constellation is an organized aggregate, a moving and changing network of indeterminate size that is constituted by virtue of its inner interconnections and its connections with other constellations. However, this fluid constellation does have a nucleus, a signifying core, a central concept around which meaning is organized and that allows new elements to become linked. A semantic constellation may be defined as a dynamical and evolving network of meanings and related processes, organized around a nucleus. The nucleus, the central meaning, ties together interrelated concepts, internal sensations, images, sounds, colors, gestures, acts, attitudes, behaviors, moods, and so forth, while the SeCo is the ensemble, the network implicating all these various elements.[10]

Meaning: Beyond Language

Some of a person's semantic constellations are concepts, and their nucleus is generally the name the individual assigns to them. However, names or, more generally, linguistic items are not the only kind of nucleus. Imagine an explorer lost in the wilderness who needs to dig a hole in the ground in order to make an overnight shelter. He finds a fine, solid piece of wood that has obviously been cut and shaped. Perhaps it is a tool left by a native of the area—but at this point, whether or not the stick is a particular kind of tool and has a name is irrelevant to the explorer, who is thinking only about its usefulness for digging a hole. The meaning-generative nucleus here is the envisioned shelter-to-be, which necessitates digging a hole; the object our explorer uses thus takes on meaning in relation to the "Shelter" SeCo; it is a cluster or subconstellation of "Shelter." Now, suppose that the next day our hero comes across a similar stick in a village. This stick reactivates his whole memory of the shelter scene. To his surprise, he now finds out that this stick is in fact a long whistle for attracting certain birds. Suddenly, the significations associated with yesterday's transient tool are now modified and extended; the object, which still has no name, takes on new meanings and may even become, if further used, a constellation in its own right with links both to "Shelter" SeCo and to constellations associated with musical instruments.

Even sounds, having no names attached to them, may constitute the nucleus of a constellation. For example, a bird song heard while on a far-away journey may have made such a deep impression that this sound has become the nucleus of a very rich SeCo without the subject even knowing the name of the bird. This sound may specify an atmosphere, a particular ambiance, or it may evoke the experienced situations and interactions with a traveling companion or perhaps the landscape surrounding the house where the person first heard it; all of these aggregated elements may form subconstellations. If the SeCo is reactivated (for instance, by hearing the bird song in a musical sequence or while talking about the journey), it will continue to evoke meaning and perhaps "constellate" new significations.

This leads us to understand that sensorimotor processes are loaded with meaning, far beyond their connection with language; in the same way, affects and feelings—some of the most meaningful individual experiences—are largely beyond language. For most of us, love and passion are a depth of experience and meaning that words cannot adequately describe.

Thus, what makes sense for an individual—her or his set of concepts—is not limited to language, or even to signs. For example, the bird song is not a sign since it has nothing consensually referential about it; rather, it is the meaning a person attributes to it that renders it the nucleus of a constellation and thus generative of new meanings. Similarly, a poet may endow a word—however meaningless for most people—with an extremely meaningful symbolism; in the same way a painter may develop entire SeCos dealing with the experience of specific hues or color harmonies for which he or she has no specific names. The nucleus can act both as a sink (attracting new materials) and as a semantic source (generating activations)—whether or not it is linguistic in nature.

Meaning also eludes and defies some of the usual dichotomies, such as personal versus collective frameworks. Clearly, a particular set of meanings could be highly idiosyncratic, specific to an individual. The meaning of the bird song above involves just one person, or it may be shared by a traveling companion—in which case the two similar (but not identical) SeCos are intertwined. On the other hand, in many cases SeCos are strongly influenced by culture and reflect social or collective viewpoints. A concept can possess an enormous power of fascination at a certain epoch, for certain people; when new concepts are recognized and adopted by many people, they are integrated into the culture and may even become key concepts of that culture. Thus, a new expression of love feelings, developed in a novel or film, could suddenly become a model or meaningful reference for a whole generation. For example, when Johann Goethe's novel *The Sorrows of Young Werther* was published, a wave of suicides followed among romantic youth who resonated with the desperate hero.

When interacting with cultural concepts, individuals build their own world vision; they generally do not simply accept or reject them, but rather modify or remold the associated meanings, adapting them to their needs or feelings through their own experiences and understandings.

The essential characteristic of meaning lies in its dynamic generation: it belongs to consciousness as a whole, and it expresses a living, integrative process. Human beings generate meaning while drawing upon experiences and exchanges, contexts and perceptions, feelings and affects, needs and intentions—through a dynamic being-in-the-world involving other subjects who are themselves sources of meaning. Although language and signs are among the richest supports and sources of meaning, they certainly are not the only ones: feelings, mental imagery, affective and sensorimotor processes are all woven into the semantic networks. Consequently, in this book I will not be spending much time discussing linguistic issues. Instead, I will be looking toward the dynamics of meaning-generation itself, both within and between individuals.

The Many Levels of Meaning

The creation of meaning is complex and multidimensional, bringing together all levels of being. It continuously forms connections and points to implications; it is a constant flux, embedded in communication and exchange processes. This is why there is no such thing as a simple, fixed semantic entity, even in what seems to be the simplest of all contexts, the lexical definitions of meaning. In order to be understood, words demand other words—which are themselves complex concepts. How can the mere definition of a word compare to the richness of a meaningful experience? It can do so only very poorly because there is no such thing as isolated meanings; everything has meaning in relation to other meaningful entities.

First and foremost, meaning consists of linking, connecting, and bringing into relation. This is why the basic structure I make use of here is that of a dynamic and organized network. If we want to study living meaning, our fundamental system must be a complex and diversified constellation with an ongoing history, binding together specific images, sensations, feelings, words, ideas, memories, experiences, and so forth through a nucleus or seed-meaning.

The constellation is the simplest, most "elementary" semantic entity. An individual may contain millions of them, both great and small, in hierarchies or in parallel structures. SeCos are capable of splitting or merging, of interpenetrating and engulfing each other. As in the case of neurons, they are distinct entities (each having a specific organization and identity) and members of larger groupings or wholes. Semantic constellations are integrated within broader constellations that envelop them while they themselves contain yet other constellations. Thus, the sensations, gestures, mental procedures, and so forth that are linked in a SeCo are themselves connected in very specific ways to extensive neurological and organic processes. SeCos are instantiated through processes ranging from the most abstract knowledge levels to basic functional and physiological levels. Therefore, part of each constellation remains in nonconscious cognitive and neurological levels while another part moves in and out of awareness.

At the highest, most global level of any individual, we may consider the network organization of the whole mind-psyche as a *semantic lattice*, an ensemble of major SeCos containing subconstellations, intertwined in very complex ways, mostly interacting and evolving but sometimes frozen into closed ensembles. As will be developed in later chapters, whether we are dealing with large or small SeCos, they are linked by networks of mutual influence; a single process within a large constellation can sometimes modify the entire structure while the whole SeCo influences the organization of linked elements.

The semantic lattice houses all of a person's knowledge, sensoriality, affectivity, and behavior patterns—both as memory clusters and as a living, growing experience; it constitutes the totality of an individual's cognitive/affective dynamics, grounding the capacity for global consciousness. Consciousness, then, is viewed here as the global semantic individuality and quality of a person's lattice; it is both that which organizes the generation of meaning (through conscious *and* nonconscious dynamics) and the end product of meaning-generation.[11] "Semantic lattice" and "consciousness" are two sides of the same coin: while lattice points to the dynamical organization, consciousness involves its qualitative experiential process. The linked processes and experiences create the lattice/consciousness system. This same lattice/consciousness system influences that which it envelops or contains—a process referred to as autopoiesis, or self-creation.[12]

The *noo-semantic field* or *noo-field* of an individual (from the Greek *noesis* signifying the act of thinking) is the activated part of the lattice. While the lattice contains all the memory and potentials of the mind, the noo-field, the ensemble of activated SeCos, is its current instantiation. As we will see, the noo-field shows a somewhat stable organization over a given time period and displays specific field properties.[13]

Although the lattice is characterized by a degree of closure that allows for its self-organizing properties, I posit that it extends beyond the individual, interchanging with semantic fields of the environment or of objects—what I call *eco-fields*.

Furthermore, if we were to look beyond the individual, we find that constellations of meaning also exist on a collective level, as in ideologies, cultures, great currents of thought, arts, and so forth—what I call *collective SeCos*. At this level, collective SeCos are composed of numerous nested and overlapping constellations (including those of individuals) that are thereby linked to each other.

The many levels of meaning defy categories. We find ourselves in a multidimensional universe in which every entity is both container and contained, influencing and being influenced. It is both part and whole, local and nonlocal, existing in space and time and beyond them. In considering meaning, we are at the very core of complexity.

NOTES

1. D. Bohm (1986), A new theory of the relationship of mind and matter, *Journal of the American Society for Psychical Research, 80* (2), 113–36. D. Bohm (1980), *Wholeness and the implicate order*, London: Routledge & Kegan Paul.

2. My choice of words for this model takes the word "semantic" in its etymological sense from the Greek "semantikos": a signification, an act of signifying.

3. N. A. Stillings, M. H. Feinstein, J. L. Garfield, E. L. Rissland, D. A. Rosenbaum, S. E Weisler, & L. Baker-Ward (1987), *Cognitive science: An introduction,* Cambridge, MA: Bradford Books, MIT Press, Chapter 3.

4. The learning capacity of neural nets is accrued in multilayered networks that use back-propagation and allow for the spontaneous self-organization of hidden units. At each step, the actual state of the network is compared to the expected outputs (or goal), and the error-signal is back-propagated; the network

then lowers the weights of the links that concur to create the error.

For example, McClelland and Rumelhart (1986) present a three-layered network (input-layer, hidden units layer, and output layer) that permits learning of the XOR (exclusive OR) logical function. It contains two input units, two hidden units (intermediary layer), and one output unit. While the stimulus patterns are presented repeatedly, the two hidden units learn to specialize spontaneously. Thus, after 210 sweeps, the first unit becomes a detector of the OR logical function, while the second one is able to detect the AND. After 289 sweeps, the second unit becomes a detector of XOR. Finally, for the network to be able to recognize the negation of XOR, that is the IF and ONLY IF, nearly twice as many sweeps are necessary, that is about 540 training epochs. Yves Chauvin, working with the Parallel Distributed Processing (PDP) Group, systematically varied the number of hidden units and found that with 32 hidden units, only 120 presentations were necessary for the network to solve the XOR problem. See D. E. Rumelhart, J. L. McClelland, & the PDP Research Group (1986), *Explorations in the microstructure of cognition: Vol. 1. Foundations*, Cambridge, MA: MIT Press/Bradford Books. (Chapter 8)

As for the memorization of learning procedures, Sejnowski and Rosenberg (1988) say about their "network that learns to read aloud" or NETtalk, that "relearning was about ten times faster than the original learning starting from the same level of performance." See T. J. Sejnowski, & C. R. Rosenberg (1988), NETtalk: A parallel network that learns to read aloud, in J. A. Anderson & E. Rosenfeld (Eds.), *Neurocomputing: Foundations of research* (pp. 663–72). Cambridge, MA: The MIT Press. See also McClelland, Rumelhart, & the PDP Research Group (1986); Bechtel & Abrahamsen (1990).

5. F. Varela (1989), *Autonomie et connaissance,* Paris: Seuil. See also H. Maturana & F. Varela (1980), *Autopoiesis and cognition*, Boston: D.Reidel.

6. A. Combs (1996), *The radiance of being. Complexity, chaos and the evolution of consciousness*, St Paul, MN: Paragon House. In *The radiance of being*, Allan Combs elaborated a process-view of consciousness, stressing its dynamical aspects.

7. I. Prigogine, & Stengers, I. (1984). *Order out of chaos*. New York: Bantam Books.

8. L. Smith (1995), Stability and variability: The geometry of children's novel-word interpretations, in F. D. Abraham & A. R. Gilgen (Eds.), *Chaos theory in psychology,* Westport, CT: Praeger Publishers.

9. I. Stengers (Ed.) (1987), *D'une science à l'autre; des concepts nomades*, Paris: Seuil.

10. As discussed at length in this chapter, there is no such thing as a simple unitary and independent semantic "element"; I use the term "element" not in its atomistic sense, but only to signify "part of something." Thus, SeCo elements need not be simple at all; as we have seen, they can be anything from processes to complex concepts. In general, thus, the semantic element is itself a cluster.

11. My understanding of the term "consciousness" is closest to that of

Jungian depth psychology and transpersonal psychology: it covers both the conscious mind and the unconscious—the perspective of the latter on things can be quite distinct from that of the conscious mind (as witnessed in dreams).

Note, however, that my focus, in the semantic fields model, is not upon psychic dynamics per se (as in psychoanalysis or depth psychology), but upon thought-processes and the manner in which they interweave with psychic dynamics. I make use of the term "mind-psyche" insofar as processes viewed as psychic are integrated with the more intellectual facets of the mind. Thus the semantic fields model proposes that mental, psychic/emotional, and neurological processes are all bound together by a unique organizational process, the SeCo. The dynamics observed by depth psychology are consequently part of the thinking mind; indeed, all psychic and mental processes concur to the building of consciousness, as an ongoing dynamic of meaning generation. This is why I consider that nonconscious processes, unconscious psychic clusters, as well as the more neurological cognitive unconscious, are all part of, and interact in, the individual's consciousness.

12. Maturana & Varela (1980).

13. In this model , I am using the term *field* in its mathematical (as opposed to physical) sense—as an ensemble of mathematical objects or processes sharing certain distinct properties. Thus I do not assume semantic fields behave like physical fields (e.g., electromagnetic fields); this permits us to approach semantic fields without any preconceptions and to determine their specific internal properties.

2

CONSCIOUS EXPERIENCE

My goal in this chapter is to describe some of the major issues confronting modern cognitive sciences, and the present semantic fields model, in their attempt to understand conscious experience and the cohesion of the self.

Subjectively, we experience what William James termed a "stream of consciousness," a flow of experiences that seems to take place within a private, "personal" context: the unitary self. The self appears to be the "observer" or subject of experience, seemingly independent of changes in the contents of consciousness and persisting across periods in which we have no consciousness at all (e.g., sleep). Our experience, on the other hand, seems to be a varied but linear, one-dimensional flow, focusing on just one object at a time. The attentional object may be internal (ideas, images, feelings, reactions, intuitions, etc.) or external (our physical or social environment, what we are working on, the people we are exchanging with, etc.), but in either case the "beam" of consciousness—attention—seems to move sequentially from one object to the next.

A variety of research data, however, suggests a far more complex picture than depicted in the preceeding paragraph. For one thing, conscious mental experience seems to build on a large array of mostly nonconscious neural and biological processes that are both distributed and massively parallel; it also draws on numerous nonconscious mental processes that are linguistic and cognitive in nature. Equally important, the subject of conscious experience may not be what it seems to be—as different depth-psychological frameworks unveil the complexity of the mind and challenge the idea of a unitary, cohesive self.

PHILOSOPHICAL BACKGROUND

The diverse questions that arise concerning the self and consciousness are very complex; many of these touch on the age-old debates between monistic and dualistic views of the mind and their import on the mind/brain relationship. René Descartes saw the mind as a *res cogitans*, a thought-substance different from, and independent of, material substance, which is extended in space (*res extensa*). Despite these differences, though, he held that the mental and the material substances interact with each other. His own research on the visual system led him to posit an intermediate level, related to sensory inputs and processed by the brain, that determined perception, imagination, and feeling. Nevertheless, he was convinced that the intellect—a purely rational, self-conscious entity—did not need the brain for its own workings. Descartes was thus instrumental in instilling in science a concept that would dominate over the next three centuries: that of the unitary and wholly rational mind.

Brain scientist Sir John Eccles was an important modern proponent of interactionist dualism; he suggested that the mind, viewed as a unique, self-conscious entity, constantly scans the neuronal activity of the brain, focusing on and influencing specific modules of interest. The cortex acts mainly as a detector of these subtle mental "fields of influence," that modify patterns of neural network activity.[1] Thus, from Eccles's point of view, the organization, unity, and coherence of conscious experience is accounted for strictly at a mental level; there is no theoretical necessity for explanations on a biological level. As Eccles expressed it: "The unity of conscious experience is provided by the self-conscious mind and not by the neural machinery of the liaison areas of the cerebral hemispheres."[2]

This strong dualist-interactionist position has some clear-cut shortcomings. The Cartesian doctrine fails because even the higher, more abstract thought processes are strongly interconnected with numerous neuronal and subneuronal processes. As we can see in split-brain persons, or through the effects of chemical substances on cognition, brain or bodily alterations go much deeper than simply depriving the mind of information: they can alter the very manner in which we think—the process itself and its evolution.

Another major shortcoming of the dualistic position is its weakness in accounting for nonconscious cognitive processes; indeed, insofar as the mind is defined as a self-conscious entity, dualism may be seen as excluding, by definition, nonconscious cognitive processes.

In the opposite doctrine of radical monism, the mind is either identical to biological processes or a mere epiphenomenon; consciousness and all mental events can either be accounted for by more elementary processes (at the molecular, neuronal or subatomic levels) or dismissed as having no causal import. The task of cognitive sciences, in this view, is to convincingly account for all apparently mental processes in computational or, preferably, neurochemical terms.

In the philosophy of mind, this trend gave rise, in the 1950s, to what was termed "identity theory" or "central-state materialism," which posited the identity of mental states (or events) with brain states (or events). For the most part, this strong identity doctrine has been abandoned. Philosopher Alan Gauld has pointed out two of its main shortcomings.[3] The first—the "multiple correspondences" problem—focuses on the claimed one-to-one correspondence between mind states and brain states. As Gauld observed, in any one individual, a number of different mental states may correspond to a given brain state; conversely, similar mental states can be found in different individuals despite their idiosyncratic brain structures. Thus, an identity between brain and mental states seems highly implausible, and insistence upon a formal mental-neural identity has been mostly abandoned. Nevertheless, the idea of a one-to-one *causal* linkage is still widely held and is the preferred explanation of mind-brain interaction, despite conspicuous philosophical weaknesses.

Gauld's second objection refers to the wide "explanatory gap"[4] between accounts based upon neuronal processes and those based upon subjective experience (involving qualities or *qualia*). Indeed, explaining the subjective experience of *qualia* has been dubbed "the hard problem" of cognitive sciences by David Chalmers[5]; the chasm runs deep, as it involves differences not only in assertions but also in epistemology and language.[6] An interesting insight into this issue is given by Güven Güzeldere, who noted that neuronal processes are described from a third-person perspective, as causal laws, while conscious experience is described in first-person terms, as a phenomenal process.[7]

While most contemporary scientists find the dualistic stand unacceptable, they nevertheless increasingly recognize that consciousness and mental experience cannot be reduced to specific brain processes. An intermediate, compromise position seems to be more appealing than either extremes. Indeed, dualist and monist philosophies have found common ground in certain versions of emergentism[8] that view the mind as emerging from the brain's functioning—a necessary consequence of the complexification of neural processes. The emergentist position considers that consciousness involves genuine new properties, distinct from those of the physical or biological realms. Equally important, it acknowledges both *top-down* and *bottom-up* exchanges: consciousness may cause brain events, just as neurophysiological processes may cause mental events.

I readily agree with Frederic Myers's assessment: "We are now pretty well agreed that such concomitance [of mind and matter] does always and inevitably exist within us." Myers then concluded that "our notions of mind and matter must pass through many a phase as yet unimagined."[9] As with many other illustrious and vehement debates of history, it may turn out that there is no clear-cut winner in the dualist-monist conflict; rather, the conflict itself will somehow be displaced or transcended.

Today, the mind-body problem tends to be recast in a number of specific issues. The ones I am going to address are those dealing with semantic processes, such as: What is the nature of conscious experience? In what ways does it differ from—and interact with—nonconscious mental processes and with neuronal and bodily processes? What gives rise to our sense of a homogenous, unitary self? Is it indeed homogenous?

My approach, starting with this chapter and continuing throughout the rest of the book, is to attempt to address these issues through the dynamical network architecture that I have proposed in semantic fields theory.

THE FLOW OF CONSCIOUSNESS

When we speak of a "stream of consciousness," it sounds like our mental life consists of a single tranquil sequence of thoughts, a sort of linear, constant flow of mental events, following the focus of attention. In the cognitivist or symbolic paradigm, which was dominant in the 1970s and 1980s, this metaphor is pushed to the extreme: the mind is viewed as a computer, and thought is the sequential processing of symbolic representations in accordance to sets of rules.

By contrast, a growing number of scientists are adopting the connectionist paradigm, which underlies neural networks research; it posits that thought and the generation of meaning are equated to the emergence of global properties out of a vast connective network of distributed information.[10] Several neurological discoveries have shown unequivocal evidence for parallel and distributed neural processes. One major milestone was Karl Lashley's demonstration (from 1920 to 1951) that memory is not localized in specific areas of the brain, but is, rather, distributed throughout the brain.[11] Similarly, an important discovery was that perception of visual stimuli is based on highly distributed and parallel processing; indeed, it involves 20 or so visual maps located in various brain areas, each one dealing with a specific parameter (e.g., contrast).[12] What is puzzling, however, is the fact that there seems to be no brain area where these maps' outputs are coordinated. At this basic organizational level, the challenge is to understand the *binding* together of such widely distributed information-processing systems.[13]

It is true that, despite evidence for massive parallelism in the brain, we can still posit the existence of logical processes taking place at higher organizational levels. However, the very concept of linear and sequential rule-driven symbol manipulation is simply not powerful enough to deal with the flexibility and evolving capacities of the mind; the self-organization and learning that neural networks and dynamical systems exhibit seem to be a much more powerful explanatory tool. Thus, higher-level logical processing has to be thought of as a hybrid type of computation, involving logical rules, network properties, and nonlinear dynamics (more on this in chapter 6).

Nonconscious Cognitive Processes

As many researchers have pointed out, natural thought processes are mostly nonlogical or, as Arthur Reber put it, "arational"[14]; the main spontaneous mental processes are grounded on associations, as well as analogical and metaphorical thinking, which are much more rapid and global than linear computations. Studies on decision making show that even experts make far more use of nonrational or intuitive mental processes than is apparent at first glance. In the domain of creativity research, a great deal of data show that symbolic, analogical, or metaphoric thinking does not follow a linear logic, and does not result from application of fixed rules; it involves true qualitative leaps and abrupt shifts in reasoning.[15]

Numerous phenomena also point to the existence of nonconscious parallel thought-processes. Even our day-to-day problem-solving, seemingly the most linear of mental activities, clearly reveals that thought-processes keep evolving while we are no longer conscious of them. For example, we have spent some time looking for a solution to a given problem; we have checked out diverse possibilities, but none of them seems to offer a good answer. We then get involved in something else. The next morning, upon awakening, the perfect solution suddenly pops out of nowhere. The conscious mind, which introduced the problem, was no longer working on it—yet the solution emerged of its own will, so to speak. How could this occur? Obviously, the semantic search for a solution and processing were still going on further down in our semantic lattice even though we were unaware of them; this supposes the existence of nonconscious thought-processes, operating in parallel to the conscious stream of thought.

Dreams themselves—or dreamlike states, in general—have long been known to bring forth solutions to complex problems; the history of science and technology is filled with examples of insights that came through a dream or reverie and sometimes implied solutions to complex mathematical or physics problems. Here is a beautiful example: for a long time Friedrich von Kekule had pondered over the possible molecular structure of benzene without finding a workable solution. One afternoon everything became clear. He wrote:

> I turned my chair to the fire and dozed . . . . Again the atoms were gamboling before my eyes. My mental eye, rendered more acute by repeated visions of this kind, could distinguish larger structures, of manifold conformation; long rows, sometimes more closely fitted together; all twining and twisting in snakelike motion. But look! What was that? One of the snakes had seized hold of its own tail, and the form whirled mockingly before my eyes. As if by a flash of lightning, I awoke . . . . Let us learn to dream, gentlemen.[16]

Dreams are particularly helpful in the area of emotional intelligence. Over the course of three centuries, the prevalent rationalist paradigm has separated the intellect, seen as purely rational, from the psyche. As a consequence, we have failed to appreciate the intelligence instantiated by emotions, feelings, and social relationships—a state of affairs that researchers like Howard Gardner and Daniel Goleman have set out to correct.[17] Indeed dreams, while nonrational, often display great intelligence in the understanding of interrelationships. As noted by several psychoanalysts, they generally provide a much deeper outlook on our own feelings and priorities. For example, I have personally had dreams in which a short-sighted, egocentric, waking behavior of mine was replayed in a comic book–like setting, critically highlighting my handling of the situation. As most psychologists would agree, dreams present us with very different viewpoints than the ones we hold in waking life; this alone reveals that some divergent semantic processes are at work in the psyche.

Nonconscious processes have been the subject of much recent research, particularly in the domain of perception. It is now established that sensory pathways can be activated in the brain even though the individual is totally unaware of the presence of a stimulus. While conscious attention comes into play whenever significant changes are introduced into the environment (e. g., the opening of a door); it seems that pre-attentive perceptual processes, requiring neither focused attention nor analysis, tacitly keep an ongoing check on incoming stimuli; they constitute the ground of automatic and reflex responses. Stable perceptual inputs (visual, auditory, tactile, etc.) are thus processed through very economical and rapid routines; according to Cristof Koch, preconscious stimuli are registered through an extremely short-term precategorical and preconceptual form of memory, which he calls "iconic memory" (involving durations from 250 to 500 milliseconds).[18]

Another example of nonconscious process is the well-documented phenomenon of *subliminal perception*—perception below the awareness threshold. To study this, an image is flashed too rapidly (or a sound played at too low a volume) for subjects to be able to consciously perceive it. Their reaction time to a subsequent related stimulus is then compared to trials without the subliminal stimulus. Subjects' reaction times are indeed found to be reliably different following subliminal exposure to a menacing versus a neutral image. In general, these studies show that subliminal stimuli instantiate a *priming* effect, meaning that the subsequent behavior or mental process of the subject vis-à-vis a related stimulus is modified.[19]

Subliminal perception and priming are examples of what is called *implicit memory*.[20] Contrary to preconscious iconic memory, subliminal perception studies suggest a processing of basic emotional contents (e.g., threatening or friendly stimuli). One possibility here is that they are processed by the limbic system (also called the emotional brain), that is, without implication of the cortex. For example, patients suffering from brain damage that impedes conscious memory nevertheless responded appropriately to the friendly or unfriendly way people had related to them in previous encounters: the memory was there, but not consciously accessible. Another dramatic example is given by amnesiac patients who are suffering from an extreme inability to consciously recall events. The patients were primed with a group of related words (or word-stems) and immediately forgot the experience. Nonetheless, when they were later asked to complete word associations, they consistently chose words to which they had already been exposed. These latter experiments definitely suggest that implicit memory involves mental—and not just emotional—processing.

A related area of research is *implicit learning*. A person generally learns a task with difficulty and then reaches a point where the whole task is accomplished quite automatically, without any need for awareness (just as in walking or typing). In the mid-nineteenth century, such behaviors were already well established; today, they are referred to as *procedural knowledge*—an unconscious control of complex tasks—and contrasted to conscious *declarative knowledge*.[21]

The study of experts' problem-solving is similarly informative. While experts seemingly used reasoning and inference, they were in fact relying on implicit heuristic knowledge. Their own conscious description of how they had reached a solution was found to be quite removed from the actual processes involved. Arthur Reber, who has conducted a great deal of experimental research in this area, stated: "Implicit learning came to be viewed as a rather general information acquisition process . . . . acquired largely independently of the subjects' awareness of either the process of acquisition, or the knowledge base ultimately acquired."[22]

Implicit mental processes, increasingly recognized by cognitive scientists, are often referred to as the *cognitive unconscious*.[23] As is often pointed out, the simplest mental act—for example a statement during a dialogue—relies on numerous nonconscious processes, both at the semantic and at the neural level (e.g., search for the right words, the building of a grammatically correct sentence, tones and gestures, quasi-automatic adaptation to the other person's style of communication, etc.). At the neuromotor level, it involves activation of neural pathways and brain areas, psychomotor coordination of the larynx muscles, coordination of diverse sensory maps, control of posture and spatial orientation, and so on. In short, even in the simple act of forming a single statement, the mind triggers—and somehow directs—extensive nonconscious processes, searches, and computations at both neural and linguistic levels. In critical situations, we may experience extremely rapid and intelligent reflex actions that have not been consciously thought out or decided upon—for example, bringing a car out of a dangerous skid without ever having been in that situation before (or ever being instructed in the proper way to control a skid). Unlike a mere automatism (e.g., jerking one's hand away from a very hot surface), such actions involve a complex assessment of the situation and rapid adjustments and error correction. They thus underscore the existence of processes that, although lying beyond the conscious self, are nevertheless intelligent and goal-directed.

Parallel Mental Processes

Some of us may be very uncomfortable with the idea of "nonconscious thought processes"—judging this to be a contradiction in terms.

Nevertheless, it is contradictory *only* if we assume that thought is a reasoning process that necessitates a rational mind to produce it. If we take the whole semantic lattice of an individual to be a dynamical self-organizing system, then conscious thought is the end product of the internal connective processes at work in the whole network and its constant dynamical self-organization. In this framework, what constitutes the bulk of the flow of consciousness is the specific SeCo on which the self decides to focus on—a thought-train constantly interrupted by emergences of parallel nonconscious processing, coming from deeper in the noo-field. Focusing attention on one topic does not preclude the self from launching other searches and processing activities in the lattice. These will follow their own dynamics until their results are brought back into the main thought-stream.

To verify this, try the following experiment: make a list of what has occupied your mind in the last three hours. I have played the game myself several times. What I discovered was a load of unrelated thoughts surrounding the main task—thoughts about things I did in the past few days, or ones which remain to be done, or new ideas or insights, spontaneously popping up in consciousness. I noted affective emergences (feelings, memories, intentions) and occasional sensory and interoceptive perceptions (hunger, cold, pain, etc.). I found that my mind was weaving the present context into my main train of thought while constantly turning to the past and to the future (reliving events, making plans, imagining actions, etc.).

Such unexpected intrusions into the flow of consciousness are not just random events; rather, they derive from *ongoing parallel processing within activated constellations*. At times, the thoughts or images that "pop" into consciousness are clearly a response to a mental activity initiated some time earlier—for example, in the tip-of-the-tongue phenomenon, we unexpectedly recall a word we had been seeking earlier. Sometimes, though, the reemergence is more than just a straightforward response: the thought process has evolved well beyond the point where we consciously "left off," and a full-blown solution pops up into consciousness, as in the "aha!" experience described by Koestler.[24] This definitely shows that a semantic activation was sustained, unfolding and working in parallel to the conscious flow. It is also coherent with the incubation phase mathematician Henri Poincaré spoke of in his study of creativity in science—the period between the conscious analysis of a problem and the moment when the solution springs forth, unexpectedly and totally out of context.[25]

"Near death experiences" (NDEs) are mental phenomena that une-quivocally point to parallel thought-processing within the flow of consciousness itself. These hyperlucid mental states occur in a variety of contexts, such as terminal illness, suicide attempts, seconds prior to a serious accident, and so forth. Besides the famous tunnel and light experiences, a number of subjective content-types have been identified. Indeed, it seems that particular contexts favor certain experiences over other ones. Car accidents (where several seconds might elapse between the person's realization of what is coming and the actual impact) and mountain-climbing accidents (where long moments of sliding may precede the final fall) are especially favorable for states of hyperlucidity in which the subject experiences several simultaneous trains of thought.

Albert Heim, a geology professor at the University of Zurich, survived a long fall down a glacier while in the mountains. He reported that a part of his mind was busy trying to slow down his body's slide, while thinking about the inevitable fall and its consequences, whereas another part of his mind was thinking of his wife and family; simultaneously, another thought-train was reviewing his entire life, in minute detail—all of this within a few seconds. Astonished by his experience, Heim conducted an inquiry among climbers and members of the Alpine Club and found marked similarities with his own experience:

> In nearly 95% of the victims, there occurred, independent of the degree of their education, thoroughly similar phenomena, experienced with only slight differences. . . . Mental activity became enormous, rising to a hun-dred-fold velocity or intensity. The relationships of events and their prob-able outcomes were overviewed with objective clarity. No confusion en-tered at all. Time became greatly expanded. The individual acted with lightning-quickness in accord with accurate judgment of his situation. In many cases, there followed a sudden review of the individual's entire past.[26]

Of course, such occurrences, in which the flow of consciousness divides into several simultaneous and coherent trains of thought, are relatively rare. Nevertheless, less dramatic forms of parallel mental-processing are quite frequent, even if we rarely notice them. For example, we might catch ourselves simultaneously following two trains of thought, as when we listen to someone speaking while pursuing our own thoughts. Another example is deeply reflecting on something while driving; although, of course, I do not recommend it (unless you take full responsi-bility for yourself!), such deep reflection generally does not hinder us in dealing with the complex navigational necessities of city traffic.

Let us summarize the points of major importance regarding the flow of consciousness:

1. The ordinary waking state is itself quite complex and variable; as we move through the day, we constantly shift between professional or familial task-oriented activities, affective states, states of relaxation or leisure, and so forth. At a finer grain, we distinguish transient states that are woven inside the main cycle of activities: joy, sadness, fatigue, boredom, hunger, pain, anger, reverie, fleeting thoughts, sudden insights, and so forth.

2. Some processes activated within diverse SeCos may keep evolving in a nonconscious manner, in parallel with the conscious flow. They may generate meanings and solutions that occasionally emerge into the flow of consciousness.

3. The conscious flow as experienced by the individual is not a linear sequential process, but is rather a complex overlapping and weaving of multiple semantic activities—some intentional or volitional, others unintentional, emerging from deeper in the noo-field.

CONSCIOUS EXPERIENCE AND THE SELF

It is clear, from the above, that the thinking process implies not only conscious and intentional processes, but also nonconscious processes that evolve somewhat independently of the flow of consciousness. From the perspective of the model developed here, there are no clear-cut partitions or boundaries between these conscious and nonconscious semantic processes (apart from the impenetrable layers where semantic processes mingle with neural and somatic processes).

Given the complex and multilayered nature of conscious experience, how is it we feel so coherent and unitary, a unique "I"? To put it a bit more lightly, "Where are all my other selves? And why am I stuck in this particular one—neither the most exciting nor the most pleasant of them all?"

The short, common-sensical answer is that there is a clear-cut difference between the varied experiences or contents of the mind and the subject who has those experiences; we distinguish between the I (or self), and that which the self observes, feels, states, and so forth.

The very structure of language itself—"I" being the subject of linguistic propositions—reinforces the impression that the self is radically different from its experience.

Formally, the roots of this point of view can be found in the rationalist/idealist paradigm of Descartes and his school of thought, which attributed a primordial importance to the rational subject referred to in *cogito ergo sum* (I think, therefore I am). The cognitivist approach, based on the computer metaphor, is essentially an extension of the rationalist paradigm in the way it gives prominence to the rational self; but it shows a major shortcoming: insofar as thought is the processing of symbolic representations, according to rules, it necessitates the existence of a higher-level entity, one who can decide which rules apply and, above all, how to interpret the symbols. Nevertheless, in order to think, this entity must also use symbols that then must be interpreted by yet another conscious entity, and so forth. The resulting infinite regress has been described by a number of researchers as "the specter of the homunculus."[27]

The Cartesian split feels good. Each of us tends to perceive our own self as fairly coherent and consistent. Contradictions and inconsistencies are all so readily obvious in others, but, surely, when it comes to our own self, we have full claim to reason and rationality! Yet it seems difficult to accept that the self—the subject of experience—can be completely distinct from the contents of experience. It is clear that states of extreme sensory intensity (such as pain, sexual excitation, hunger and thirst, extreme discomfort from cold and heat, fatigue, etc.) invariably disturb all thought processes. Similarly, it would be difficult to ignore the influence upon the mind of all those rare but valuable cognitive and affective states—falling in love, being mesmerized by an aesthetic experience, sudden intuitive understanding, the "aha!" experience in science, abrupt doubts and reexaminations, changes of perspective that lead to radically new possibilities, the occasional psychological rebellion against one's everyday lot, with all its compromises and constraints upon individual desires and ideals. Even the most rational person cannot entirely escape such "irrational" states. Do we remain blissfully the same self throughout these turbulences, or must we say that substantive changes occur and that we may not be quite the same person we usually are?

The Improbable Existence of a Unitary Self

In contrast to the Cartesian outlook and its descendants, a number of alternative representations of the mind start from the assumption that the psyche is not unitary and simple, but rather is complex and multilayered; its structure, to some extent, reflects the multifaceted dynamics of conscious experience.

Psychoanalysis and depth psychology replace the concept of a conscious self with that of the ego—an ensemble of dynamics and representations associated with the self-image. These dynamics and representations, however, are shaped by materials stemming from other parts of the psyche—such as, in Freudian terminology, the impulsive "id," or the "superego," that yoke of the socialized personality.[28] Thus, in psychoanalytic thought, the self is far from unitary and coherent, and the flow of consciousness is not necessarily one-dimensional: psychic contents from the unconscious can well up into the flow of experience, resulting in such phenomena as the famous Freudian slips and lapses.

While Carl Jung's mapping of the psyche differs from that of Freud, he maintains the concept of psychic clusters. The "ego" is the conscious subject, while the "Self" is the broader, wiser and more comprehensive subject of the unconscious; the "persona" is the embodiment of social roles and the "anima/animus" are the unconscious complements of the person's explicit sexual identity (masculine or feminine). Consciousness, in Jung's view, includes both the conscious and the unconscious; it is seen as influenced and organized by the "archetypes," those common psychological roots linking all human beings through the collective unconscious.[29] Archetypes refer to primeval concepts—such as "hero," "mother," "sun," and so forth—the symbolic meaning of which is often unraveled by myths, legends, and art, and which is the underlying fabric of many dreams. Thus, in Jung's framework, not only is consciousness organized into several major clusters, but additionally, the self is considered to be more than a "closed," independent system: the personal unconscious opens to the collective unconscious.

Whether in Freudian or Jungian perspective, the personality is viewed as multilayered and complex. However well-organized, conscious experience reflects a fundamental lack of homogeneity: feelings, impulses, desires, imaginations, projections, and so forth intermingle throughout conscious experience. Far from being dominant, the rational self is seen as being more in a permanent state of siege in the Freudian viewpoint, or as embedded in, and nurtured by, unconscious meaningful forces in the Jungian perspective.

Transpersonal psychology also challenges the view of a unique, coherent self by emphasizing the existence of different states of consciousness and, consequently, of distinct behavioral and experiential clusters within the same individual. In the transpersonal approach, the content of the subject's conscious experience is essentially seen as a function of his or her state of consciousness. The ordinary (or "baseline") state is defined and stabilized by the familiarity of the tasks and activities in which the person engages, as well as her or his immediate physical and social surroundings. Insofar as individuals detach themselves from their usual preoccupations and surroundings, they shift from their ordinary state into an altered state of consciousness (ASC).[30] The most obvious examples, of course, are sleep and dreams; but this shift can also occur by other means, for example, by practicing some mental technique (such as meditation or auto-hypnosis), by drug induction or by music and dance (as in ritual trance states).[31]

Although it is lived episodically, interrupted by the emergence of other states, each ASC has its own internal consistency. While in their ordinary state people tend to "live through" their usual self, in ASCs they express facets of their being that generally tend to be otherwise suppressed or silenced. Charles Tart, one of the pioneers of transpersonal psychology, has shown that particular states of consciousness reach deep into the psyche, and that we exhibit "state specific" memory, perception, and ways of relating to the world.[32] In other words, ASCs modify not only the content of consciousness but also the thinking process and its modalities. In a meditation practice, for example, individuals may discover a facet of their self never experienced before, or feel like they have tuned in to their "deep self." These commonly reported experiences point to the fact that the "I" we ordinarily identify with may not be all there is to the self, but just that part that is activated and stabilized by our current activities. This theme was also developed by Jung; in discussing what he termed the "individuation process," he referred to the possibility of the conscious gradually coming in touch with, and attuning to, the Self, thus opening the latent potentials of the psyche.[33]

Anthropological data are consistent with and reinforce the views of transpersonal psychology. In ritual possession trances, widely practiced in a number of traditional cultures all over the world, entranced "initiates" report that a god or goddess has possessed their body during the trance and acts and talks through them. In some rituals, like the Haitian voodoo, or the Holey rituals of the Songhai of Mali, the initiate may be possessed by any of several gods or spirits.[34] Indeed, intentionally induced possession episodes also exist in some shamanistic rituals, as with the Sangoma shamans of South Africa[35]: for these shamans (mostly women), the number of spirits they are able to impersonate is a sign of the extent of their knowledge. In some other possession rituals, such as that of the Brazilian Macumba, the initiate can incorporate only one god (the priestess Maria-José states that this god represents "the deep nature" of the initiate[36]). Anthropologist Erika Bourguignon saw the main characteristic of possession trance as being "a discontinuity to the person's identity," one which is condoned by the culture and also offers the initiate intense personal satisfaction.[37]

Impersonations of spirits have their counterpart in the Occident, in the mediumnistic trances in which a deceased person seemingly speaks through the mouth of the medium. The voice, features, and linguistic style of the medium may be drastically altered, and cases of glossolalia (fluently speaking an unknown language) have been reported by reliable researchers.[38]

As with cases of multiple personality disorders and schizophrenia that have been studied by psychiatrists, these ritual impersonations show that the self may house more than one personality (or quasi-personality) cluster. At the very least, this reveals the complexity of the self; but, as I understand it, it points to the fact that the cohesiveness of the self is not so much a given, but is rather an ongoing process of construction that may be channeled toward specific types of organizations, either by culture or by the individual.

Building the Coherence of the "I"

I believe that, try as we may, we must conclude that the purely unitary, homogenous "I" is nowhere to be found. Anyway, let us face it: the purely rational self is hardly the ideal it has been cooked up to be. In fact, it could only exist at the cost of all spontaneity and flexibility and would necessitate sacrificing any possibility of creative exploration—not only of the latent facets of the psyche, but also of different conceptual frameworks and alternative mental states.

The next question, then, is whether we must completely abandon the concept of the self. Some researchers, like Francisco Varela, have argued in favor of this perspective.[39] Hinayana Buddhist doctrine states that all we experience are only transient consciousness aggregates, driven by sensory objects, each one different and unrelated to the other one. Drawing on these concepts, Varela proposed the self's only reality is in the desire of people to believe in it.

This is a radical position; it is a big jump from denying the existence of a purely rational, Cartesian self, to denying all forms of selfhood. Claiming that the psyche is a multitude of unrelated psychological events, drifting in incoherence, does not fit our subjective experience. It also does not account for individuals' need for a sense of self or for their lifelong struggle to discover and integrate the latent facets of their being.

Clinicians in practically every psychological school of thought consider this lifelong work—what Jung referred to as individuation—as healthy and sane; it would be quite surprising if all this amounted to mere illusion.

In fact, there is no necessity for the cohesion of the psyche-mind to depend on the existence of a unitary, homogenous entity; there exist alternative ways to achieve cohesiveness. As I will develop later on, a cognitive architecture based on diversified and specialized SeCos does not necessarily lack organization as a whole. We simply need to think of it as a modular form of organization. The self may be more like a traditional village, consisting of families, with each one having developed a particular art or craft. Several families may have the same craft expertise, say that of weavers, but what they produce is still different. They then may exchange the products of their artwork, and the village as a whole benefits from the rich diversity of all that is produced by the different families.

The individual's whole mind, the semantic lattice, has to be seen as a system containing other systems. The sheer diversity, specialization, competition, and redundancy of SeCos that constitute the lattice are what ensure its dynamical and evolutionary quality. Homogeneity, as we know well, leads to increased entropy and stability. This is the death of the mind.

In considering the structure of the self, I believe that the frameworks of Jungian depth psychology and transpersonal psychology come closest to the experienced reality; but we need to integrate these two approaches into a model that is dynamic, and not just conceptual. Rather than being seen as pure illusion, the coherent "I" can be considered to be an ongoing construction, a process. It is not a given, an a priori, but a striving, fueled by the individual's urge for coherence, consistency, and continuity of being. Individuals believe in their self, and they need to experience and present to others a coherent identity. (Even a hedonist, who would live only by the pleasure of each moment, would cling to his or her own hedonist credo.) As we evolve, we constantly bring into being and shape our own cohesiveness: avoiding self-contradiction, seeking consistency in our ways of being, maintaining personal habits, aligning deeds with beliefs and values, and so forth. We organize our actions according to our current self-model, so as to build our integrity—interpreting and rationalizing both consonances and dissonances, and thereby constructing our coherence, along with our personal history.

The psyche is thus constantly and dynamically being pulled between order and disorder. On the one hand, we are invariably confronted with diversity, multiplicity, and complexity—particularly in our modern societies, where we are constantly exposed to a wealth of ideas and worldviews, and must frequently adapt to new environments or contexts. We also have the means to develop new talents and indulge in novel hobbies, thereby exploring our latent potentials. Inevitably, personality moves toward complexity, exhibiting multiple facets and even competing constellations.

On the other hand, given our profound need for consistency and continuity, and given the constraints imposed on us by society, we are strongly motivated to create a coherent identity, the unity of a self. The creation of meaning is what allows us to construct and weave our own identity vis-à-vis others and society. This nonhomogenous, systemic identity, constantly self-created and emerging out of the dynamic pull between diversity and continuity, is reflected in the idiosyncratic organization of the semantic lattice; it constitutes the fundamental fabric of experience, the ground for decoding and creating meanings.

NOTES

1. K. R. Popper & J. C. Eccles (1977), *The self and its brain: An argument for interactionism*, Berlin: Springer-Verlag. Eccles further argues that when the mind is deprived of data—that is when "there is nothing to read out," as in sleep—then this brings about unconsciousness. This seems quite weak, insofar as in dreams, and even in non-REM sleep, the mind continues to function.

2. Ibid., p. 362.

3. A. Gauld (1989), Cognitive psychology, entrapment and the philosophy of the mind, in J. R. Smithies & J. Beloff (Eds.), *The case for dualism*, Charlottesville: University Press of Virginia.

4. J. Levine (1983), Materialism and qualia: The explanatory gap, *Pacific Philosophical Quarterly, 64,* 354–61.

5. D. Chalmers (1996), Facing up to the problem of consciousness, in S. R. Hameroff, A. W. Kasazniak & A. C. Scott (Eds.), *Toward a science of consciousness,* Cambridge, MA: MIT Press/Bradford Books.

See also the discussion about the "hard problem" in the *Journal of Consciousness Studies.* Special issue: The hard problem. Parts 1–4. This specific topic was running through 1995 and 1996.

6. Gauld (1989) exposed the impossibility of bridging the gap between the concept-set of psychology and the concept-set of physical sciences in order to establish the identity between assertions about mental events and assertions about brain states. While stable global correlations between brain states and mental states can be found, it is logically incorrect to state that a given brain pattern refers to the same object as the mental or qualitative experience of the

subject exhibiting that brain pattern. Joe Levine (1983) considers the difficulty of bridging neuronal mechanisms and qualitative experience to be an epistemological—as opposed to ontological—problem, that is an issue mostly stemming from our mental representations and knowledge-systems, rather than from a fundamental gap between subjective and neural processes.

7. G. Güzeldere (1995), Problems of consciousness: A perspective on contemporary issues, current debates, *Journal of Consciousness Studies, 2* (2), 112–43, p. 141.

In Güzeldere's view, the solution could lie in a "cross-fertilization of the first-person and the third-person perspectives which would allow us to talk about the *causal efficacy of how consciousness feels* and the *phenomenal quality of what consciousness does.*"

8. W. Sperry (1976), Mental phenomena as causal determinants in brain functions, in G. Globus, G. Maxwell, & I. Savodnic (Eds.), *Consciousness and the brain*, New York: Plenum.

9. F. W. H. Myers (1886), On telepathic hypnotism, and its relation to other forms of hypnotic suggestion, *Proceedings of the Society for Psychical Research, 4,* 127–88. Cited by Cook (1994).

10. J. A. Anderson & E. Rosenfeld (Eds.), *Neurocomputing: Foundations of research,* Cambridge, MA: The MIT Press (First printed in 1950).

See also Rumelhart, McClelland & the PDP Research Group (1986); McClelland, Rumelhart & the PDP Research Group (1986); Bechtel & Abrahamsen (1990).

11. K. S. Lashley (1988), In search of the engram, in Anderson & Rosenfeld (1988).

12. J. P. Changeux (1997), *Neuronal man: The biology of mind*, Princeton, NJ: Princeton University Press (First printed in 1983).

13. A deeper facet of the binding problem is associated with the discovery of oscillatory cortical patterns within the 40–70 hertz range (i.e., exceeding typical EEG frequencies). Milner suggested in 1974 that neurons activated by a specific visual stimulus would fire synchronously. In 1975 Freeman discovered oscillations around 40 Hz in the olfactory system. Then, in 1989, working on the cat's visual cortex, Gray showed that neurons that are quite far apart (relative to the scale of the brain) oscillate synchronously at 40 Hz in response to a particular visual stimulus, such as a stripe.

This connection of distant neurons points to a higher-level organization of the brain. Thus, Crick & Koch (1990) proposed that the synchronous firing of neurons provided the basis for coherent mental representations and ultimately for the sense of a unitary self. Given that electrochemical links are too slow to explain this distant synchronization, several interesting alternatives have been proposed, based on either quantum, holonomic, or neural network processes. (More on the subject in chapter 8). See Crick, F., & Koch, C. (1990). Toward a neurobiological theory of consciousness. *Seminars in the neurosciences*, 2, 263–75.

The repeated observations centering around the 40 Hz frequency does indeed seem of interest: as it turns out, anesthesia, which provokes loss of consciousness, also inhibits 40 Hz cortical oscillations. Nevertheless, while these discoveries and their neurological implications are fascinating, it seems a bit stretched to present them as an explanation for consciousness and the self. As Güzeldere (1995) pointed out: "The discovery of an empirical correlation does not suffice to bridge the explanatory gap between the phenomenon as it appears to the subject, and what its underlying mechanism does."

On synchronous firing, see also Freeman (1995b); Hameroff (1994); Koch (1996).

14. A. S. Reber (1993), *Implicit learning and tacit knowledge*, New York: Oxford University Press. See also Minsky (1985).

15. I. Stengers & J. Schlanger (1988), *Les concepts scientifiques*, Paris: La découverte. On creativity, see De Bono (1970); Parnes (1988).

16. Kekule as cited in Robertson (1995), pp. 162–3.

17. H. Gardner (1983), *Frames of mind. The theory of multiple intelligences*, New York: Harper Collins/Basic Books. See also D. Goleman (1995), *Emotional intelligence*, New York: Bantam.

18. C. Koch (1996), Toward the neuronal substrate of visual consciousness, in S. R. Hameroff, A. W. Kaszniak, & A. C. Scott (Eds.), *Toward a science of consciousness*. Cambridge, MA: MIT Press/Bradford Books.

19. D. L. Schacter (1987), Implicit memory: History and current status, *Journal of Experimental Psychology: Learning, Memory, and Cognition, 13,* 501–18. See also N. Dixon (1981), *Preconscious processing,* Chichester: John Wiley & Sons.

20. Popper (1977) proposed to distinguish between implicit and explicit memory: *implicit memory* implies deeply ingrained linguistic-semantic and psychomotor processes (such as gestures, speech, writing, reading, walking, common tool handling, etc.) and is relatively unaffected by events; *explicit memory* is linked to specific events and objects (such as faces, patterns, different kinds of conceptual information, etc.) and needs repetition to be sustained. A somewhat analogous scheme distinguishes between *procedural memory*, organizing psychomotor processes as procedures that have become automatic and nonconscious, and *declarative memory*—the conscious enunciation of precise memories and the recognition of objects and events as expressed through language. See Popper & Eccles (1977).

21. J. R. Anderson (1976), *Language, memory and thought*, Hillsdale, NJ: Erlbaum.

22. Reber (1993) held that the robustness of implicit cognitive functions, despite conscious dysfunctions, shows that they have distinct properties; in his view, they antedate the apparition of conscious mental processes in human evolution.

23. Of course, recognition of the existence of the cognitive unconscious does not imply acceptance of the Freudian concept of the unconscious, formed by

repressed drives.

24. A. Koestler (1989), *The act of creation*, New York: Penguin.

25. H. Poincaré (1952), *Science and method*, New York: Dover Publications.

26. A. Heim (1892/1972), The experience of dying from fall, *Omega, 3,* 45–52. See also D. Lorimer, *Whole in one,* London, UK : Arkana.

27. G. M. Edelman (1992), *Bright air, brilliant fire: On the matter of mind,* New York: Basic Books.

28. S. Freud (1988), *The essentials of psychoanalysis*, New York: Penguin.

29. C. G. Jung (1966), *The collected works of C. G. Jung: Vol. 7. Two essays on analytical psychology* (Bollingen Series, XX), Adler, G., & Hull, R. F. (Eds.). Princeton, NJ: Princeton University Press. C. G. Jung (1964), *Man and his symbols*, Garden City, NY: Windfall Books/DoubleDay. R. Robertson (1995), *Jungian Archetypes. Jung, Gödel and the history of archetypes*, York Beach: Nicolas-Hays.

30. C. Tart (Ed.), (1969), *Altered states of consciousness,* New York: John Wiley & Sons. A. Ludwig (1969), Altered states of consciousness, in C. Tart (Ed.). C. Hardy (1988), *La science et les états frontières*, Paris: Rocher.

31. C. Hardy (1991), *Le vécu de la transe*, Paris: Le Dauphin. S. Krippner & P. Welch (1992), *Spiritual dimensions of healing,* New York: Irvington.

32. C. Tart (1975), *States of consciousness*, New York: Dutton.

33. C. G. Jung (1967), *The collected works of C. G. Jung: Vol. 13. Alchemical studies* (Bollingen Series, XX), Adler, G., & Hull, R. F. (Eds.), Princeton, NJ: Princeton University Press.

34. A. Métraux (1958), *Le vaudou haïtien*, Paris: Gallimard. J. Rouch (1989), *La religion et la magie Songhaï*, Ed. de l'Université de Bruxelles (First printed in 1960).

35. A. Boshier (1973), African apprenticeship, in A. Angoff, & D. Barth (Eds.), *Parapsychology and anthropology*, New York: Parapsychology Foundation.

36. S. Bramly (1981), *Macumba, forces noires du Brésil*, Paris: Albin Michel.

37. E. Bourguignon (1976), *Possession*, Corte Madera, CA: Chandler & Sharp.

38. C.G. Jung (1970), On the psychology and pathology of so-called occult phenomena, in Jung, C. G., *The collected works of C. G. Jung: Vol. 1. Psychiatric studies* (2d Ed., Bollingen Series, XX), Adler, G., & Hull, R. F. (Eds.). Princeton, NJ: Princeton University Press. See also F. Myers, O. Lodge, W. Leaf, & W. James (1890), A record of observation of certain phenomena of trance, *Proc. of the Society for Psychical Research, 6,* 436-695.

39. F. Varela, E. Thompson, & E. Rosch (1991), *The embodied mind,* Cambridge, MA: The MIT Press.

3

THE MIND'S ARCHITECTURE

The high level of integrative functioning of the human mind calls for a particular view of the mind's "architecture," or structural organization. The currently dominant framework, functionalism, partitions functions into diverse global work-systems that quite mysteriously manage to yield an integrated end product. Drawing on a computational or AI perspective, the mind is viewed as a huge set of software modules, each module accomplishing a specific task (or function). One of the main drawbacks here is the well-known "homunculus" problem: Who is the agent selecting and activating particular software modules, and how does this agent then integrate the results of all the operations into a coherent experience?

Michael Gazzaniga proposed a possible solution. He envisioned a large number of brain modules working somewhat independently, while "the interpreter," a module based in the left hemisphere, receives all information from the other ones and interprets it.[1] In Gazzaniga's view, consciousness hardly knows anything at all about these operations, having access only to their results.

THE SECOS ARCHITECTURE

The semantic fields model is based upon an alternative modular architecture, deriving from a dynamical systems view. It posits the interdependence of modules, which are seen as sets of dynamical processes; self-organization, generativity, and hence the emergence of new states are thus inherent to the system.

This kind of architecture involves highly integrated SeCos, ones in which functions work in a specialized and cooperative manner.

A Modular Network

A number of cognitive scientists are now presenting either distributed or dynamical modular theories of the mind. Bernard Baars has proposed that numerous brain modules respond to the contents of the flow of consciousness.[2] He viewed the conscious mind as a work area called the "Global Workspace" (GWS), which acts as a "broadcasting" agency, distributing information throughout the brain. Diverse brain processors work in a parallel and distributed fashion, and move into action whenever their symbol appears in the Workspace. The most dominant information streams—for example, those reinforced by feedback loops—gain access to the GWS; from there they are redistributed throughout the brain, thus activating other processors.

It is tempting to adopt the concept of a neural system that "understands" everything that happens in the stream of consciousness (the GWS), with each agent responding by itself to a specific signal, rather than being "ordered" to perform an operation. Nevertheless, this whole approach has a major drawback: the symbol-agent pairs are too tightly coupled, and the entire system is entirely deterministic. There is little room in this model for self-organization, generativity, and innovation.[3]

Adopting a dynamical-systems approach, Allan Combs viewed the mind as an ensemble of modules, each one constituting a set of dynamical processes; Allan Combs also underscored the organizing quality of consciousness.[4] In his *Dual Network Theory*, Ben Goertzel proposed the superposition of two networks—a memory network, having an associative organization, and a control network, showing a hierarchical structure.[5] Both Combs and Goertzel view the mind as a giant system housing many modules, which would be dynamically organized as a giant attractor with subsystems.

Let us now turn to the semantic fields model. As we have already seen, the SeCos bind together a plurality of interconnected processes and semantic contents—memories, sensory patterns, judgments, beliefs, behavioral patterns, and so forth. We thus have a modular-network organization: through experience, SeCos become highly specialized networks, each one involving a unique cooperative ensemble of "elements" and processes.[6] The SeCos, as "modules," are complex self-organizing networks; each major network has integrated a complex array of processes, knowledge, feelings, behaviors, and so forth.[7]

Now, this cognitive architecture, based on diversified and specialized SeCos, does not necessarily imply a lack of organization as a whole. The mind-psyche can be compared to the structural organization of a traditional village. Each family in the village (each SeCo) has developed a particular craft. While several families may have the same profession, say, that of potter, what they produce is still different—from basic cooking pots to art objects. In other words, even if certain SeCos are similar, or competitive, they generate different processes. Even if they branch into the same low-level neuronal processes (e.g., all potters using the same basic forest clay), they still integrate and use these processes in idiosyncratic ways.

The rich complexity and innovative productivity of the village stems from the specialization of its families and the diversity of their art products. Similarly, the complexity of the mind-psyche stems from the idiosyncrasy and diversity of the SeCos. On the other hand, the coherence and organization of the mind-psyche (the village), derives from the dense, continuous exchanges of very specific forms of know-how between the SeCos (the families).

The individual's whole mind, the semantic lattice, should thus be seen as a system containing other systems—its cohesiveness derives from an intense interdependence, rather than a centralized authority. The sheer diversity, specialization, competition, and redundancy of the SeCos constituting the lattice is what ensures its dynamical and evolutionary quality. Homogeneity, as we know well, leads to increased entropy and stability; it is the death of the mind.

Given a SeCo-based cognitive architecture, it follows that concepts are linked to a whole array of sub-SeCos or clusters, representing not only visual schemas (frames), procedural schemas (scripts), propositional knowledge, and language-set, but also clusters of qualia, memories, feelings, values, desires and intentions, and states of consciousness. Within each SeCo, these clusters are linked to specific neurological, physiological, and somatic processes; at the same time, the sub-SeCos maintain a high degree of connectivity between themselves—largely because they have co-evolved and developed in conjunction with each other, creating and informing the SeCo in the process.

Thus, each SeCo is the locus of a unique self-organizing process in which the elements that have been linked together, through experience, cooperate and co-evolve. At any given moment, each SeCo displays a specific cooperative network of semantic and biological clusters that are engaged in an ongoing interactive and integrative process.

Of course, depending on the manner in which they have formed,

SeCos will show different levels of lability and adaptive capacity. Some are more rigid, others extremely malleable. A trauma is a particularly rigid and closed SeCo—somewhat like a cyst. Its closedness and low level of lability tend to preclude the creation of new links that could modify its internal organization. On the other end of the spectrum, a SeCo built up through ongoing creative activities, like musical improvisation or innovative team building, is subject to constant modifications (whether through cooperative improvements or linkage of new clusters).

The SeCos architecture is well suited to account for creative insights that are often based on a juxtaposition or interlacing of two unrelated domains. A given SeCo may express a particular viewpoint on the world, a framework, a way of looking at specific issues. Formed by experience, education, and training, the SeCo, as a set, expresses a specific logic, or style of connectivity; for example, one SeCo could constitute the individual's personal integration of a given scientific domain. What is interesting, then, is to consider what happens when two such SeCos, each constituting a complex framework or outlook, collide with each other.

Say a researcher is trying to solve problem P. Like any scientist, she has learned to view problems in her field through a specific formalization, deriving from the framework of her science—and instantiated in a huge SeCo ("S" SeCo). Now, what happens if problem P, usually embedded in SeCo S, pops up in our researcher's mind while she is temporarily preoccupied with a very different framework—say, while reading a science fiction novel ("SF" SeCo)? The meeting of S and SF may translate into her spontaneously applying the SF framework to problem P and coming up with an unexpected insight.[8] The rich diversity of activated SeCos is thus a major source of innovations and breakthroughs.

What I am getting at is that a system such as the lattice can be "self-organized" without being "logically coherent." Just as we might have, even within a single SeCo, a large diversity of links, including inconsistent or conflictual ones, in the same way the lattice can include highly diversified SeCos; some of these will be closely related, others totally unrelated, yet others antithetical or competing. This kind of organization permits a high level of lability and flexibility; it allows for the ongoing adaptive and creative evolution and transformation of consciousness.

Customized Functions

The cognitive architecture presented here, then, is not based upon compartmentalized, independent functions, like memory, perception, sensorimotor processes, learning, and so forth. Rather, highly specialized subsets of functions may evolve within specific SeCos if their own particular development is tightly tied to the development of the SeCo.

Cognitive functions have traditionally been viewed as specific, well-differentiated structures, localized in particular brain zones. The long search for brain localization was initially stimulated by Paul Broca's discovery of brain areas corresponding to language and speech. It received a major blow when Karl Lashley demonstrated the distributed organization of memory,[9] and when it was later found that perception involves highly distributed perceptual maps in the brain.[10] The issue is still not settled; evidence for very fine function specialization of groups of neurons continues to accumulate while evidence for widely distributed processes is itself overwhelming. One suspects we may have another instance of paradoxes and conflicts arising from the dichotomous manner in which the problem was originally posed.[11]

Functionalism offered a workable framework for getting around all this, rendering the issue of localization irrelevant. Insofar as cognitive functions could be performed by several different mechanisms—whether neuron-based (wetware) or chip-based (hardware)—it no longer seemed necessary to discover how the mental language-set can "talk" to the brain language-set. The issue reduced to an understanding of the "programs" that correspond to particular functions (such as memorizing). Following the still widely used computational metaphor, mental functions could thus be considered analogous to diverse computer tasks (exec programs, databases, task-oriented auxiliaries, etc.).

Even if framed in terms of functions, rather than localized brain structures, the general trend has still been toward a compartmentalization of mental functions. For example, the concept of "belief-set" is seen as referring to the whole declarative knowledge of an individual, expressed in terms of propositions and implying an ordered ensemble—a distinct entity that is somehow detached from other functions. From this, it follows that any symbol-coded proposition within the belief-set group must be as readily accessible and subject to computations as symbols in a Turing machine (a symbol-based computational machine like digital computers).

The problem, of course, is that the mind just does not seem to work like a Turing machine, as has been confirmed by numerous empirical data. For example, the retrieval of a specific propositional or linguistic item is greatly facilitated by a semantically associated context. Similarly, in the well-known priming effect, we find that pre-exposure to a subliminal stimulus or particular context influences the interpretation of related items.[12] Functionalism has great difficulty modeling such findings; by contrast, they are quite adequately modeled by a network-type organization, such as the SeCos architecture.[13]

Take the common situation of people who have learned the rudiments of a foreign language while in a remote country and then return home; typically, they will quickly forget much of what they learned. If they venture back for a second visit, just a few words casually overheard at the airport might trigger recall of a number of other words and expressions. The same kind of dynamic applies to the long-forgotten rudiments of a specific science, or of a rule-driven game we may have played in our childhood.

All this clearly shows the extent to which knowledge grows within a network of interrelated concepts and processes, and thus remains tied to it. Knowledge is organized in semantic clusters and the retrieval of specific items is greatly helped by first activating (or priming) the embedding network.

Note, also, that from a semantic fields perspective, knowledge cannot be partitioned into declarative and procedural sets. In terms of declarative knowledge, as we have seen, concepts are no longer uniquely equated with propositions; while some knowledge can take on a propositional form,[14] these propositions do not even come close to representing the totality of the linked elements and processes that truly constitute knowledge. Similarly, we cannot posit a fixed set comprising all of the individual's procedural knowledge; rather than belonging to an abstract procedural set, any learned procedure has to be viewed as an integrated, interactive cluster within the SeCo(s).

In place of the functionalist framework that divides the person into distinct functions, the present model posits a modular network-architecture in which a particular SeCo may have custom-tailored the main function(s) it needs to be efficient. Subsets of functions may develop into very specialized clusters that are network-linked within specific SeCos: the customized function evolves out of the original function. So here we have a whole SeCo (say, a professional's musical skill) that while growing, requires and triggers the specialized development of a function (like hearing). In this case, the function develops a more complex, customized version of itself.

Of course, I am not claiming that all functions, even the most elementary ones, are necessarily customized and distributed; this depends both on the nature of the function and upon the degree of specialized use that has developed over time. For example, if we learn a new language using the familiar Latin alphabet, we obviously do not need to develop a specialized function for reading that particular language; on the other hand, we may need a specialized reading function to read, say, Japanese script. In other words, at one extreme, a function may constitute a distinct low-level cluster, to which other SeCos branch as needed; at the other extreme, the function is fully adapted to and integrated within a given SeCo. Let us illustrate with some examples.

Walking-running Function. Walking-running is used in an infinite set of situations or goals. We can sort out five quite distinct states of organization from walking to running: walking slowly, walking quickly, speedy half-running, jogging, and running. If we view these organizational states from the viewpoint of dynamical systems, we can envision representing them through the "attractor with wings" proposed by Walter Freeman to explain the sense of smell.[15] This attractor looks like a flower with petals; basically, it has subattractors, or wings (the petals), that instantiate specific organizational states. Depending on the requirements of the situation, it is simply a question of the activated SeCo branching onto one of the walking-running wings and specifying added requirements (cautious to the left, light on the wounded toe, and so forth.).

Let us say we find ourselves in a situation that calls for attention to the way we walk. We are at a very elegant gathering, and we find it necessary to modify our usual trot, nudging ourselves into a more graceful walk than normal. So far, so good: we simply make use of the usual organization of the walking cluster and all its neuromotor processes while adding some extra requirements (like, be graceful!). No customization of the function is necessary here: there is no sustained, specialized learning process to trigger its development.

Now, however, imagine a professional runner: his long-term training and experience in fast-running has produced a huge SeCo that has developed its own neuromotor pathways and organization (P), on top of the original running "wing" or organization (O). In P, the running function has developed a specific, complex organization, network-linked to the professional "Running" SeCo. P may then be considered a *customized subset* of O. Though it grew out of O, P has taken on such importance in the runner's life that it now predominates: in all situations calling for "running," the person will tend to fall into the "professional runner" mode.

Hearing Function. Of course, the original attractor's wing can co-exist with the new "specialized" one, and can be used in non specific occasions, as in the following example.

Let us take a professional violinist, whose artistic hearing function is tied into his whole "Music" SeCo. The latter is an extremely complex weaving of musical concepts, vocabulary, sensitivity and feelings, memories, procedural knowledge, gestures and know-how, and so forth—all these elements being network-linked to specific sensorimotor and neuronal processes.

Here, then, through training, the hearing function has grown a new, specialized attractor wing. The original wing, though, is still in use in non musical situations. Indeed, the usual hearing function (on the phone, in the street) has hardly changed; it may display a pronounced sensitivity to sounds in general, but for the most part, it is not tied to the artistic hearing function per se. Whenever in a musical context (that is, when the "Music" SeCo is activated) hearing will involve a particular sensory-affective-mental state that permits both emotional appreciation and a more analytic attention to the performer's art. The auditory sensorimotor pathways thus get to be enormously more numerous and complex, and involve larger brain areas, insofar as they are connected, early on, with huge areas of the associative cortex.[16]

These examples thus show the extent to which particular psychomental SeCos are network-linked in very specialized ways to functional neuromotor processes; and inversely, the extent to which the development of neuromotor pathways is influenced by psychomental facets of the SeCo network. This leads me to propose that a customized function develops whenever sustained learning or training—involving a whole semantic constellation of knowledge and processes—uses an original function in a new, specialized manner. The mind-psyche thus takes on a distributed organization, in the sense that customized functions are, in some cases, integrated within different SeCos; they are then organized and activated according to the SeCo in which they are embedded.

NOO-SEMANTIC FIELD AND LATTICE

Insofar as the semantic lattice is the ensemble of all the SeCos ever constructed in one's life, its organization reflects everything the person has ever experienced and learned. Over a given time period, only a fraction of the existing SeCos are actually activated, depending on the major activities and preoccupations in the person's current life (profession, family ties, relationships, and so forth.). These SeCos, which are constantly primed or activated—hence, changing and evolving—"stick out" from the background of the lattice and generate a rather stable organization: the *noo-semantic field* (or *noo-field*).[17]

The noo-field should not be confused with concepts such as "the conscious mind" or the "flow of consciousness." Given the diverse nonconscious processes that are associated with SeCos (see chapter 2), the ensemble of activated SeCos are necessarily much broader than the mental contents of awareness.

Essentially, the noo-field reflects the general activities and trends of the person for that time period. It may be viewed as a self-organizing system that has a distinct set of properties and self-organizes according to a semantic linkage process. (We will discuss the linkage process in the next chapter.)

The noo-field's configuration will change if major changes or significant events arrive in our life (e.g., getting a new job). Generally, the noo-field is relatively stable, insofar as most of our main activated SeCos tend to remain the same within a given time period (same work, same relationships, same house, and so forth). Despite their relative overall stability, activated SeCos are constantly going through a dynamical evolution, involving minute changes or more oscillatory states. Furthermore, all kinds of SeCos may be activated or created at any moment, and thus become part of the noo-field—as a result of new encounters and situations, discoveries, exploratory and innovative endeavors, news, data, and so forth. These SeCos remain in the person's noo-field as long as they are activated, then they gradually subside into the background—the lattice—until a new source reactivates them.

The passage of other SeCos through awareness may be even more transient, and thus not become part of the noo-field at all. Given the numerous sensory and intellectual events on a given day, fleeting links and currents of activation may run through some of the lattice's inactive SeCos as well, arousing brief linkages between elements. In the absence of a strong, prolonged, or repeated arousal that would trigger chain-linkages, the lattice-SeCo quickly returns to its inactive state. This, for example would be the case when, while reading a newspaper, we quickly browse through headlines, recognizing but discarding all kinds of topics or remarks that do not interest us. On the contrary, as soon as something of psychological import grabs our attention (translating into a substantial linkage process) the related SeCos become activated—at which point they may be reorganized, trigger the activation of associated SeCos, or even create new ones.

In general, then, the emergence of a SeCo into the noo-field is a function of:

• The psychological import of the content;
• The volume of elements simultaneously activated within the SeCo;
• The quantity of new links formed with existing elements;
• The number of elements added to the SeCos; and
• The degree to which the SeCos' organization is modified.

Thus, from a global perspective, we can distinguish three operational systems in the mind-psyche.

First there is the *flow of consciousness*, what we are aware of moment by moment, hour by hour. The flow of consciousness reflects the activity of the conscious mind vis-à-vis the attentional object of the moment—which, in the present model, corresponds to the currently activated SeCos. As we have seen, the results of operations from several SeCos keep intruding into consciousness.

A second, more global, system is the *noo-field*, the ensemble of activated SeCos in a given period—what we are intermittently aware of in a larger time span, rather than just momentarily. A number of SeCos, though not at the center of attentional focus, will tend to be more active, or primed in a given period or situation. For example, for a fan of skiing, the approach of winter and snow will tend to activate the "Ski" SeCo. Thus the noo-field includes all SeCos that intermittently may become the focus of attention.

Finally, *the lattice* is the totality of the person's SeCos, and thus includes those SeCos that, over time, have become inactive. For example, for an adult who has dropped all interest in playing the piano, "Piano Lessons" is a deactivated SeCo that has dropped out from the noo-field into the further reaches of the lattice.

Because it contains the activated SeCos, a certain portion of the noo-field is constantly dealing with our exchanges with the human and physical environment. Indeed, it is mainly through the noo-field that we interact with our environment (both natural and cultural). As we shall see in the next chapter, the environment is one of the triggers of the semantic linkage process: it is an "eco-semantic source," directly or indirectly activating SeCos and eliciting links that modify and influence the noo-field. The environment also exerts a more subtle but continuous influence on the psyche, stabilizing the ordinary state of consciousness and thus affecting the organizational state of the noo-field.

The inverse is also true: the noo-field influences and changes the environment. We are constantly—consciously and/or physiologically—interacting with the environment (even if this simply boils down to an armchair and a book!). In fact, insofar as the process of meaning-generation is itself an organizing process, both internally and externally, it follows that the noo-field must play a major role in the shaping of our environment—not only by our actions in and upon the world, but also at a semantic level. (More on this in chapter 9.) This makes the noo-field the privileged locus of mind-matter interaction, or, more precisely, of the interaction between semantic and physical dimensions.

NOTES

1. M. Gazzaniga (1985), *The social brain: Discovering the networks of the mind*, New York: Basic Books.

2. B. J. Baars (1988), *A cognitive theory of consciousness,* Cambridge, MA: Cambridge University Press.

3. A. Newell (1973), Productions systems. Models of control structures, in W. Chase (Ed.), *Visual information processing*, New York: Academic Press.

The GWS concept was first developed by Newell in 1973, as an artificial intelligence (AI) formalism. Newell proposed a new formal structure for symbolic logic operations, which he named a "production system." This AI system, or computer, is divided into two structures. The first is a Workspace, analogous to a bulletin board, where symbols are posted. The second is a Production structure that houses condition/action pairs (the bureaucrats). Each bureaucrat constantly watches the symbols on the bulletin board, and when it sees it, goes into action. For instance, if the symbol A shows up (meaning, condition A has been fulfilled), then the corresponding A-production is evoked, and A-action is executed.

In this production system, no orders are ever given. It is a data-driven system, insofar as the symbols are responsible for evoking operations. It is also a environment-driven system, because the symbols may derive either from the production or from the environment. Furthermore, it is distributive and modular, as new symbol/production pairs may be added without modifying the rest of the system (Haugeland, 1985). Such properties, which are typical of neural networks and parallel distributive systems, are quite astonishing for a symbol-based system.

What I find most interesting is the fact that actions are not directed centrally, but are triggered by different parts of the system. Nevertheless, there are some major drawbacks to this model. Although the environment is taken into account, it is viewed in a most deterministic fashion, since no generative work is done on the raw environmental data; its only effect, "evoked" though it may be, is the execution of whatever action is a priori associated with it. In other words, even if "evoked," rather than being "ordered" (as in classical symbolic systems), the outcome still has an inevitable quality about it. Basically, we are back to the old stimulus/response coupling.

As Pylyshyn (1981) pointed out, the central system (WS) is incapable of control: it cannot change a process that has been initiated or even agree on a particular procedure. Similarly, there is little room in this approach for generativity. The stream of consciousness (the bulletin board) is not supposed to perform any work itself on these symbolic expressions. Similarly, we cannot look toward the "bureaucrats" for choice or generativity. Actions performed at the distributed production level do not allow for the slightest initiative or decision. The whole system is completely deterministic in its tight coupling of production-action pairs. Whatever its merits in artificial intelligence, when it comes to human cognition, this model seems to be extremely deterministic, as this system cannot produce anything new. Z. Pylyshyn (1981), Complexity and the study of artificial and human intelligence, in J. Haugeland (Ed.), *Mind design,* Cambridge, MA: MIT Press. See also Haugeland (1981).

4. Combs (1996).

5. B. Goertzel (1994), *Chaotic logic. Language, thought and reality from the perspective of complex systems science,* New York: Plenum Press.

Goertzel viewed the mind as consisting of two interlaced and superposed networks, each one having its specific organization and dynamics: the *structurally associative memory* (or heterarchical network), and the *multilevel control hierarchy* (hierarchical network, or perceptual-motor hierarchy). The organization of the control network is a pyramidal hierarchy of networks/ processes, where commands are passed down from higher levels to the ones underneath. In their turn, each level gives feedback to the level above as to the efficiency achieved. Thus control moves down the network while feedback moves upward. For example, in motor actions, the order to raise an arm is given by the higher level, and then increasingly specialized and local instructions are passed down to the minute muscle tensions of the lower level.

As for the memory network, assimilated to a long-term memory, it is structured through associative processes and relies upon contiguity of similar entities. Goertzel viewed the dynamical properties of both control and memory networks as governed by trial and error: subnetworks are swapped or copied, and the larger network tests the effectiveness of the new hierarchical organization. The evolution of the dual network is based on the implementation of nonlinear algorithms, which he called "the cognitive equation," allowing for the emergence of new, higher level processes. In his model, though, it is difficult to figure out the integration of the two types of properties—control and associativity—insofar as they are supported by two different organizational structures.

6. Let us recall that there is no such thing as a unitary element in the psyche. I use the term "element" as a shortcut to represent specific clusters; these are generally quite complex, involving both processes and concepts.

7. As mentioned earlier, this modular SeCos architecture is consistent with a number of observations in clinical psychology, and with the general frameworks of both transpersonal psychology and psychoanalysis.

8. Several well known creativity techniques, such as Synectics and Bionics, are in fact based upon purposeful juxtapositions of distant domains. Whether used in business, technological, or scientific applications, these creativity techniques use concepts that are seemingly remote from the problem at hand in order to trigger novel insights.

9. Lashley (1988).

10. Changeux (1997).

11. This competition between localization and distribution frameworks resembles, in my opinion, the competition between corpuscular and wave theories of light, which dominated theoretical physics until Louis de Broglie proposed a framework for the fundamentally dual nature of light. Just as in the case of the two physics paradigms, proponents of brain localization find more

and more finely localized brain constraints (in specific zones, or groups of neurons), bearing on the proper working of functions; while proponents of distributed parallel processing have based their arguments on functions like memory or perception.

12. Schacter (1987).

13. On priming in networks, see chapter 1.

14. See the Technotalk example, chapters 5 and 6.

15. C. A. Skarda & W. J. Freeman (1987), How brains make chaos in order to make sense of the world, *Behavioral and brain sciences, 10,* 161–95.

16. Studies have indeed shown that dedicated brain areas are very appreciably enlarged with specific learning.

17. "Noo," from the Greek *noesis*, refers to "the act of thinking." Noo-semantic thus signifies thinking that makes sense, thinking that confers meaning.

4

THE MIND'S DYNAMICS

Having described the mind's architecture, we now turn to its dynamics. What kind of mechanisms or processes can account for the mind's exquisite flexibility and its capacity to transform itself? AI formalisms have introduced the classical hardware/software division to distinguish between architecture and processing. They have also introduced the distinction between processing rules and the data to which these rules are applied. Nevertheless, the astonishing processing feats of intelligent computers should not lead us into thinking that mental computations abide by similar constraints; in fact, there is good reason to question the pertinence of such partitionings as far as living systems are concerned.

In this chapter, I propose a basic connective dynamic that functions as an activation process. While activating and linking semantic elements, it also modifies the structure of semantic constellations—all the way down to neural organization. Inversely the SeCos' architecture influences the activation process, as the latter will tend to follow the most weighted paths in the SeCo. Thus, there is a strong mutual influence and co-dependence between structure and dynamics.

DYNAMIC ACTIVATION

Mind-brain Interactions

The mental processes involved in complex intuitive problem solving are certainly among the most challenging for any model of human cognition. In this context, the first issue worth reflecting upon is how conscious thought is able to trigger and precisely orient nonconscious linguistic, semantic, and neurological processes, once the individual decides to tackle a mental problem. For example, how do we seek out a precise memory that contains information relevant to the problem at hand? More generally, how does intentional thought selectively activate relevant neural pathways and processes in several different areas of the brain, independently of an external stimulus?

The symbolic or computational hypothesis—that a command (or a program) executes a fixed set of algorithmic operations—seems especially inadequate here. To send a specific order, in the sense of implementing a logical operation according to predetermined rules, the brain/mind would have to

1. know in advance the exact rules that apply to this specific problem, that is, the appropriate logical operations (this is only possible in a small number of cases, such as certain mathematical problems); or

2. know all possible responses, thus only needing to select the appropriate one (given applicable rules or constraints); or

3. know the solution, and only need to determine the rule that applies in the particular case.

These three situations presuppose a logical system that would be complete and self-consistent (i.e., one in which all propositions are necessarily true). Such a system would permit neither fuzziness, nor error, nor competition between rules or possible solutions. Furthermore, it could not itself evaluate its own propositions (as true/false), and therefore it could not judge the validity of its own operations. According to John Searle, such a system could not have any understanding of the operations it is performing[1]; it would be even less capable of accounting for *human* self-reflection.[2]

Note that in rule-based systems, all activities are command-driven. By contrast, in neural nets or dynamical systems, we do have rules as well, but they are just activation rules. These nonlinear activation rules (nonlinear algorithms) just set up the way a system is going to self-organize: for example, in a network, they define how weights are going to be adjusted.[3]

Rule-bound symbolic operations cannot adequately deal with even common problem-solving. Humans typically improvise solutions from materials or methods that either did not exist before or were not used in similar ways; we often grope toward a goal that is itself vague or ill-defined and that only becomes clear during the problem-solving process.

Also, as shown by studies done in view of the elaboration of expert systems, human experts appreciate a situation and behave according to heuristic rules of thumb that are far from clearly defined. This led Roger Penrose to propose that the mind makes use of non-algorithmic processes.[4] Indeed several non-algorithmic alternatives have been proposed to model the mind's processing—quantum processes (quantum potentials, interference patterns, quantum void, quantum computers), topology and morphogenetic fields.[5]

As we have seen, even in the simple act of forming a single statement, the mind triggers—and somehow directs—extensive nonconscious processes, searches and computations, at neural and semantic levels. This brings us to another mental feat worth reflecting upon: the mind is able to maintain a semantic-neural coherence, even though part of the semantic process may drift in and out of awareness. This demands both a coherent connection between divergent processes and the action of convergent processes that would bring the results of the divergent linkages back to the flow of consciousness.

One-to-one Correspondence. In my opinion, none of these mental traits can be addressed through models positing a strict linear-causal linkage between brain and mind—as assumed by theories positing a "one-to-one" correspondence between neural and mental events. For one thing, I doubt whether we can really single out "events," either on the neural or the mental side, as it is impossible to sort out which level of complexity defines a supposed event.

For example, in forming a phrase during a dialogue, what is the key mental event? a single word? the sum of the words? the image in the person's mind to which the words are referring? As we have seen, even a single word has complex meanings that are entirely dependent upon the context.

If we turn now to the neural side, what is the supposed corresponding event? a single neuron firing? a group of neurons? a pattern of activity? Neural processes are themselves part of, or contain, other systems: so, where do we stop and delimit "the" neuronal pattern? Also, fixed patterns do not really exist, as such, in the functioning brain: they are snapshots of processes that continuously evolve in time and mingle with other processes. It is just as difficult to single out a pattern in a time frame as it is in a spatial or structural frame.

A yet trickier problem arises with the concept of a one-to-one causal principle: a strictly linear causality between two definite terms (whatever they may be) would in no way be able to account for the interpretational flexibility we display, for example, our capacity for subtle or abrupt shifts in outlook or perspective. If each word is tied to a specific neural pattern, how does a subtle change of *context* trigger abundant laughter—as in jokes?

The linear-causal representation of mental-neural interactions fails because it assumes the application of a strictly causal event—a *command*—to strongly delimited and *invariant* items. In other words, it poses a partition between a command system (the rules or algorithms) and a system of data on which the rules apply. By contrast, mental processes point to nonlinear dynamics and self-transforming systems, the subsystems being in mutual interaction and co-evolving.[6] As Karl Pribram proposes, "The mind-brain connection is composed of intimate reciprocal self-organizing procedures at every level of neural organization. High-level psychological processes such as those involved in cognition are therefore the result of cascades of biopsychological bootstrapping operations."[7]

The mind-brain shows self-organization, that is, the capacity to reorganize itself internally. In such self-organizing and self-transforming systems, the dynamics are an integral part of what constitutes the system itself: *elements of the system are themselves transformed by the dynamical process*. This is what we saw with concepts: by interacting with each other, concepts not only produce new concepts but are themselves transformed.

A Transversal Mental-neural Network

Many brain scientists, as I have pointed out earlier, now view the brain's neuronal and subneuronal activity in terms of network dynamics. For example, Pribram distinguishes between a "surface structure" (the circuitry of neural pathways) and a "deep structure" (the distributed, network-type web of connections at the synaptodendritic level).[8] This framework is somewhat analogous to the two levels of mental functioning I have proposed: a high-level logical and rational thinking process, and a low-level connective architecture and dynamics, instantiated in the semantic constellations.

I posit a transversal network-type organization between semantic and neural levels of organization. This underlying, network-based level of semantic processes is hypothesized to interconnect with neuronal and subneuronal networks—whereby semantic networks branch into neuronal networks in a distributed, parallel and dynamical fashion. We thus have two interlaced and interwoven dynamical-network systems. Each system's configuration, and their common interlacing, are both products of self-organizing dynamics. This, indeed, is what I mean by *transversal mental-neural network:* the interlacing of mental and neural networks into a single, comprehensive whole.

In this transversal mental-neural network, links between neural networks and semantic processes (sensations, qualia, judments, names, etc.) are instantiated through the subject's experience. Thus, while these mental-neural links do follow genetically weighted brain pathways, experience enriches and complexifies them enormously; as well-recognized, each person's fine-grained brain organization ends up being highly unique (even if, at a coarser grain, we find global similarities between brain structures).

The self-organization of coupled mental-neural systems which interact with and influence each other, leads to co-evolution: the two systems respond to one another through coupled processes, and the links are generally reinforced over time. Just as an artificial hidden-units network may organize itself to respond to—and recognize—a specific shape, in the same way a brain's neural network may organize itself to respond to a specific semantic cluster (and vice-versa). Thus, a SeCo may have numerous branchings into neuronal and subneuronal networks, spread out throughout different brain areas. Once specific links are made between mental and neural processes, they may complexify with time, but basically they remain accessible as paths that will be more or less weighted by further experience. A chain-linkage activating one of the linked clusters (whether neuronal or semantic) will automatically trigger the activation of the coupled system, unless an alternative or competitive path has been established.

In order to account for the human ability to choose and modify one's behavior or ideas, as well as mental evolution, innovation, and intelligent adaptation to context, I suggest we need four things.

First, there must be *network-type links* between neural and mental clusters and processes—that is densely woven two-way pathways and many orthogonal, crisscrossing junctions, thus allowing for alternative or even competing routes.

Second, we need a *lattice of linked systems, organized into subsystems*. These must be complex enough to include clusters of alternative or competitive options—a variety of possible viewpoints or perspectives, and a range of possible neural organizations and processes. Such a network organization, with various densely intersecting clusters, would account for adaptive variations—and, hence, learning. It would also entail the creation of specific subnetworks, as well as the evolution of the organization of the lattice as a whole. This kind of architecture may also allow us to understand some of the more astonishing feats of mental reorganization—for example, when a young child loses one cerebral hemisphere, the other one reorganizes itself to assume the missing brain functions.

This complex structure must also involve complex dynamics. So, the third thing we need is a *nonlinear activation process* that must fulfill two conditions: (1) nonlinearity and sensitivity to initial conditions, leading to a wide array of possible developments; and (2) self-transformation, in that the entities undergoing the activation process must *themselves* change along the way.

The fourth attribute needed is *self-organization*. This must be a property of the clusters themselves, grounding the self-organization of the whole lattice.

Integrating these four features, I propose we view mind-brain interactions through *a dynamical linkage process that plays on a dense transversal mental-neural network organization*. Given the SeCos cognitive architecture, it is posited that whole semantic clusters within each SeCo are idiosyncratically network-linked (not causally tied) to neural clusters. Furthermore, these SeCos' networks are so complex that they contain the diverse meaning-clusters of a concept, alternative behaviors, as well as an array of neural and sensorimotor processes. Thus, when a SeCo is activated, the mind is presented with an array of previously experienced mental *and* neural behaviors, as alternative weighted paths *within* a single SeCo. At the same time, the posited connective activation process, which is of a dynamical-network type, permits self-organization, distribution of processes, retroactive learning, and functional customization through gradual adaptive dynamics. The system's diversity and complexity would thus readily allow for the creation of a novel mental-neural behavior whenever the context brings new activation triggers.

The Semantic Linkage Process

Having reviewed the architectural organization of the lattice (see chapter 3), let us now turn to the activation process.

In the semantic fields model, mental processes such as thinking, meaning-creation, and choice all basically depend upon the activation and linkage of different SeCos. An understanding of the dynamics of SeCo activation, and of the different sources responsible for such activation, is therefore crucial to our understanding of the mind.

I propose the existence of a spontaneous dynamical process creating or activating links between semantic elements. I call it the *semantic linkage process*.

The semantic linkage process is set into motion by a set of similarities between the triggering impulse and a SeCo in the person's noo-field. This dynamic, however, is bound to simultaneously activate all kinds of linked elements in the SeCo—some of which will be quite dissimilar or even contradictory to the original trigger.

The linkage dynamic is a low-level process, working conjointly with consciously driven thought processes; it is connective and divergent in nature. As we shall see, it can be triggered by various sources: percepts, the conscious flow of thoughts, and nonintentional mental processes. In all cases, the initial activation impulse (intention, feeling, percept) remains attached to the dynamical activation process; even if attention drifts to another topic (or SeCo), the linkage process follows its course in the noo-field, activating elements coherent with the initial impulse, or related, emotionally charged contents.

It is clear that we cannot explore this spontaneous linkage process directly; but we *can* infer its dynamics indirectly, for example, through an analysis of spontaneously occurring associations. This approach is reminiscent of psychoanalysts' potent methods for surfacing clusters of psychic contents (e.g., complexes) through patients' free associations or through analysis of spontaneous symbolic linkages in dreams or "waking dreams."[9] I assume, then, that by analyzing just a simple train of thought (excluding logical or procedural tasks), we can highlight the basic connective workings of the mind—that is, *spontaneous chain-linkages*.

"Saint Bernard" SeCo. An example will suffice. Loh's currently activated SeCo is "Go buy the newspaper." On the way, she sees a person walking a beautiful gray-blue, long-haired dog. The dog reminds her of a Saint Bernard; yet she knows that is not its breed. Loh starts thinking, "It would be nice to have a dog, a beautiful and calm dog, just like this one." She remembers her flat was broken into recently, and reflects that such a dog could protect her flat from robbers. She also recalls a story about a Saint Bernard that saved a person lost in the snow-covered peaks of the Swiss Alps.

Let us analyze the chain-linkages triggered by the perception of the dog.

• Elements of percept include: big dog, long-haired, calm.

- These activate a "Saint Bernard" cluster of elements in the "Dog" SeCo.
- This brings on the interpretation: he is like a Saint Bernard.
- The cluster also highlights discrepant elements like different shape and color and hence the interpretation: this is not a Saint Bernard.
- In the "Dog" SeCo, the concepts "Dogs as Guardian of House" and "Dogs as Protection" are activated; this occurs because the recent robbery is still an active cluster in the noo-field, and it evokes a highly charged feeling of "need to protect myself." Thus the cluster "Robbery" within the "My Flat" SeCo is activated simultaneously.
- This leads to the conclusion: a dog could be a good solution, and it would be nice if it were such a calm and beautiful one.
- The concept "Protection" linked to Saint Bernard dogs activates the story contained in the "Saint Bernard" SeCo and linked to the Swiss Alps.

In this case, where the activation source is a set of sensory data, the linkage process activates semantic clusters that show maximal matches with the perceived features and/or some related, highly charged content.

Of course, not *all* existing dog clusters are activated; that would lead to a very unmanageable flood of links (reminiscent of what happens when you trigger a search on the World Wide Web, using a very broad substantive like "computers" or "psychology"). Instead, the process instantiated here is quite specific: based on a maximum number of matches (as in a pattern-recognition network), it evokes only the closest dog-type contained in the lattice. The new links then spring forth from that precise concept, based on the concept's most noticed (i.e., highly weighted) qualities, or based on similarities to a highly charged cluster.

It thus seems likely that specific properties or qualities of the initial impulse (e.g., an objective, a feeling, or an emotional state) will be retained and passed along the activation process. This serves to maintain the initial semantic dynamic, avoiding too much divergence and inefficient branching and consequently helping to build coherency into the process.

At the same time, while the linkage process connects clusters showing some similarities, it is likely that these same clusters (or embedding SeCos) will also contain dissimilarities, divergences, and discrepancies. As a result, this brings into the thinking process diversified elements and links that specify and modulate comparisons and distinctions, thus grounding an intelligent discriminative process (e.g., this dog looks like, but is not, a Saint Bernard). The more diversified and dissimilar the elements, the longer the SeCo remains in an unstable state, sorting out comparisons and thus triggering new chain-linkages. Inversely, the more similar the elements, the quicker the mind achieves a stable recognition or judgment, and the quicker the activation process settles down.

Through diverse experiences, then, our thought-processes create and implement specific links between diversified elements/processes and help "mold" the SeCos' general configuration.

If the subject lives a truly novel experience (for example, one with very paradoxical contextual elements), then new links and, therefore, new paths will be created through the activated SeCos (or previously unrelated SeCos will suddenly be linked). The whole system thus reorganizes itself and adopts a novel configuration, its diversity and complexity readily allowing for the creation of novel mental-neural linkages.

On the other hand, SeCos may show an already organized configuration of elements and links that have been constructed through repeated experiences. A SeCo then acts as an *attractor* that influences and organizes subsequent experiences, in the sense that its internal processes or states will tend to be reenacted in similar situations.[10] Thus "familiar" experiences have specific habitual pathways for moving through that SeCo. Patterned behaviors might be seen as weighted paths in the SeCo-network, or, in dynamical terms, as trajectories in the attractor basin. Repetition of similar experiences in similar contexts presumably reinforces these paths.

Likewise, paths are affected by the "qualifiers" that express different relationships between the clusters. For example, in his mind, George does not link John to Raymond in the way he links him to Hal; he sees John as Raymond's colleague of but as Hal's competitor. Such qualifiers of links can be represented as *semantic relators* (e.g., friend of, opposite to, preceding, leading to, etc.) that are retained or memorized during the linkage process. Two clusters, then, may be related by an indefinite number of links.

Working conjointly with higher-level consciously driven thought-processes, this fine-grained, low-level, spontaneous linkage process can apply to any form of semantic interaction—between internal SeCos, between the mind and eco-fields, between two persons' noo-fields. We can formulate the semantic linkage process as follows: Given an activation source (percept, concept, or process), if any cluster of currently activated semantic elements presents precise similarities with another cluster (contained in any internal constellation or surrounding semantic field), then the clusters have a certain probability to form a link. The more numerous or highly charged the similarities, the greater the likelihood that a linkage will be generated. Once the link is made between two clusters, then the more specific or highly charged the discrepancies, the more dynamical and generative the linkage process.

Through its great flexibility and plasticity, as well as its capacity for associating and recombining, the linkage process renders the semantic lattice as a highly dynamic system, showing continuous cross-connections and interactions. The dynamics involved are thus perfectly suited to form the basis of creative and evolving mental processes.

The major points can be summarized as follows:

1. The linkage process either creates new links and reorganizes the whole SeCo, or it follows existing links; in the latter case, the path followed depends on (a) the weights attributed to links, as in current neural nets (the higher weight showing the most probable trajectory) and (b) the coherency with the initial impulse. These two parameters modulate each other.

2. A semantic cluster is activated on the basis of the maximum number of matches with the activation source (concept, percept, or process), or on the basis of the high charge of one specific match.

3. The linkage process remains coherent with the initial impulse (internal or contextual); it keeps track of the links formed and also memorizes the specific semantic relators attached to the links.

4. In general, the process appears as a building of coherency and a creation of meaning. It dynamically sustains the activation beyond primary perceptual (pattern-recognition) processes to induce further activations and links. It also organizes the ensemble of newly linked elements into a new SeCo. In this sense, it is a dynamic self-organizing process, oriented toward the building of meaning.

Given this framework, we can now turn to an analysis of the sources of SeCo activation, that is, the diverse triggers of linkage processes.

SEMANTIC ACTIVATION SOURCES

Internal versus External Activation

In classical cognitive psychology, mental processes are viewed as internal computations on invariant memorized concepts that take on transient qualifications as a function of a given experience. In this "constructed theory of perception," the stimulus is seen simply as a trigger of complex internal processes. Perception, essentially, is a constructed process involving the building of representations internal to the subject. By contrast, the "direct perception" model rejects the concepts of internal construction and of internal representations altogether. It states perception is directly determined by the surfaces and optical features of the environment. Thus, in his *ecological theory,* James Gibson viewed the environment as a rich source of structured information that offers opportunities (or "affordances") for actions and attitudes to the members of a species.[11] (There is more on Gibson's theory in chapter 6.)

Several researchers have proposed intermediate positions that admit both constructed internal processes and a structured input from external events. Indeed, the inherent limitations of both extreme positions are becoming increasingly evident. First, brain scientists are discovering the extreme complexity of processes triggered by the activation of sensory pathways while also noting their wide distribution in diverse brain areas; this shows that stimuli and their effects are of a highly complex nature. At the same time, the enormous connectivity between sensory pathways and the associative cortex clearly points to a "construction" of sensory experience, building on previous experiences and implying analysis of the stimuli. Finally, psychologists and sociologists are establishing the major influence of both context and object-attributes upon perception— while also noting the real time adaptation of behavioral responses to a specific context.

In short, diverse lines of research lend credence to *both* hypotheses concerning the nature of perception. The most sound position, it would seem, would be to admit both the influence of the environment and the reality of internally constructed processes. This is the position taken by brain scientist Karl Pribram in his *holonomic theory.*[12] For Pribram, form recognition is influenced both by internal processes, reflecting the subject's past experiences and by sensory inputs. He proposes that the receptive fields of neurons in the visual cortex are sensitive to a specific frequency bandwidth. Sensory receptors are metaphorically akin to a piano keyboard and maintain a specific connection to neurons' receptive fields, just as piano keys are linked to strings attuned to a particular frequency. Pribram states that neuronal networks, in addition to their inherent capacity of self-organization, are subject to two different sources of constraints: those derived from sensory inputs (bottom-up processes) and those generated internally (acting as top-down procedures).[13]

Taking a rather different approach, Francisco Varela suggests that cognition is a constructive process that develops in conjunction with perceptual processes and motor acts. Cognition is "embodied": it involves a participation in the world, which Varela describes as *enaction.*[14] The cognitive subject and its milieu are linked through a coupling dynamic, and perturbations arising from the environment continuously force the cognitive system to reorganize itself. Note, though, that in this theory, no information is exchanged through the coupling process. Varela is strongly opposed to the cognitivist paradigm, involving commands and information transfer. The environment exerts no causal influence, except as a perturbation that forces the system to reorganize itself in order to maintain its own individuality. Rather than exchanging information, the two coupled systems adjust to each other in a continual process of internal reorganization. Maturana and Varela have proposed the concept of *autopoiesis* (or self-creation) to signify a system re-creating its own organization, thus maintaining its individuality, its specificity, and its separateness from the background.[15]

Another interesting approach is Pierre Lévy's *cognitive ecology*, which develops the concept of a "human/machine thinking collective"—in which subjects and objects are both seen as agents in a social-cognitive network.[16] For Lévy, the thinking subject is, by definition, a collective subject, using "transpersonal" modes of thinking. The human/machine thinking collectives include not only individuals but also social organisms and objects (such as books and libraries, computers, information storage devices, simulation systems, and so forth). For example, computer technologies, Lévy states, "structure the collective cognitive network and contribute in determining its properties."[17] Thus in Lévy's framework, objects and subjects, as well as social organisms, are seen as agents co-creating a cognitive network.

It is encouraging that at least some researchers (such as Gibson and Lévy) explicitly recognize that the environment has been in-formed by meaning and thus constitutes organized information, influencing or participating in the semantic organization of individuals. From my own perspective, it seems self-evident that a theory should account not only for the person's internal meaning construction but also for the meaning embodied in social structures and objects, as well as this meaning's influence on the mental processes of a person. It also seems to me that a simple binary categorization, in terms of internal versus external sources of semantic activation, does not do justice to the complexity of the processes involved. I propose to consider four activation sources: three internal—intentional, procedural processes, and nonintentional—and one originating in the environment itself. (See Figure 4.1)

Four Activation Sources

Intentional Activation Source (I-S). Earlier, we saw that nonconscious mental processes remain coherent with the initial intention: thematically related ideas keep surfacing, even though the conscious mind is preoccupied with other tasks. Let us examine this in more detail.

The central dynamic is a spontaneous activation of links between semantic clusters of the intention and clusters from other SeCos. The consciously activated constellation triggers new links, activating specific constellations, and further spreading the semantic connectivities.

Far from being a simple command, the intentional source triggers complex divergent processes that may fall out of the flow of consciousness. Simultaneously, the intentional source acts as the center, or focus, of a convergent process; linking elements of diverse constellations in a novel way, it spontaneously constitutes a new semantic path or cluster that remains organized around its original impulse, thus weaving part of the train of thought as long as attention remains focused on it.[18]

This would explain why results of nonconscious processing return to the flow of consciousness. Since the original source is an intention, the nucleus of the newly formed constellation remains within the larger scope of the noo-field. As meanings generated from spontaneous linkages remain connected to the initial impulse, and to the cluster's nucleus, they will thus tend to re-emerge into the flow of consciousness.

Furthermore, since the cluster is formed from both consciously and nonconsciously assembled elements and connections, it remains in an unstable yet active state that may produce new and spontaneous emergences of meaning over an indefinite period of time. This might help explain how sudden problem-solving ideas and flashes of intuition can still occur although we have stopped thinking about a problem.

The hypothesized dynamic may also account for the efficacy of self-suggestion, whereby one tends to obtain the desired effect or result even when the intermediate mental processes remain completely nonconscious—as in the well-known example of successfully programming oneself to wake up at an inhabitual time. (An example of an I-S process is given at the end of this chapter: "Synergy" SeCo.)

Procedural Processing (P-P). Linear or sequential information processing, which is procedural in nature, is another internal source of semantic activation.

Procedural knowledge has been equated to the automatic, nonconscious performance of procedures that have been overlearned—for example, walking or typing. Note that even in these cases, the automatic behavior may be triggered by an intention (go to the garden, type this sentence, etc.).

Figure 4.1
Sources of Semantic Activation

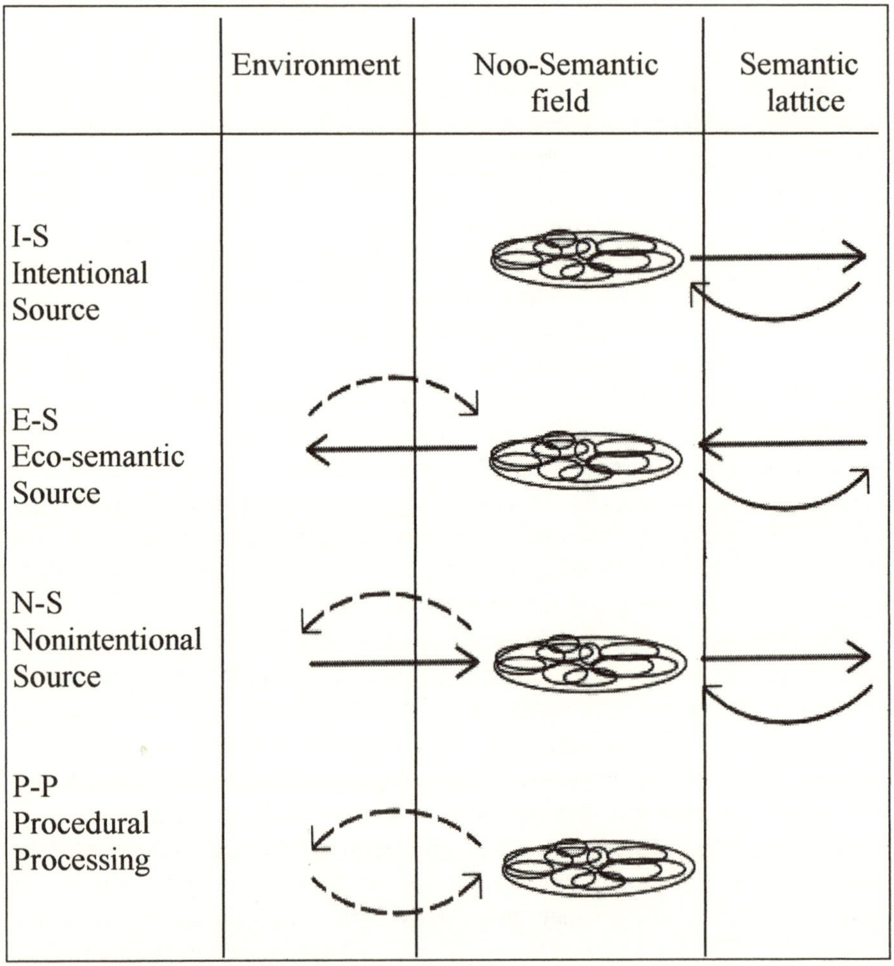

	Environment	Noo-Semantic field	Semantic lattice
I-S Intentional Source			
E-S Eco-semantic Source			
N-S Nonintentional Source			
P-P Procedural Processing			

In the context of the semantic fields model, procedural processing implies any series of actions that follow a procedure or preselected rule. It could involve swimming toward a goal, building a table, assembling a machine, but it also includes a game played according to rules or a mathematical operation. Thus depending upon where one is at in the learning process, procedural processing may be wholly automatic, semiautomatic, or still needing the person's full attention.

In the present model, P-P is viewed as a subset of intentional activation sources (I-S). Its difference from I-S is that P-P activations, while intentionally triggered, follow predefined rules, procedures, or links, thereby minimizing spontaneous divergence processes. Thus, if nothing unusual happens during the procedure to differentiate it from earlier occurrences, then the constellation will undergo only minimal modifications.

These are the mental operations that are most readily explicable in computational terms. On the other hand, what appears to be strictly computational in nature could, in fact, involve far more complex processes. It is clear that countless novel semantic and neurological treatments *could* be triggered in the course of P-P processing. Nothing strictly precludes spontaneous activations of links of the I-S type. Although attention may be focused on the application of the procedure, auxiliary links may still be generated. For example, a musician performing from a written score—a procedural activity—is nevertheless in an intensely generative state of mind. However unlikely it may seem, even a mathematician in the midst of rule-bound mathematical operations may experience aesthetic and meaningful insights, thus generating processes of the I-S type in the midst of procedural processing. (We will review an example of the acquisition of a skill in chapter 6: the "Drawing Skill" SeCo.)

Nonintentional Activation Source (N-S). An activation source does not need to be a specific objective, intention, or problem to be solved. The noo-field includes a large number of SeCos that may not be the current focus of attention, but that are nevertheless sensitized or "primed." A relatively minor trigger may then activate one of these SeCos, thus initiating a nonconscious semantic linkage process. In such cases, the chain-linkage has little to do with the stimulus itself; it is mostly based on existing internal constellations.

For example, consider the case of a photographer who specializes on ecological issues and is on vacation in some foreign country. After unpacking, she and her friends are on the way to a bar, discussing their travel plans. Though not thinking about her profession in any way, her mind keeps nonconsciously registering all kinds of subtle details about the environment, triggering chain-linkages. Later on, the results of this nonconscious processing may emerge as an insight or understanding about ecological issues in the country.

Another instance of N-S is based on the existence of unconscious clusters that people have incorporated from their family or culture at an early age. In other words, the psyche has been "contaminated" by these value/behavior clusters that are like fixated or encysted SeCos and resist transformation. People are then prone to fall into particular patterns of behavior and thought as soon as a trigger activates these SeCos. We will analyze an example of this type of N-S at the end of the chapter: the "Synergy" SeCo.

The N-S may also be a recent situation or experience that has had a strong impact—a remark made by someone, a word, a place, a film, and so forth. An activation process is triggered precisely because the individual's semantic lattice is already "sensitized" to the stimulus as it contains similar, and highly charged, materials. Here we encounter a fundamental dynamic known in psychoanalysis—a person who has been traumatized by a semantic element (situation, behavior, object) reacts very strongly when again confronted by this element, or a similar situation.

In the case of an experience that has been particularly traumatic, the corresponding SeCo is so strongly fixated, and the path through it so heavily weighted, that we will probably encounter pathological behaviors. Overreactions to a seemingly innocuous statement, projection mechanisms, and obsessive-compulsive syndromes all belong to this category.

Eco-semantic Source (E-S). In every situation we face highly organized systems—persons, work groups, buildings, holiday resorts, institutions— that can be viewed as semantic fields. In the present model the environment is seen as imbued with meaning, implying both collective and personal significations. Thus, the environment constitutes a fourth activation source, over and above the three internal ones. We will call it an "eco-semantic" source.

Though external to the individual, the eco-semantic source is by no means synonymous to the concept of "stimulus" as used in behaviorist psychology. In fact, I think it is misguided to try to model the complexities of human behavior using the most simplistic of concepts. After all, human beings rarely find themselves in situations like these of a mouse that is rewarded with food for certain behavior (and even mice themselves rarely experience such simplistic situations in nature!). It may be convenient, and easier, to illustrate cognitive processes with the simplest perceptual stimuli (a tree, a red ball); but if we were to systematically consider complex perceptual and cognitive tasks, perhaps we would avoid oversimplifications, such as the concept of stimulus, and give the environment its due.

For example, take a newly released graphic design program. Clearly, meaning is already organized within this tool by its author, and its semantic organization includes complex mental constraints upon users who need to understand its functioning and its architecture, as well as its possibilities. It is much more than a collection of discrete stimuli, or a mere trigger for internal cognitive processes. On the other hand, users will tend to manipulate the tool according to their own needs and desires; they will develop their own rapport with it, they will make it their own—perhaps going so far as to modify it, or use it in a way not intended by the author.

"Film" SeCo. So let us reflect on a "real" eco-semantic source, that is, a semantically complex situation. Consider a person going to see a movie. A film is a very complex semantic constellation because it reflects a highly organized web of significations. The plot, the scenes, the setting, the actions and dialogue, the musical score—all these have been put together in such a way as to produce a certain impact, to deliver a particular message, or, at any rate, to instill a certain state of mind in spectators. Each viewer, of course, will react somewhat differently, his or her interpretation being a function of his or her own semantic lattice. However, this interpretative process is neither voluntary nor intentional. The film's semantic constellation, with all its rich elements and implicit connections, spontaneously activates resonant and connective elements in the spectator's semantic lattice.

Actually, only some of the links that are spontaneously formed will be grasped in "real time" by the viewer's conscious mind; whatever the degree of conscious creative participation, a much broader "Film" SeCo is formed in the viewer's psyche. Connective processing within this constellation may continue for hours or even days, bringing forth new emergents of meaning into the flow of consciousness.

Here we have a complex organized constellation in the environment acting as a source; the resulting specific semantic activation blends with the pre-existing, internal constellations, and thus constructs the overall meaning that the spectator attributes to the film. In the particular case of watching a film—which leaves little time for the conscious mind to reflect—the flow of consciousness is mostly a transitional space, and the external constellations are powerful activation sources. In other circumstances, as in an exchange with another person, internal and external sources of activation are more balanced. (More on this in chapter 11.)

SELF-REFLECTION AND TRANSFORMATION

The challenge, for any cognitive theory, is to understand how a mental process can be activated internally, solely on the basis of the person's intentions, decisions, or affective state, and how this process may thus lead to the creation of new significations and values. In terms of the present theory, this means understanding how an intention or a state of consciousness can bring about a radical modification of the internal state of the system (a bifurcation), leading to a major reorganization of existing SeCos or the creation of new ones.

Dreams certainly constitute a mental process that is wholly internal to the person, and that can nevertheless help generate new meanings. Although, with some notable exceptions, dreams are nonintentional,[19] conative processes (such as intention) can come into play through the person's later analysis of the dream and subsequent actions. The following example highlights a self-transformative process, confronting a fixated constellation; it will enable us to study both intentional and nonintentional activation sources.

"Synergy" SeCo

Take the example of David, who one fine summer night had a powerful dream. While analyzing it, he realizes that social interrelations based on authority and social hierarchies are highly inefficient and that they often lead to negative results. He comes to recognize that synergistic interrelations—based on cooperative exchange—are a good alternative to hierarchical relationships. He thus decides to consciously pursue and develop these latter kinds of relationships in his life. His reflection on "hierarchy versus synergy" also leads him to nurture and evolve a new set of values, one appropriate to the synergistic actions and behaviors he is looking to adopt.

Let us say that all concepts and behaviors associated with the issue of interpersonal style, and based on hierarchical values, form the earlier, fixated SeCo "Authority." While evolving a new set of values, David is thus creating, in himself, the seed of a new SeCo—let us call it "Synergy." On the basis of these new concepts, he begins to experiment and explore the world in a quite different way and to develop new interpersonal styles. In the process, his multiple experiential discoveries lead to the evolution and expansion of the SeCo's elements, thus strengthening the association between synergy concepts and his new interpersonal attitudes.

In short, the process of dream analysis has led to:

1. A critique of the concepts of authority and hierarchy, leading to a mostly nonconscious reorganization of the internal SeCo "Authority";

2. The conscious creation of a new SeCo "Synergy," organized around the basic

concept of Synergy, and linking the dream experience, its interpretation, new relational values, and novel relational experiences;

3. A voluntary decision to nurture and promote synergistic values and attitudes in life.

A very similar process has been described by David Feinstein and Stanley Krippner as a way to liberate oneself from the entanglement of fixed, outdated schemas, which they call "old myths." The authors suggest discarding these old myths and consciously creating a "counter-myth" for oneself.[20]

Now let us imagine that at some point, while confronting a particular situation X, David reacts with a violent outburst of anger, with disastrous consequences for his personal life. Later, while pondering on X and analyzing his behavior, he evaluates his impulsive reaction in view of the synergistic values he had been seeking to nurture. He realizes that his angry reaction is identical to the one his father used to show in this type of situation; he also sees that his father's style was definitely based upon an ensemble of values implicitly accepted by his generation's society (the father's role in the family, authority as a supreme value in social and familial relationships, and so forth.). Thus, he now realizes the existence of an old authority constellation (the "Authority" SeCo), and he sees his angry behavior as a direct product of it.

While mentally replaying scene X, David is now imagining other possible reactions, words, and behaviors that would have spared him the disaster and the guilt. At the same time, each "replay" of the X situation also renews the violent anger that he felt originally. (As many of us have discovered, in our mental reconstruction of past exchanges with others we can simultaneously feel remorse over the way things went, yet persist in our affective reactions of anger, frustration, or whatever.)

So, in David's semantic lattice, the values he had unconsciously incorporated from his father, and the specific behaviors associated with it, are part of the SeCo "Authority." He is beginning to become aware of its existence, largely because of the newly established "Synergy" SeCo, which points to an alternative set of possibilities. In other words, David's awareness and understanding of the "Authority" contents emerges out of their confrontation to—and distinction from—the more recent values of the "Synergy" SeCo. By retrospectively imagining alternatives to his angry reactions, David is essentially enriching the "X Situation" cluster with new behavioral possibilities. The "X Situation" is now being connected to several virtual alternative reactions and to the "Synergy"

SeCo; and the memorized reaction of anger (linked to both SeCos) is now marked with a big "to be avoided" flag.

David's analysis of his angry reaction thus has three distinct consequences:

1. The previously opaque "Authority" SeCo is brought to light and is being put into question and modified (if not altogether dispersed).

2. The "X Situation" cluster is reorganized with an adjunct of judgments and virtual links to alternative behaviors.

3. The "Synergy" SeCo is expanded with novel significations, values, attitudes, and experiences while its import and intensity are reinforced.

David's example illustrates how internal mental acts may not only create a novel semantic constellation but also radically modify existing ones—along with their corresponding value-judgments and behavioral attitudes—even if the latter have grown out of early conditioning or semantic "contamination."

The example also points to the clear distinction between choice, or free will, and reactive behaviors, S-R chains and the like. David's violent reaction is brought about by a nonintentional activation of the fixated SeCo, triggered by a minor stimulus (the X situation).

By contrast, his reflections and resolutions are part of a self-generated transformation; they are in no way traceable to any external input, or to any already fixed value/behavior cluster. Indeed, it is only to the extent to which he can shift his attention away from the X situation, and toward the internally generated "Synergy" SeCo, that he can perceive that situation from a new angle and entertain alternative possibilities. This is clearly a process implying self-reflection and self-awareness, both of which are the grounds of free will.

The above example highlights the dynamics of self-transformation, grounded both on a specific type of activation process and on a modular architecture. On the one hand, the spontaneous connective and generative activation process, working at a low level, is what grounds the self-organization of coherent, operant networks. On the other hand, only a multiplicity of self-organized systems (the SeCos), constituting a larger system (the lattice), can display the flexibility, fluidity, and redundancy needed for competitive semantic organizations to exist. This plurality of SeCos, expressing divergent viewpoints and competitive values and behaviors, is the basis for the person's intelligent choice between diverse possibilities and her or his selection of appropriate behavior.[21]

In short, competitive or nearly redundant SeCos permit the plurality of perspectives, behaviors, and neuromotor processes, and allow for the existence of self-reflection. Self-reflection necessitates multiple and divergent viewpoints in the individual's semantic lattice; such divergence is based on a multiplicity of SeCos, each displaying its own self-organization and coherency.

NOTES

1. J. R. Searle (1992), *The rediscovery of the mind,* Cambridge, MA: Bradford Books, MIT Press.

2. M. Conrad (1992), Molecular computing: The lock-key pradigm, *Computer,* Nov. 1992, 11–20. M. Conrad (1996), Percolation and collapse of quantum parallelism: A model of qualia and choice, in S. R. Hameroff, A. W. Kaszniak, & A. C. Scott (Eds.), *Toward a science of consciousness,* Cambridge, MA: MIT Press/Bradford Books.

This is a very complex issue. Without getting into a long discussion here, it is clear that a one-level, rule-bound system can neither correct its own errors nor assess the validity of what it is doing. On the other hand, I do not exclude the possibility that far more sophisticated future computers may eventually do so. We can imagine computers instantiating a blend of rule-bound operations with neural nets, topological and quantum types of computing, while exhibiting nonlinear dynamics. I have toyed around with these possibilities in a science fiction novel—a much more conducive setting for discussing such issues. On a more concrete level, Michael Conrad (1992) envisioned exploiting "powerful computational synergies," between electronic machines and biomolecular technologies. The shape-recognition of macromolecules (e.g., proteins) would permit a "shape-based mode of computing." It would also display dynamical system properties, such as sensitive dependence on physiochemical context and self-organization (e.g., the self-assembly of macromolecules). Conrad (1996) held that complex computers based on quantum superposition and biomolecular computing (and displaying self-enclosure) would allow choice and qualia to be "referents" for their system processes; in short, they would display qualia-like and choice-like properties—while Turing machines *would not*.

My own position here is that such complex, multileveled, and modular computing systems could well have an understanding of their own operations. However, we should not equate *computer* understanding with *human* understanding: the two systems would have quite distinct types of semantic fields.

3. The distinction between the constraining implementation of algorithms or rules in a computational framework and their use as a trigger of self-organizing processes even in simple networks was made clear by Terrence Sejnowski and Charles Rosenberg. Rumelhart and McClelland (1986) had taught a network of just one layer to recognize the past tenses of English verbs. Sejnowski and Rosenberg (1988) wrote: "The verb-learning network is rule-following but not

rule-based in the sense that no rules are explicitly programmed in the network."
(p. 663) Furthermore, in back-propagation networks, the input/ouput function is nonlinear.

T. J. Sejnowski & C. R. Rosenberg (1988), NETtalk: A parallel network that learns to read aloud, in J. A. Anderson, & E. Rosenfeld (Eds.), *Neurocomputing: Foundations of research,* Cambridge, MA: The MIT Press. 663-672.

D. E. Rumelhart & J. L. McClelland (1986), On learning the past tense of english verbs, in J. L. McClelland, D. E. Rumelhart, & the PDP Research Group, *Explorations in the microstructure of cognition. Vol. 2. Psychological and biological models.* Chapter 18. Cambridge, MA: MIT Press/Bradford Books.

4. R. Penrose (1989), *The emperor's new mind,* Oxford, UK: Oxford University Press.

5. On quantum processes, see chapter 8. On topology, see Penrose (1989); Conrad (1992). On morphogenetic fields, see Sheldrake (1981).

6. F. Abraham (1997), Nonlinear coherence in multivariate research: Invariants and the reconstruction of attractors, *Nonlinear Dynamics, Psychology and Life Sciences, 1* (1).

Nonlinearity can be inferred when, if we apply to a system a force that is either constant or increasing linearly, the system does not respond in a constant or linear way. At some thresholds, called *bifurcation points*, it shows a rather abrupt change of behavior and global configuration. Over the course of time, with continued application of the same forces, it may go through a cascade of bifurcations, eventually exhibiting a chaotic (or apparently unpatterned) behavior. As Feigenbaum discovered, a system may show a "doubling of periods": it evolves from a point-attractor (step1) to a periodic one (step 2), and then goes through two more sequences of period-doubling until at step 5 it enters a chaotic behavior.

The simplest example of a nonlinear system is Benard cells: large vertical rotational movements appearing in a liquid when heated by a constant source, and replacing the random collisions of water molecules. In other words, while the energy input (heat) remains constant and the liquid's temperature rises, at a certain threshold, a new organization within the system is brought about: the system self-organizes. Self-organization, in this context, is the creation of new organizational states or global orders (see the development on self-organization, chapter 5).

First thought to be a rare behavior of specific systems under limit conditions, nonlinearity, according to Sally Goerner, may actually be the general case in most natural systems (i.e., in systems that are not artificially constrained or closed).

Linearity seems less and less adequate for modeling the behavior of natural systems. Indeed, according to Stephen Guastello, when nonlinear models were tested for their predictive accuracy against conventional linear models, they steadily performed twice as well.

S. Goerner (1995), Chaos, evolution and deep ecology, in R. Robertson &

A. Combs (Eds.), *Chaos theory in psychology and the life sciences,* Mahwah, NJ: Lawrence Erlbaum. See also S. Guastello (1995), *Chaos, catastrophe, and human affairs*, Mahwah, NJ: Lawrence Erlbaum Associates.

7. K. H. Pribram (1997), The deep and surface structure of memory and conscious learning: Toward a 21st-century model, in R. L. Solso (ed.), *Mind and brain sciences in the 21st century*, Cambridge, MA: The MIT Press (pp. 127–56), p. 145.

8. Ibid.

9. Jung, C.G. (1968), *The collected works of C.G. Jung, Vol 12: Psychology and Alchemy*. (2d ed., Bollingen Series, XX), Adler, G. & Hull, R.F. (Eds.), Princeton, NJ: Princeton University Press. See also Jung (1964).

Adopting a somewhat different method, Carl Jung tracked down the weaving of meaningful symbols in art and myths. He showed it involved the same organizing process as in dreams: powerful collective symbols, the archetypes, act as an organizing force, drawing to them a range of semantic elements and processes, and constellating them.

10. F. Abraham, R. Abraham, & C. Shaw (1990), *A visual introduction to dynamical systems theory for psychology*, Santa Cruz, CA: Aerial Press.

In a dynamical system, an attractor is a limit-set to which all trajectories tend. The state-space is the geometric space containing all the possible states of the system. The region in the state-space enclosing all trajectories is called the attractor basin.

There are three main types of attractors: static, periodic, and chaotic.

• *Static attractors* may be fixed point attractors (trajectories converge toward a point), or spiral attractors (trajectories spiral toward the point attractor).

• *Periodic (or cyclic) attractors* display a trajectory that repeats itself in a cyclical fashion.

• *Chaotic attractors* display trajectories diverging, then converging; the trajectories never repeat exactly, but instead fill more and more of the attractor basin space. Chaotic attractors also show sensitive dependence on initial conditions as a very small difference at the starting point (e.g., on two nearby trajectories) may become very large at a later moment (at which point the trajectories may then be wide apart from each other). See also Guastello (1995).

11. J. J. Gibson (1986), *An ecological approach to visual perception*, Hillsdale, NJ: Lawrence Erlbaum. (First printed in 1979).

12. K. H. Pribram (1991), *Brain and perception: Holonomy and structure in figural processing*, Hillsdale, NJ: Lawrence Erlbaum.

13. Pribram (1991) assumed that perceptual "features" (such as lines, movements, colors) are in fact emergent characteristics of the global perceptual form; according to Pribram, these features would be activated either within the central brain structure, or by sensory inputs: "Features such as oriented lines, movement and color are best conceived as identifiable emergents of form, because they are already conjoined in the receptive field. Furthermore, such features become activated either by sensory input or by central process to configure a percept" (Pribram, 1991, p. 14.). Furthermore, these two activation sources impose their

own constraints on network—neuronal and subneuronal—thus permitting a pre-processing of data according to past experiences. Indeed, for Pribram, even if networks, by virtue of their "cooperativity," adequately account for self-organization and for the development of "perceptual constancies," they still cannot explain the whole range of mental computations, notably top-down procedures such as interpretation, or conative processes (decision, intention, etc.).

14. F. Varela (1989), *Autonomie et connaissance*, Paris: Seuil. See also Varela, Thompson, & Rosch (1991).

15. H. Maturana & F. Varela (1980), *Autopoiesis and cognition*, Boston: D.Reidel.

16. P. Lévy (1990), *Les technologies de l'intelligence,* Paris: La découverte. Lévy used the term "un collectif pensant hommes-choses," p.11.

17. Ibid., p. 197.

18. Some semantic links are explicitly instantiated and woven into the flow of consciousness ("That reminds me of . . ."); with others, only the result of the chain-linkage emerges while the analogous or linked event is not consciously recognized ("I am not sure why, but I believe it works like this . . .").

19. One such exception is lucid dreaming, dreams during which the person becomes aware that she or he is dreaming, and may succeed in intentionally transforming the contents or the unfolding of the dream. See LaBerge (1980).

20. D. Feinstein & S. Krippner (1997), *The mythic path,* New York: Tarcher/Putnam.

Feinstein and Krippner see personal myths acting as "attractors" that organize personality clusters. As far as I can tell, this is similar to the concept of SeCos—particularly insofar as they stress that personal myths modify behaviors, perception, and neurophysiological activities (all processes linked within a SeCo).

21. C. Hardy (1996), Théorie des champs sémantiques: Dynamiques de l'interprétation et de la création de sens, *Biomath, 34* (135). Paris.

5

CONNECTIVE LEARNING

Learning is certainly among the foundational topics of modern psychology. The framework developed here is based on the network and dynamical properties of semantic constellations (SeCos). As we will see, the semantic fields model equates learning to a connective process that generates new SeCos. From this perspective, any thought or activity implying a SeCo triggers its reactivation within somewhat different internal and external contexts. Thus, recall, action and reflection involve identical dynamical processes of activation and modification of a constellation.

In this chapter and the following one, a number of examples will permit us to analyze different types of learning so as to construct a general framework.

THE MANY PATHS OF MEMORY

Any model of learning automatically implies a specific model of memory (such as models distinguishing between iconic, short-term and long-term memory).[1] A particularly interesting model is Karl Pribram's well-known holographic model, whereby memory is distributed and instantiates quantum interference patterns. More recently, Pribram has proposed that memory comprises two embedded structures.[2] The "surface structure" is encompassed in specific brain circuits and shows patterned propagation of signals; these brain circuits may have been formed either genetically or through experience. The "deep structure" is "distributed in the connection web of brain tissue," at the synaptodendritic level of processing.[3] The surface structure allows for automatic processing, whereas conscious processing engages the deep subneuronal distributed structure.[4]

For Pribram, the map or representation of the environment in the brain is not geometrically isomorphic, but rather holographic-like (holonomic); this quantum process takes place in the deep structure, in the dendritic arborizations of neurons.[5] The surface structure, on the other hand, allows another type of encoding, in the space-time domain, instantiated in the brain circuits. According to Pribram, both types of encoding—quantum holonomic and patterned in space and time—may work conjointly in the brain (e.g., in the hippocampus).[6]

Whereas memory, as a function, is traditionally distinguished from learning, the network approach can coherently represent learning and memory as two facets of the same process. Thus, in Marvin Minsky's framework the learning process involves the formation of a particular network of cognitive processes (or "mental agents," to use Minsky's term)—while recall or recognition are simply the reactivation of that same network.[7]

While interesting, Minsky's framework encounters a major problem: if, in recall, agents connected through a given network get back into the very same state they were in during the original experience, then the mind would have no ground for distinguishing between the experience itself and recall of the experience.[8]

The network concept is further elaborated upon in the present model to integrate the proposed SeCos architecture. The nucleus of a SeCo is a semantic element (a concept, process, word, sensation, and so forth) that, through the semantic linkage process, spontaneously attracts new elements (the ensemble forming the constellation). Let us call "basic Link" the element taking the role of nucleus; and let us call a "Link" whatever semantic element is attracted to a nucleus, and thus added in a SeCo. In other words, for the sake of clarity, the term Link includes both the node (proposition, concept, process), and the link specification or relator (if any).[9]

The ongoing process of semantic linkage is viewed here as the foundation of cognition: semantic Links, qualified by different types of relators (differentiation, analogy, and so forth), are generated either through the experience of the world or internally. I thus propose that semantic constellations (SeCos) self-organize the ensemble of Links in a way that is at the same time coherent and sensitive to fluctuations.

"Dog Bite" SeCo

Let us take the example of a very young child who, following a quarrel with his playmates, angrily takes off. Wandering alone, he reaches a lake, where, as bad luck would have it, he encounters a nasty dog and gets bitten. The central experience—the traumatic dog bite—now becomes the nucleus of a constellation (the SeCo "Dog Bite"); fueled by the impact of the trauma, it links together the fear of the dog and its attack, the walk near the lake, the quarrel, and angrily taking off alone (Figure 5.1a).

Figure 5.1a
Original "Dog Bite" SeCo

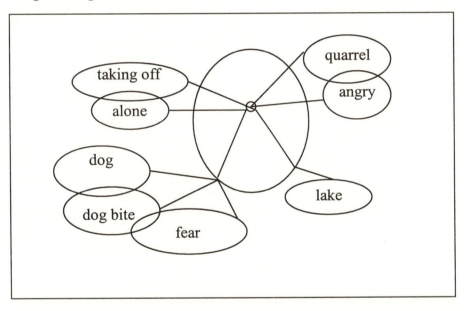

For some time afterward, the sight of any dog will probably reactivate the initial "Dog Bite" SeCo and arouse fear in the child. To a lesser degree, after any new quarrel, he may avoid taking off alone (especially if there is a lake nearby!). To a still lesser degree, the sight of any lake may evoke some uneasiness in him, even when he is accompanied by others.

It is altogether conceivable that this "Dog Bite" SeCo remains relatively stable over a certain period of time. Indeed, certain circumstances—for instance, a second, similar experience with a dog—could reinforce the weights of Links to the point of rendering the SeCo impervious to changes and to new inputs, like a cyst (Figure 5.1b).

Figure 5.1b
Encysted "Dog Bite" Trauma

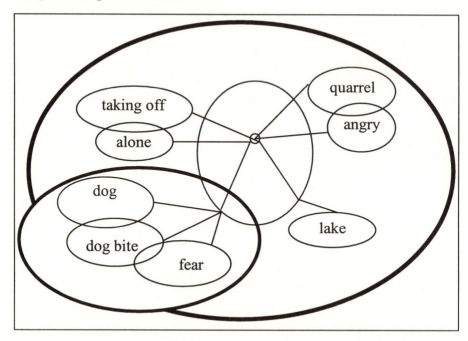

The trauma—the fixed and reinforced SeCo—would then implicitly shape the person's behaviors and thoughts for years, until perhaps therapy or some strong experience renders it accessible and challenges its organization.

Normally, however, a more natural development occurs: the SeCo "Dog Bite" will gradually be modified by the adjunction of new meanings to its elements, stemming from new experiences with dogs, quarrels, and lakes—whether real or imaginary (as in reading, seeing films, and so forth.). Over the course of successive experiences, the initial semantic constellation is reorganized and may split into several different SeCos—the nucleus of which is composed of some of the elements of the initial SeCo (see Figure 5.1c).

For example, a constellation "Dog" will form, grouping experiences linked to dogs, while other SeCos will bind together the experiences of lakes, of loneliness, of quarrels. If things do evolve in this way, then the initial trauma will largely be dispersed—its elements having been regrouped into new semantic organizations that link them with quite different mind-sets and affective states.

Figure 5.1c
Healthy Learning: Formation of New SeCos

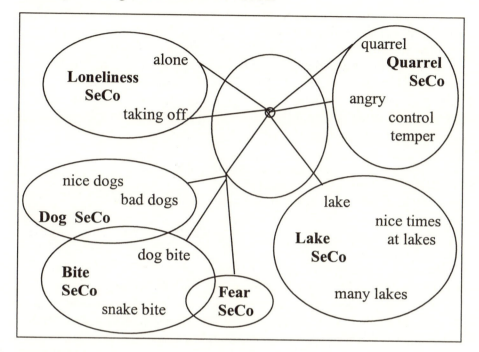

Figure 5.1d
Fractal Memories of "Dog Bite"

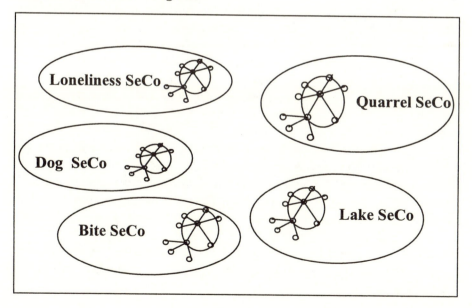

Memory Fractals

A fractalization process occurs here, in the sense that the initial "Dog Bite" experience (and SeCo) will duplicate itself in a fractal form (a self-similar form on a smaller scale)[10]; these memory fractals will remain attached to the main elements, and consequently to the newly formed SeCos. Thus the memorized "Dog Bite" experience, in a fractal form, may still remain accessible through the new SeCos "Dog," "Quarrel," "Lake," etc. (see Figure 5.1d). Indeed, the memory of a strong experience can be reconstituted through several "entry points":

- < nice dog > opposed to < bad dog > ==> dog bite>
- < snake bite > analogous to < dog bite >
- < friends' quarrel > analogous to < quarrel near lake> ==> dog bite>

It is clear that, by the time we reach adulthood, the networks of intertwined SeCos will attain a stupendous degree of complexity. For instance, in the above example, the nucleus of the SeCo "Lake" may also be an element in hundreds of other SeCos. In fact, the SeCo "Lake" will be linked to a multitude of other SeCos, both through its nucleus (basic Link) and through all of its diverse elements (boat, picnic, and so forth.). This clearly increases the complexity and richness of recall: apart from direct paths, there exist numerous indirect paths for recalling a particular memorized experience.

Due to the fractalization of memories into several SeCos, the earlier the memory or concept, the more distributed it is and the greater the number of links to that memory; it is to be expected, then, that it will also show a greater degree of robustness. This is fully in accordance with evidence from neurological studies, suggesting that memory is highly distributed[11]; It also is coherent with observations that earlier memories are the ones least affected by brain damage and the last to fade with senility.

Also worthy of note, in the present model, is the role of context in recall. In each SeCo reactivation (potentially leading to recollection of linked experiences) a new set of Links is constructed between this reactivated SeCo, the more general semantic state of the person, and the current external context. Insofar as a memory-content is tied to both internal and external contexts, it is always reactivated in a different network. This explicitly accounts for the difference between direct experience and recollection of that experience—a distinction lacking in Minsky's theory.

In summary, the semantic lattice must be seen as an extremely diversified landscape with myriads of connected and overlapping constellations, fluctuating and evolving in quite varied ways. Certain clusters progressively change and develop with the influx of new experiences, while others evolve through purely internal mental processes—as in dreams, imagination, meditation, introspection. Some SeCos may result from conscious reflection and choice, while others are absorbed at an early age from the familial and social milieu and tend to remain like fixed structures throughout life—their contents never explicitly questioned or analyzed by the person; ideologies, cultural stereotypes, and certain personality traits may fall into this category. Again, certain SeCos may develop in an ordered way and show internal consistency; other ones may spring up in apparent disorder, emerging out of spontaneous Links and remappings, and containing affective and intellectual inconsistencies.

Yet, the latter's lack of logical coherence does not mean that they are devoid of semantic coherence, or without a hidden order. Just as unregulated construction in a township may lack central planning, yet reflect the needs and desires of different individuals and groups, so too the spontaneous development and evolution of Links within SeCos reflect an underlying order, intelligent and coherent in a semantic sense. Indeed, the creative emergence of change and innovation are mainly the fruit of this chaotic semantic growth.

The semantic fields model underscores the dynamic, ever active nature of memory, insofar as memorized experiences are continually linked with an expanding network of SeCos and sub-SeCos. It is this kind of semantic dynamic that allows people to adopt new perspectives on their own past experiences or ideas, to change outlooks, to modify past judgments, even to radically shift belief and value-systems, as in conversion experiences. What we have, in other words, are semantic linkage processes that organize a *living memory*—itself an active force in the ceaseless generation of meaning, the essence of intelligent mental life.

Let us turn now to a more precise analysis of the learning process.

CONNECTIVE LEARNING

Learning, one of the central topics of psychology over the past century, has traditionally been approached through conditioning models. In classical conditioning, learning is considered a fairly passive, mechanical process; it reduces to the sum of stimulus-response pairs, formed over the subject's history. In operant conditioning, the subject is considered more active, engaging in trial-and-error explorations and memorizing action-chains that have led to success in achieving particular objectives or rewards. Both models share a similar basic logic. Whether expressed in stimulus ==> response terms, or in terms of trial ==> error/success, conditioning models are based upon a cause ==> effect form of reasoning, implying linear-causal, sequential logic.

Whatever the merits of such models, their limitations are now well recognized: much of our real-life acquisition of skills and knowledge engages far more complex and multilayered processes. For example, how do we come to "know" someone else, to have an understanding of his or her personality, or of the way he or she will speak or act in specific settings and situations? Such knowledge does not necessarily depend just upon the person's reactions to our own behaviors (a "stimulus-response" kind of logic). Much of what we learn about the person comes from observing them in varied situations, involving complex and diversified relationships and exchanges. The learning process, in such instances, is based upon the enrichment, multiplication, and diversification of the Links and connections that form the SeCo referring to that person. Learning is largely based upon what I will call *Connective logic,* which embeds *Connective learning* processes.

"Technotalk Effects" SeCo

Consider the case of Carol, a young doctoral candidate in applied physics who designed an ambitious engineering project and now must present it to a group of potential investors. She is well aware of the fact that approval of her project depends on the quality of her presentation and the ensuing discussion. She is extremely attentive to the overall atmosphere, continually analyzing the discussion to see whether it is on track or digressing while also deciphering all she can about the participants' mental states. Focused and alert, she uses all she knows about implicit communication to feel the group mind-set, decode subtle signals, read faces, and adapt herself to the people present; for example, noting that T looks sullen and withdrawn, Carol directs a question to him so as to engage his interest.

Her vigilance is such that, following the meeting, Carol can give her friends a detailed, blow-by-blow account of the vicissitudes of the meeting—the sequence of questions and answers, the reactions and arguments of all participants, even their gestures, grimaces, and body postures.

For Carol, this situation clearly has been a learning experience; it is rich with the observations, heuristic inferences, and understanding which we normally associate with learning. For example, during the meeting, Carol notes the following:

- E and R always agree with each other
            (=> they must have a real good relationship).

- P tends to counter what E says
            (=> P must feel antagonistic toward E).

- When T speaks, R leans back, rolling his eyes upward
            (=> R cannot stand T).

- When C speaks, everyone listens
            (=> C is very influential in this circle of people).

- They always laugh together, except for T
            (=> T is an outsider).

How, then, do we best represent the cognitive processes involved in this learning experience? We often make use of cause-effect types of assertions as a convenient shorthand to codify or summarize observations and inferences (as in Carol's reflections, above); yet this is far too simplistic an approach to *model the interactions* between participants, or Carol's perception and analysis of them. For example, R's reaction to T certainly cannot be explained in cause-effect terms (T does not mechanically "force" a particular reaction in R); and Carol correctly perceives this as essentially a relational, rather than "causal," issue (she realizes that R and T have a poor relationship, i.e., that R tends to reject T). Connective logic seems far more appropriate to model an understanding of interrelationships, of relational modes between members or facets of a system. In particular, such logic allows for a wide range of *relators*, specifying any qualitative relationship between two elements (e.g., partial agreement, complementarity, antithesis, and so forth.). Connective logic enables us to formalize learning in its full complexity and richness and gives us a better grasp as to how people come to understand the following:

- relational and affective dynamics;
- groups of complex, nested interactions;
- the position and function of an entity in a system;
- qualitative distinctions.

It is likely that different kinds of situations and conditions call for different types of learning processes (as well as different kinds of behavioral attitudes). The formation and reinforcement of stimulus ==> response pairs, in classical conditioning, is construed as a quasi-automatic reflex-like event; it does not depend on sophisticated mental processing to take hold. Similarly, in operant conditioning, trial-and-error learning requires only transient forms of mental engagement, for example, momentary attention to assess whether an action has led to the desired objective or reward. By contrast, connective learning seems to be far more demanding, engaging more of the subject's mental resources. It depends upon a sustained mental vigilance, involving real-time assessments of the observed system (the situation, dialogue, and so forth.), complex analyses of its different states, its organization, its functioning and evolution, and so forth.

A person's focus may also be much more inclusive and broad than in linear-causal learning. There need not be a single "stimulus" that solicits the subject's immediate attention; rather, learning may be based upon the initial intentions and objectives of the person, coupled with an alert mental state, a state of lucidity that triggers connective enrichment. For example, a child stands in front of a construction site, fascinated by the cranes, the workers, the noises and movements, the chain of events, and so forth. At no time during this process does the child engage in trial-and-error explorations, or experience any intention to accomplish any objective—yet a learning process is undoubtedly underway as the child's understanding of building construction is being enormously enriched.

In general, linear-causal logic can usefully model learning processes in certain well circumscribed situations (e.g., the conditioning of laboratory rats). It also serves as a convenient shortcut to codify knowledge of stable sequential processes or of cause-effect and action-reaction relationships. In short, linear-causal learning may be seen as a subset of connective learning, a particularly efficient way of inferring linear-causal relations in a given sequence of events. However, attempts to apply such logic to the complex situations of everyday life invariably lead to oversimplifications and errors.

Let us go back to Carol and one of the dimmer moments of her meeting. At some point, in accordance with her plan, Carol begins to give a detailed explanation of a certain technical mechanism in the project. She quickly notices her audience's attention and interest have taken a nosedive. Some begin to look at their watches, others engage in small talk, still others go blurry eyed and start nodding out. Besides the obvious inference ("I'd better shift topics, fast!"), Carol also makes a more long-term inference, in the form of the following "if-then" proposition:

A: Technotalk ==> boredom for nonspecialists.

Here we have an apparently clear-cut case of linear-causal learning. Based on the threat of a failed meeting (the potential punishment), Carol has learned that a certain stimulus (technotalk) will lead to an undesirable result (boredom) in a particular system (nonspecialists).

Yet, even in this seemingly typical instance of operant conditioning, things turn out to be much more complex. Let us say that, some time after the meeting, Carol is walking down the hall when she's approached by Iris, a young administrative assistant she cannot stand. Suddenly she has a brilliant idea: "I know how to get rid of her! I'll just hit her with the driest Technotalk I can muster; that should do the trick." Looks like a straightforward application of linear-causal learning. When examined more closely, however, we see that Carol's ploy (which worked like a charm), is puzzling from a conditioning perspective: what represented "failure" or punishment in the first situation (i.e., alienating a nonspecialist with technical jargon) has now come to signify "success" or reward.[12] A model of learning based on memorization of strategies that have succeeded or failed simply cannot work here. Carol obviously can separate the logical cause-effect sequence from the success/failure judgment that had been associated with that sequence. By shifting her goal, and inverting the punishment/reward contingencies, she has essentially reversed proposition A to:

-A: To bore a nonspecialist ==> use technotalk.

Many such shifts and modifications are possible, each posing additional challenges to a linear-causal representation of the learning process. Thus, two days later, Carol runs into Luc, a friend who has been persistently trying to get a date with her. She is in no mood for this, and, armed with her latest analyses of technotalk and nonspecialists, she starts complaining at length about her difficulties with partial differential equations. Contrary to expectation, Luc shows great interest, going as far as to ask her to tell him more about differential equations. Initially perplexed (-A is not working!), Carol is now led to a new inference:

A2: Technotalk ==> boredom for nonspecialists
             UNLESS they have an overriding objective.

Meanwhile, the conversation is moving right along when Luc abruptly becomes restless and changes the topic. Carol realizes that proposition A2 is not entirely valid either, leading her to yet a new inference:

A3: Technotalk ==> boredom for nonspecialists
                   AND they will fake interest
                   IF they have an overriding objective.

Some time later, after her project has been accepted, Carol is looking to get Michel interested in it. He is a specialist in a different domain and she is wondering how to present the project to him without boring him with technical details. She hits on the idea of presenting this collaboration as an exploration in a new multidisciplinary domain. She figures that his enthusiasm for multidisciplinary research will tip the scales in her favor ("After all," she reflects, "that was the hook that got me into this area!"). It works. Michel is hooked and ready to try it out. Triumphantly, Carol has now reached a new understanding:

A4: Technotalk ==> boredom for specialists
                   UNLESS presented with enthusiasm.

Development and Transformation of a SeCo

Carol's experience illustrates the fluidity, complexity, and evolutionary nature of real-life learning. The simplistic and rough initial understanding associated with proposition A progressively evolves and changes with experience, that is, as Carol encounters exceptions to it or even contradictions in her interactions with different persons. The initial judgment is thus sharpened and refined and becomes a more complex system of knowledge. For example, during Carol's encounter with Luc, the resulting A2 proposition (technotalk does not bore nonspecialists if they have higher priorities) reduces the universality of the initial propositions (A and -A). Proposition A2, however, is itself quickly replaced by the new inference A3 (technotalk does bore nonspecialists after all, but they will conceal this in view of an overriding objective). The modification process, in other words, can be almost immediate and may entail a bracketing or perhaps a denial of earlier judgments.

Such shifts and changes in understanding, which are natural facets of our day-to-day interactions with the world, can be efficiently accounted for through a connective logic and the evolution of SeCos. Carol's experience may be seen as a progressive formation and growth of an internal constellation that becomes more dense and complex according to the situations encountered. It quickly begins to function as a whole system that uses differentiated Links, forming relations between the factors present in each developmental situation and thus deriving new propositions.

Let us take a more global look at the organization of the SeCo "Technotalk Effects" (or "T.T. Effects") (see Figure 5.2).

Figure 5.2
"Technotalk Effects" SeCo: Semantic Self-organization

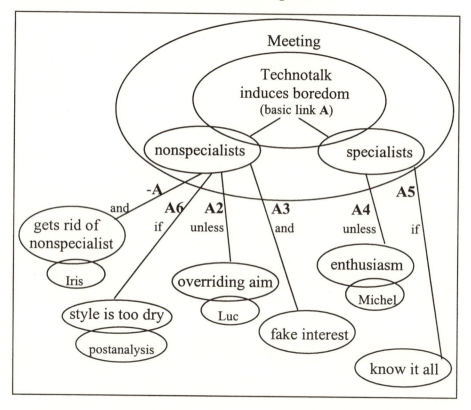

This SeCo is activated whenever Carol finds herself in a situation that mixes some sort of technical talk with nonexperts. Gradually, with time and experience, a greater number of propositions are added to the SeCo, and knowledge relating to a Technotalk's effect on nonspecialists becomes more refined and complex. Furthermore, the SeCo might expand to include categories other than just "nonspecialists." Thus, although initially "T.T. Effects" is not activated in the presence of specialists (e.g., her colleagues), during an interaction with a particular colleague, some event or thought could intervene and trigger one or more elements of the

SeCo, thus bringing the constellation into focus. For example, during a particular exchange, a specialist might show signs of impatience or boredom. Since "boredom" is an element of the "T.T. Effects" SeCo, and "specialist" is the opposite of "nonspecialist," these two semantic Links may suddenly reactivate the SeCo, leading to its further elaboration and enrichment:

A5: Technotalk ==> boredom for specialists
        IF they have heard it all before.

Given the dynamic interconnectedness that characterizes SeCos, it is easy to understand how modifications in certain concepts can bring about changes in other ones, and how new knowledge can retroactively be applied to earlier propositions and modify them. In other words, at one time or another, a past situation may be re-evoked with the whole SeCo reactivated along with its attendant propositions, and reassessed in light of subsequent experiences. This refinement process brings new clarifications, alterations, specifications, and contexts that are added to—or integrated with—the initial propositions, modifying or perhaps even canceling them. For example, a retrospective analysis of the original meeting with the investors may allow Carol to understand that the boredom she noticed was probably due to her style of presentation, rather than just the "technotalk." This leads her to recognize the need to develop certain relational skills that (as her experience with Michel has shown) can counteract boredom and lack of interest. Thus, the retrospective analysis enriches and refines the seed proposition (A) of the "T.T. Effects" SeCo, shifting it from

A: Technotalk ==> boredom for nonspecialists.
to
   A6: Technotalk ==> boredom for nonspecialists
        IF style too dry.

SELF-ORGANIZATION WITHIN SECOS

At this point it is important to address a problem brought up by James Gibson in his critiques of theories of "constructed perception."[13] Gibson stated that it is implausible that, in order to perceive an object, the subject has to reactivate the whole chain of experiences involving that particular object, all the way back to the first perception/experience of it. This would simply be too long and inefficient a process—particularly in view of the subjective immediacy of perception.

I believe this is a sound criticism; however, the semantic fields model avoids this problem. Any SeCo (or part of it) is reorganized through each new perception/experience, leading to the creation of new Links, or the reinforcement, weakening, or deactivation of existing ones. As a consequence, when reactivated, a SeCo displays its latest organization, which represents the overall state of its Links. This acts as a pragmatic shortcut, greatly reducing processing time while also ensuring that the person can have a fresh outlook on the issues at hand. Thus, each new experience activating a specific SeCo modifies the SeCo's organizational state— even if only minutely. Generally, a new experience instantly reactivates the most recent state of the system.

Embedded within each SeCo, then, is a self-organizing process, whereby the evolving system creates its own successive organizational states. We may define self-organization as the reorganization of a system by its own internal dynamics. In this sense, the type of dynamics involved in the process depends on the type of system itself. In the present model, self-organization in the lattice is instantiated in two ways.

First, from a global perspective, self-organization can be seen in the organizing of Links and processes into coherent constellations. This is the dynamic that creates a SeCo in the first place, and that permits its reorganization through experience—what we refer to as "learning."

Second, at a more fundamental level, the self-organizing process essentially consists of the semantic linkage process, which, as we have seen, is a dynamical activation of Links between clusters or between SeCos. The search for the maximum number of matches activates clusters that also contain dissimilar elements; this gives rise to comparative and discriminative thought-processes, while simultaneously reorganizing the SeCos.

Self-organization, then, lies in the manner in which SeCos (1) first form through experience as distinct systems and (2) keep evolving through internal modification.

The constant transformation of SeCos does not necessarily mean that the earlier states are lost, or that they become inaccessible. Indeed, this is where the fractalization process, underlying memory, occurs[14]: whenever a SeCo undergoes reorganization, its previous state becomes fractalized or "enfolded." Long-term memory consists of all the past states of a SeCo, forming a nested cluster within it.

We may imagine this as a superposition of states that recedes in time. Gradually, all states that are very similar (having evoked just minor changes in the SeCo) merge into a generic form; the process is not unlike those computer programs that superimpose many faces, flatten or average out differences, and end up with a single generic form. Eventually, as a result of this process, only quite distinct SeCo organizations are maintained within the fractal, nested clusters.[15]

Of course, even if quite distinct, early SeCo states can become so removed from active connections that they are, for all practical purposes, totally inaccessible.

On the other hand, under many circumstances the person can recall the historical evolution of the SeCo, all the way back to its initial formulation.

For example, in Carol's case, she can readily retrace her thoughts on technotalk and nonspecialists back to the original proposition. Alternatively, as we have seen in the "Dog Bite" SeCo, the fractal memory-cluster can, over time, be replicated in all the SeCos constructed from its initial elements (Lake, Dog, Quarrel, and so forth.); the memory of the event is then recoverable through several alternative pathways.

All things being equal, then, the most recent reorganization of the SeCo is the one most likely to emerge during reactivation. However, things are not always equal. When a SeCo is charged with strong affect, then the state that emerges will probably be the one associated with the most intense reaction—even if much more ancient, and even if contrary to recent experience, logic, or good sense.

Psychologists are quite familiar with such phenomena, for example, memory-distortions or pathological behavioral patterns that are based on strongly charged affects. These often arise out of value-concepts incorporated from parents, teachers, and so forth at an early age, living on in the psyche much like cysts.

Particularly in the domains of values, beliefs, and ideologies, old judgments sometimes become rigidly implanted monoliths, continuing to radiate affect and assumptions that are in flagrant contradiction with later experience. Such encysted SeCos are generally not connected to learning systems; the problem, in fact, is that they often remain immune to inputs from living experience.

The capacity to reconstruct, modulate, and enrich old data requires both mental fluidity and integrity. If intelligence is defined as the capacity to increase and use knowledge, then the ability to reexamine and modify initial suppositions and judgments constitutes the fuel of intelligence. Appearances notwithstanding, encysted constellations are not intelligent.

NOTES

1. Koch (1996) offered a succinct analysis of these three types of memory.
• *Short-term Memory* (STM)—or working memory—covering a time period in the order of 5 to 10 minutes, is of limited capacity, involving 7 items (+ or - 2). STM is involved in category-recognition and is maintained by a constant rehearsal of information. It shows good resistance to damage.
• *Iconic Memory*, which is very short term (250 to 500 milliseconds), involves a kind of quick and constant scanning of the surroundings. It is activated by preconscious stimuli and is preconceptual and prior to categorization.
• *Long-term Memory* (LTM) implies information and processes that have been memorized either through the working of attention or intention (as in explicit memory) or without them (implicit memory).

John Eccles presented a model of cognitive memory based on the discovery of the *Long Term Potentiation* (LTP). Basically, a negative potential is registered when the cell's synapses are excited using an electrode; after four excitations of 15 seconds each, the LTP remains for as long as 10 hours, as it provokes a durable depolarization of the neuron. LTP has been found in hippocampus as well as neocortex cells. We know now it necessitates the simultaneous excitation and cooperative activity of hundreds of synapses within a single neuron. Many researchers now explain cognitive memory by this potentiation, which amounts to a synaptic memory; nevertheless, Eccles said, LTP does not in itself account for memory at the global brain level. See J. C. Eccles (1989), *Evolution of the Brain: Creation of the Self,* New York: Routledge.

2. K. H. Pribram (1997), The deep and surface structure of memory and conscious learning: Toward a 21st-century model, in R. L. Solso (ed.), *Mind and brain sciences in the 21st century*, Cambridge, MA: The MIT Press. (pp. 127–56)

3. Ibid., p. 128.

4. As Pribram states, "Awareness, which provides an opportunity for conscious learning, is due to delay in processing occuring in the brain's connective web. . . . The longer the delay . . . the longer the duration of awareness and the opportunity for distributed storage. This opportunity becomes constrained as skills develop." Ibid., p. 130.

5. According to J. O'Keefe: "The representation of environment in the hippocampus is of a holographic nature; indeed, each environment is represented in many cells, while each cell cooperates to represent several environments." (Quoted by Pribram 1997, p. 134).

6. Pribram (1997), p. 136.

7. M. Minsky (1985), *The society of mind,* New York: Simon & Schuster.

Minsky (1985) viewed the mind as a society of agents organized in networks and grouped into specialized services. An experience initially activates a set of agents that form what he calls a "K line"—which is both a list of agents and an access path to those agents. Any new similar experience (e.g., seeing the same object) reactivates the K line, thus putting the same agents into a similar state. For Minsky, memory recreates anterior states of our minds; thought is the activation of a precise K line while remembering is the reactivation of that same K line. Thus thinking and memory are based on the same cognitive processes. A similar concept can be found in Lévy (1990).

8. Note also that in Minsky (1985) no interactive processes are proposed between K lines to explain mental processes of comparison, association, categorizing, and so forth—all of which are absolutely necessary for a flexible, adaptive intelligence. It seems that Minsky, who started out as a fervent adherent of the symbolic paradigm, has not used the most pertinent properties of networks, such as flexible internal connectivity and the production of emergent organizations.

9. This will make our analysis much easier, as we are going to focus on the formation and general organization of SeCos through the learning process.

10. Fractals derived from mathematical iterations, as in Benoît Mandelbrot's figures, typically show a strong self-similarity of structure across different scales, that is, they reproduce the global structure at smaller scales, albeit with minor changes. See B. Mandelbrot (1977), *The fractal geometry of nature,* New York: Freeman.

11. To account for this distributed structure of memory, Karl Pribram developed his holographic theory of memory, which is based on interference patterns and is created by coherent fields produced in dendritic networks. See K. H. Pribram (1971), *Languages of the brain: Experimental paradoxes and principles in neuropsychology,* Englewood Cliffs, NJ: Prentice-Hall.

12. Success/failure judgments can only be formulated in relation to an objective, which permits us to assess if a strategy has been effective or not. In Pavlovian and Skinnerian conditioning experiments, this initial judgment is of course formulated by experimenters, relative to their own experimental agendas. For example, if the goal is to condition a mouse to push a red lever to obtain food, "success" is judged on this basis. In other words, the objective/action/judgment sequence is considered fixed. Thus, in these models, it would be unthinkable for a "failure" sequence to later invert, spontaneously or voluntarily, to signify "success."

13. Gibson (1986). See the development on Gibson's theory in chapter 7.

14. Goertzel (1994) presented the concept of a fractal memory network. He assumed that, in his Dual Network architecture, the Control Network (a hierarchical multilayered pyramid) can only be superposed to the orthogonal Memory Network (wide associative network) if the latter is also multilayered—a property it acquires by producing fractals of itself.

15. C. Hardy (1997b), Modeling transitions between states of consciousness: The concept of nested chaos, presented at the SCTPLS annual conference in Milwaukee, WI, July 31–August 2, 1997.

6

SECOS AS DYNAMICAL NETWORKS

Viewing learning as the creation of new SeCos has led me to search for a wider framework to express connective processes, so as to dissociate these from the classical propositional framework. My aim here is to account for the dynamic and evolutionary nature of knowledge-acquisition processes. What follows, then, is an attempt to understand the process of SeCo creation and development—that is, of learning—by referring to both network and complex dynamical systems perspectives.

NETWORK AND DYNAMICAL MODELS OF LEARNING

Connectionist Models of Learning

The advent of the symbolic or cognitivist paradigm in the 1970s did not introduce any new learning theory to replace the classical and operant conditioning of the behaviorist paradigm. The whole focus of research was displaced toward the powerful computational capacities of artificial intelligence (AI) programs and the development of increasingly sophisticated rule-systems.[1] Learning returned to center stage once research on networks was resumed in the 1980s.[2] The renewed interest in learning was due to the extraordinary abilities exhibited by networks in this domain. Network learning is based on the adjustment of the weights of connections between units or neurons. Different learning algorithms are used to specify how this adjustment will be done in different types of networks. A main distinction lies in whether or not the expected outputs are specified. When they are not specified, the network learns how to extract patterns. When they are, the network calculates the error between its output at each step and the expected output, and the algorithm specifies how to reduce the error by lowering the weights of error-laden connections.[3]

One of the most interesting features of network learning is that it implies the adaptive organization of the whole network (activated units and connection weights). In other words, presented with data (the input) and with a target pattern, the network finds the most efficient internal state to code for this pattern. This has led to the idea that sophisticated "distributed networks" display a distributed representation of the target pattern that allows the network to still work efficiently despite partial damage or partial lack of information. Additionally, distributed networks can learn to recognize new patterns without loss of previous learning; furthermore, they are able to generalize, that is, to process patterns that are similar but not identical to those already learned. Altogether, this adaptive learning points to a property of dynamical self-organization within networks.

Through the spontaneous self-organization of their units, neural nets display impressive learning and pattern recognition skills. Consider for example NETtalk, conceived by Terrence Sejnowski and Charles Rosenberg.[4] This back-propagation network has demonstrated its capacity to spontaneously learn how to read the English language from a written text. The authors remarked: "Knowledge in these models is distributed over many processing units and the behavior of the network in response to a particular input pattern is a collective decision based on the exchange of information between the processing units."[5]

A particularly impressive feat here was that NETtalk showed learning behaviors quite similar to those of young children; just before it acquired a good elocution, the network went through a babbling phase, much like children do. Such parallels are also found when networks are used to simulate impairments or pathological evolution. Thus, Daniel Levine and Samuel Leven proposed that sophisticated networks could simulate pathological processes like "learned helplessness," which can be seen as a form of depression that is also exhibited by animals.[6] The authors infer that the networks would develop the known symptoms, such as showing an increasing tendency to make mistakes and a reduced learning capacity.

Networks' pattern-recognition and learning ability may well express the manner in which a brain organizes itself to recognize sensory data or internal neuronal patterns. Nevertheless, sophisticated learning in networks still depends upon comparisons with a target-pattern or goal (the expected outputs); this is what drives the internal reorganization of the network. By contrast, in human cognition neither external target-patterns nor goals are necessary, as thought processes can be generated internally, without explicit goals or known solutions.[7]

Networks' astonishing learning capacity has prompted diverse complexifications of AI programs, which now display some network features, such as microtraits coding (subsymbols) and resistance to partial damage. Powerful integrations of symbolic and connectionist approaches in hybrid systems seem to be a very promising direction for future research.[8]

Currently, a merging of neural nets and nonlinear dynamics is also under way. We already know that sophisticated neural nets make use of nonlinear algorithms. According to Michael Jordan, they also display nonlinearity through their use of thresholds (or biases) that permit classification of patterns into categories.[9]

In a far-sighted article, Prueitt et al. (1995) pointed to areas in which this integration could occur.[10] The mutual coupling of nodes is equivalent to the interaction of variables in dynamical systems, while feedback in neural nets is the equivalent of the control parameter in dynamical systems. Moreover, the nonlinear differential equations used in sophisticated networks may lead to bifurcations and chaos. The authors concluded that, while dynamics emphasize the graphical representation of "patterns of the behavior of the interacting variables over time," neural nets emphasize "the network pictures of the basic nature of the model."[11] In other words, dynamical models look at the evolution of the system's organization in time while neural nets stress its activation dynamics and processing capacity.

Dynamical Approaches to Learning

Recent investigations in learning are increasingly integrating complex dynamical systems theory. Inspired by research on natural turbulences, a number of scientists are seeking to highlight the mutual influence of diverse psychological forces as well as their interaction with the context. In their study of the interpretation of novel words in very young children, Smith, Jones and Landau have adopted this kind of approach.[12] The novel imaginary words were presented in a grammatical form (nouns, adjectives, etc.) together with shapes and colors. The responses of children, when plotted into a diagram, tend to gather into a specific region of the state space, thus revealing the presence of an attractor.[13] The experiment showed that children's interpretation of imaginary words is indeed influenced by diverse "forces": some of these reflect previously acquired knowledge (as in the type of word), others are more context-specific (as in the color or shape associated with it). For Smith, the results clearly show that an interpretation "emerges in context," with new solutions being created both from past experience and from the properties of the objects of attention. Therefore, she stated, "intelligence means adaptively fitting cognition to changing contexts."[14]

Wilson and McNaughton have also been using both network and chaos theory frameworks to explain learning and memorization.[15] Their research focused on the role of the hippocampus in memorizing space locations. They showed that the pattern of activation of particular hippocampal neurons is correlated to specific locations in space.[16] Nevertheless, they held that spatial information emerges out of the whole connective pattern of groups of neurons in the hippocampus. In their opinion, the system is not deterministic or pre-wired; to the contrary, it reorganizes itself at each new spatial exploration. During rats' sleep the researchers observed a strong reactivation of all pairs of neurons that had been interconnected during the previous exploratory experience; they thus hypothesized that, during sleep, the hippocampus's neural network reactivates the coherent states of activity that had formed during the previous experience. Wilson and McNaughton proposed that random cortical activity, while bombarding the hippocampal network, may activate patterns close to one of the memorized states. This state would then act as an attractor, pulling the system into its specific pattern (i.e., the memorized state is re-evoked). Sleep would thus strengthen the memorization process: by re-evoking its previously learned states, the hippocampus permits the neocortex to elaborate long-term representations.

ACQUIRING SKILLS: A MULTIDIMENSIONAL NETWORK

To begin with, let me emphasize again that in SeCo dynamics the elements that become linked need not be expressed as propositions, or even as words. We must allow for *all* forms of linked elements, including wordless affects, as well as sensory or motor processes.[17] In other words, our use of the term "Link" must be extended to cover linkage of all concepts and processes (images, sounds, gestures, actions, sensations, words, neuronal processes, and so forth.)—propositions being just one particular type of element contained in a SeCo, a particular shorthand expression of a heuristic knowledge.

Another point to consider is that when we are dealing with propositions, or just words, it is easy to distinguish links from nodes. For example, in the "Technotalk Effects" SeCo, <if> is the relator qualifying the link, whereas <style too dry> is the node. However, when we are dealing with complex sensorimotor learning at a global level, we want to sort out what kind of elements are clustered—and we do not know if and how the links are qualified. Hence, I use the term Link to cover both node and link.[18]

"Drawing Skill" SeCo

Mastering an artistic skill may be one of the most complex forms of learning. It involves the progressive coordination and refinement of feelings and sensitivity, states of consciousness, meaning and intention, concepts and ideas, as well as gestures and motor control. Even in the early stages of learning, pure repetition and imitation are discouraged, insofar as the emphasis is on nurturing creative states of mind. Learning an art thus integrates understanding broad patterns and trends and experiencing generative mental states.

This learning process implies the creation of a multidimensional network, a SeCo that will link widely different elements and processes into a meaningful whole. The SeCo will be reactivated, refined, or modified through each new creative process—even when artists have reached a full mastery of their art. Learning an artistic skill and creating an art form are thus one and the same process, seen at different stages. The hallmark of true creators is the generative and evolving mental dynamics, implying a mutual interaction of thinking, feeling, and acting within a meaningful whole.

For example, in learning how to draw, the "Drawing Skill" SeCo will be constructed. A spontaneous clustering of links will occur between sensations, muscle control, tools, and qualitative states (affect, intention, state of mind), as well as concepts, names, types of drawings and their characteristics.

For the beginner, for example, a Link cluster at the onset of the learning process might be quite elementary, connecting just a particular tool, its name, the gesture needed to use it, and the resulting line (see Figure 6.1a):

<Hold on tool / Name X / Hand movement Y / Perceived line Z>

Figure 6.1a
"Drawing Skill" SeCo

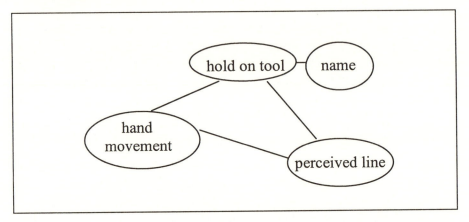

For a more advanced student, the <tool/name> recognition has long since turned automatic and implicit. As muscular control and gestures become more refined, the vague concepts are also being replaced by more precise and sophisticated ones. We may then have the emergence of a cluster of Links of this sort (see Figure 6.1b):

<Hold on tool (name X) / Wrist flexibility / Sensitive line>

Figure 6.1b
"Drawing Skill" SeCo

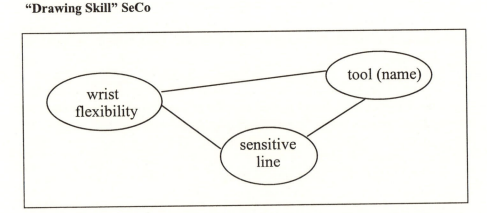

Eventually, even the skills of executing fine movements with a given tool have become semiautomatic. Meanwhile, the whole learning process is now geared toward refining the artistic expression (the quality of the drawing) to best match the artist's intention and feeling. The process then induces a further reorganization of the "Drawing Skill" SeCo into a complex cluster of numerous Links of this type (see Figure 6.1c):

<Intended expression / Meaning / Quality of drawing / (Tools/ gestures)>

Figure 6.1c
"Drawing Skill" SeCo

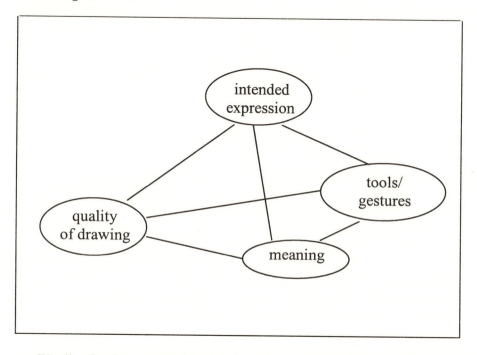

Finally, for the accomplished artist who is in the process of creation, even the mastery of fine movements has become unconscious; only the most complex and abstract Links are now created consciously, such as (see Figure 6.1d):

<Intention / Form / Quality of the drawing (Tools/gestures) / Evoked feeling / Meaning / Artistic associations / State of consciousness>

Hence in the long learning process from apprenticeship to mastery, basic concepts such as "line," or "style," inevitably undergo a series of transformations. Each correlated element can be the object of a myriad of possible new Links, modifications, and refinements, perhaps even going so far as to cancel the original SeCo outlook.

Figure 6.1d
"Drawing Skill" SeCo

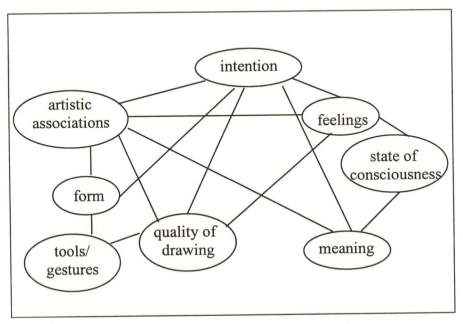

Some Links are reinforced, others undergo significant changes, while yet others may be discarded. Some later Links may progressively develop to such a high degree of complexity, with so many possible variations, that they generate a whole sub-SeCo, one which may even overshadow the original SeCo. Some clusters of Links could turn out to be so inadequate that they do not undergo any further evolution, remaining a mere souvenir of the learning process. Finally, other Links may fall into complete disuse, and eventually be dropped altogether.

As we saw earlier, in the normal course of events, the most recent SeCo state is the one that tends to be most readily accessible. In view of this, with each reactivation of the "Drawing Skill" SeCo, only the latest state of the system is generally displayed, that is, the most recent refinement of the skill. Now, if an element in the artist's train of thought, or in the newly encountered context, is in strong sync with an element or Link in a much older experience, then the sub-SeCo of this memory is going to be reactivated as well, permitting comparisons and further reflection. For example, our artist may want to try charcoal drawing, which he had abandoned years ago. The thought spontaneously reactivates the sub-SeCo of his charcoal experiences, which can now be linked to his latest refinements in drawing skills; this could bring about a qualitative leap in his charcoal-drawing ability.

Varela holds that cognition is embodied, always being both a perceiving and an acting. Here, it is the act of attributing meaning to our cognitive experiences that builds the coherence of the SeCo. The processes underlying learning are neither based on rigid stimulus-response pairings nor upon rational/sequential constructs; rather, they are connective processes that trigger the mutual interaction of many forces. As the "Drawing Skill" example illustrates, learning a skill has little to do with knowledge that has been formulated and fixed; it is the complex development of heuristic knowledge, implying continuous changes and self-organization.

Symbolic logic is simply inadequate to model the progressive changes in this development—in terms of the shifting of understanding, priorities, and focus, or the refinement of sensory impressions and motor coordination. This, perhaps, is one of the main reasons why these heuristic learning processes cannot be fully codified and passed onto someone else through words and instructions. Indeed, even when we are dealing with mental, rather than sensorimotor and artistic skills, we find a similar resistance to codification. For example, the refined thinking processes of a philosopher cannot be handed down through formal means to his students; the data, rules and formulas of a typical classroom situation are a far cry from the generative mental processes that are the hallmark of true scholars.

LEARNING AS A DYNAMICAL SYSTEM

Onset of a Connective Attractor

Recall "Technotalk Effects" (chapter 5). The SeCo began with a basic proposition (or judgment) that was then refined and elaborated through further propositions:

A: Technotalk ==> boredom for nonspecialists.
A2: Technotalk ==> boredom for nonspecialists
                   UNLESS . . .

Note first that these propositions can easily be expressed as Links, as in the following formulation:

A: < Nonspecialist + Technotalk / Boredom >
A2: < Nonspecialist + Technotalk / Boredom / UNLESS . . . >

Now, in this specific case, it so happens that all further elaborations were related to the basic Link A. A posteriori, it turns out that Link A was a rather useful tool for describing reality, inasmuch as it kept generating new Links and was never completely abandoned. However, there may be many different reasons for its apparent usefulness—its practicality, its simplicity, its adequacy in describing a range of situations, and so forth. Whether or not the judgment is "true," or the reasons for its resilience sound, is beside the point. What is of interest here is the fact that, for the subject, it served as a foundation for a whole learning process, and, more importantly, that any new encounter with the technotalk theme could be expressed as an elaboration or refinement of the basic Link A.

Using a dynamical system formalization, then, we detect the presence of one attractor, Link A, in the SeCo "T.T. Effects." The constellation's nucleus pulls new Links toward itself, thus showing a basic property of attractors—patterning new events or experiences (in this case, cognitive experiences).

The mere translation of an experience into a basic concept or judgment constitutes only a potential attractor. An actual attractor starts forming whenever this initial concept is able to generate or pull in new Links, coherent with itself. As we have already seen, the creation of new Links can stem from an internal semantic source (for example, when the initial concept is sufficiently interesting to encourage further reflection) or it can be triggered by an eco-semantic source (for example, an encounter with an external situation that reactivates the initial concept and its SeCo—as in the "T.T. Effects" example, when Carol is cornered by Iris, whom she dislikes, and hits her with "technotalk" to get rid of her!).

A Cognitive System Displaying Two Attractors

In the "T.T. Effects" SeCo, only one attractor was formed, by clustering additions, exceptions, specifications, suppositions, questions, and so forth, around the initial concept, its nucleus, and basic Link.

To analyze another type of organization, let us turn to the "Synergy" SeCo and its confrontation with the "Authority" SeCo (chapter 4). As we may recall, a dream led David to generate the "Synergy" constellation, pointing to a new style or manner of relating to others; this SeCo is

nurtured and amplified through his day-to-day experiences and reflections. At the same time, an older "Authority" SeCo is present as well,
inherited from his family and culture. Thus, two competing SeCos co-
exist in his psyche, both generally referring to the same issue (interpersonal style) and each housing distinct experiences, value-judgments,
linguistic sets, behavioral attitudes, and somatic, sensorimotor, and
neuronal processes. Between the two SeCos, some of these linked
elements will differ drastically, but many will be similar or involve
common referents (which is why they are in competition). We can thus
view the two competing SeCos—A ("Authority") and S ("Synergy")—as
a system displaying two competing attractors (A and S) that will shape
the evolutionary dynamics of interpersonal style.

For some time, all new experiences pertaining to interpersonal style
are invariably going to gravitate toward one of the two SeCos, activating
it and introducing additions, modifications, elaborations, refinements.
The two attractors will "compete" to bring new experiences (Links)
within their attractor basin, thus organizing the experiences in very
different ways. Of course, the greater the number and strength of similar
elements, between a given situation and a SeCo, the greater the likelihood
of that SeCo being the one activated. For example, in the X Situation—all
too similar to previous situations in his past—David falls into the path of
least resistance, the strongly rooted "Authority" SeCo, with its highly
weighted path toward particular mind-sets and behavior patterns.

What is interesting, however, is the follow-up: an internal process
begins, leading to a radical shift in the "Synergy" versus "Authority"
dynamic and changing the system's organization. A first bifurcation had
already occurred when David's reflection on his dream triggered the
onset of the SeCo "Synergy" ("catastrophic bifurcation," with appearance
of a new attractor).[19] Now, the reflection on his violent reaction in the X
situation produces a second bifurcation: it diverts the trajectories leading
to the "Authority" attractor, while reinforcing and strengthening the
trajectories leading to the "Synergy" attractor. The "Authority" SeCo is
undergoing an implosive bifurcation (a drastic diminution of the attractor
size and strength), while the "Synergy" SeCo goes through an explosive
bifurcation (drastic augmentation of the attractor size and strength). (Note
here the merging of network and dynamical system frameworks. The
weighted paths along links and nodes are identified with the trajectories
in an attractor basin.)

Thus we witness a very interesting dynamical system in evolution. At
first, it consists of a single attractor (the SeCo "Authority"), through
which all experiences of interpersonal style are perceived, interpreted and

dealt with. A dream and subsequent reflection then seed a new attractor ("Synergy"). For a while, the deeply rooted A attractor remains stronger. However, David's analyses and efforts progressively strengthen attractor S; this process is further reinforced as his experiences with the new concept produce a number of active Links in his social environment. At some point, attractor A no longer has a clear-cut advantage over attractor S, and it is thus the *context* itself—the number and strength of connections between any situation and each of the two attractors—that tilts the balance in one direction or the other. Finally, in the aftermath of the X Situation (at the second bifurcation), attractor A becomes radically depleted (its links toward activated SeCos being voluntarily cut) and slowly degrades. The A SeCo may then "freeze"—its past states existing only as fractalized memory-clusters. These clusters may in some cases become inaccessible; in cases such as David's, though, in which considerable conscious effort has gone into the switch from one framework to the other, it seems unlikely that the memory would become totally encysted.

SeCos and Attractors

Based on what we have seen with the Synergy example, let us analyze the dynamical evolution of SeCos.

A first attractor (A) is created whenever a concept or judgment (the basic Link A) starts clustering new elements and new Links. The self-organization of these elements form a constellation (the attractor basin) with the attractor being its nucleus. A second attractor (B) potentially exists if a new Link (B) to the topic is formulated in such a way as to imply a radical shift from—or negation of—the basic Link A. Link B could simply remain attached to attractor A if it does not itself constellate new Links. However, as soon as a new Link is made that refers explicitly to Link B, the latter becomes a new attractor, and the system as a whole thus displays two attractors. Subsequent Links relating to the initial concept will be attracted to one or the other attractor basin, while the whole system keeps growing and evolving. A similar dynamic may bring about the creation of even more attractors (and their corresponding SeCos or sub-SeCos) around the same concept.

Experientially, the existence of two competing attractors is most clearly felt when we confront data or viewpoints that conflict with our own, deeply embedded worldviews, attitudes, or habits. In these destabilizing situations of cognitive dissonance, individuals may (1) obliterate the conflict-generating data (the SeCo remains unmodified), (2) distort or rationalize the data (a proposition is added to the SeCo), or (3) accept the data (modification of the SeCo). In the last case, different types of bifurcation may occur; for example, the SeCo may display a new attractor.

Once a new potential attractor is created, four outcomes are possible. The new Link/proposition evolves as follows:

1. It stabilizes through new Links/propositions: it becomes a new attractor.
2. It is destroyed by a subsequent judgment (e.g., its basic proposition is false or irrelevant, or it was founded on false premises, such as an erroneous deduction, etc.).
3. It neither stabilizes through new Links/propositions, nor is destroyed by later judgments or events, but remains a simple Link pertaining to the first attractor (a memorized "special case").
4. It falls passively into oblivion, and at some point disappears altogether.

If a second attractor is indeed created, then the system may evolve in several ways:

1. The two attractors coexist, organizing the two SeCos or sub-SeCos, so that we have a system with two attractors.
2. The strength of the second attractor (its efficiency at constellating new Links) destroys the first attractor, absorbing and modifying all its Links/propositions so that it integrates them all in itself. At which point the system becomes unitary again.
3. Inversely, the original attractor overcomes the second one, and destroys it.
4. A third potential attractor is created, and so forth.

Viewing learning as a connective process of Links-creation allows us to account for its evolutionary, developmental qualities. In this type of model, the memorized data, far from being inert, form a dynamical network that is an integral part of any cognitive process occurring in the psyche. At the same time, the constellation architecture allows for inclusion of Links between a multiplicity of mental, affective, sensori-motor, and neuronal processes.

Links are multiform, heuristic configurations, mostly labile and adaptive, due to their extreme multiplicity and complexity. They are, furthermore, "fuzzy" rather than "crisp." Sharply defined propositions, as posited by the cognitivist paradigm are the rare exception rather than the rule—existing for example in a formal application of logic or mathematics to problem-solving. Thus, even when consciously expressed in "crisp" propositional form (as in the "T.T. Effects" example), concepts are based on far more extended, fuzzy, and complex processes in the psyche.

In the semantic fields model, then, concepts are not simple, well-defined, stable, and homogenous entities. Quite to the contrary, they are the complex, fluid, multidimensional, and evolving processes of the living mind. In general, when the constellation of a concept becomes fixed, it means that the concept is no longer generative; it is knowledge that is inert, or even encysted in a pathological way. The healthy psyche flows and evolves. The concepts themselves are an active, dynamic ingredient of any mental process, playing a generative role in the creation of meaning.

Viewing SeCos as attractor basins permits us to model learning processes in dynamical terms and to view them as SeCo-systems in evolution, presenting a specific set of states at any given point of their development. When we refer to a concept, we are then referring to a whole evolving constellation, clustering new Links around one or more attractors.

TOWARD AN INTEGRATION OF NETWORKS AND DYNAMICAL SYSTEMS

Analyzing the transformation of SeCos has allowed me to take some tentative steps toward merging a network architecture and processes with dynamical systems theory. To begin with, it seems natural to posit that SeCo-networks are systems with self-organizing properties. Obviously, the central property of SeCos is to form new Links, constellating elements/processes and organizing them. In doing so, it defines a system with its own organization and individuality—thus grounding self-organization.

A second step has been to consider SeCos both as networks and as dynamical attractor basins. The more I sorted out the network activities and properties of SeCos, the more it appeared to me that they behave like dynamical attractors: SeCos "trap" a thought-process in their idiosyncratic organization, and attract the psyche toward specific states, or trajectories through states; they thus act as convergent forces. Semantic activations thus follow the most highly weighted links between elements/processes (the nodes), or weighted paths. In dynamical terms, they follow trajectories between specific states of the system.

This brings me to a third manner in which networks and nonlinear dynamics merge in this model: weighted paths within a SeCo-network can be seen as trajectories through the SeCo–attractor basin.

Now, if the mind were limited just to these attractors, then it would have no potential for major transformation, for evolution and innovation. However, the spontaneous linkage process is a divergent force, counteracting the tendency of the mind-psyche to dwell in a SeCo's "learned" organization and giving birth to new concepts or behaviors. When it contains, as initial conditions, a different cluster of semantic elements, the linkage process burrows new paths, instantiating different chain-linkages to related elements. In doing so, it either modifies the weighted paths in a SeCo or creates new paths between SeCos. In dynamical terms, a linkage process, being sensitive to initial conditions, may instantiate new trajectories through a given SeCo–attractor basin (this means a modification of the attractor type, or "subtle bifurcation").

Other bifurcations derive from the self-generative properties I posit for the SeCo-networks—in particular, their capacity to generate new organizational clusters or subnetworks. When a SeCo-network develops a second nucleus with its own Links (link+node), the dynamical system may evolve in two ways. The first one is the creation of an independent, competitive SeCo; for example, in the "Synergy" versus "Authority" SeCo, an independent new SeCo was created, thus instantiating a "catastrophic bifurcation" (appearance of a new attractor). The second case involves the creation of a complex dual SeCo (displaying a chaotic attractor), thus instantiating a modification of the attractor type, or a subtle bifurcation; for example, in the "Breakup" or "Continuation" dilemma, two clusters (or sub-SeCos) were tightly interwoven within the "Relationship" SeCo.

To summarize, if the self-organization and generativity displayed by a SeCo-network exceeds a certain threshold, the network will change its global configuration, generating a competing network or a subnetwork.[20] Consequently, organizational thresholds in networks correspond to dynamical bifurcations. It follows, then, that the self-organization present in SeCo-networks is analogous to dynamical nonlinear self-organization.

The potential for integrating networks and dynamical systems is enormous, and can develop in a number of different directions—for example, as in the suggestion of Prueitt et al. that we view weighted links as dynamical variables.[21] My own approach has been to underscore a number of promising meeting points, even if it is too early to present a formalism for these.

To summarize, I suggest we may view the following:

- SeCo-networks as self-organizing systems;
- SeCo-networks as dynamical attractor basins;
- Weighted paths as trajectories through the SeCo–state space;
- Organizational thresholds in networks as dynamical bifurcations; and
- Network self-organization as nonlinear dynamical self-organization.

NOTES

1. Learning was a blind spot in AI until researchers began to implement programs displaying some of the properties of networks; for example, these programs use learning algorithms and parameters to control the selection of rules and their grouping into larger units (chunking).

2. The earliest research on networks dates back to 1943 with McCulloch and Pitts' formal neurons, and also with Donald Hebb's learning rule, in 1949, posing that the connection between two neurons is reinforced whenever they are activated simultaneously. Several very interesting connectionist systems were developed in the 1960s—such as Selfridge's Pandemonium, and Rosenblatt's Perceptron—but this research was overwhelmed by AI developments, and was not to re-emerge for another decade. A number of the original articles are reprinted in Anderson & Rosenfeld (1988).

3. Two basic learning procedures can be found in neural nets. In the first, termed "unsupervised learning," the network is not presented with any target solutions or expected outputs. For example, in "competitive learning," the network sorts out patterns in the input data. Generally, the learning is done on part of the data, then the remaining data is used to test the network's capacities. The process by which the network achieves the sorting out is not fully understood. We do know it involves a spontaneous sorting out of subregularities, like microtraits (one of the most powerful properties of nets).

In the second case, or "supervised learning," the network is presented with target solutions or expected outputs. In the simple, unidirectional networks, after one presentation of inputs, the network calculates the distance between the obtained and the expected outputs (the error), and lowers the weights of the connections contributing to the error. This process is then repeated until the network finally learns the right configuration of weights, leading to the expected solution.

In the more sophisticated back-propagation networks, intermediary layers of "hidden units" are added. The error calculated on the output layer is propagated backward toward the input layer, lowering the weights of error-laden connections. A very interesting feature here is the presence of a random or stochastic element in the learning algorithm (the logistic function); this prevents the network from reaching stable (forward) solutions too quickly and instead puts the burden of learning on back-propagation procedures and the adjustment of weights.

4. T. J. Sejnowski & C. R. Rosenberg (1988), NETtalk: A parallel network that learns to read aloud (First printed in 1986), in J. A. Anderson & E. Rosenfeld (Eds.), *Neurocomputing: Foundations of research*, Cambridge, MA: The MIT Press, 663–72.

In NETtalk, part of the text was presented to the network, letter by letter, while it could refer to the same text read by a child (the expected outputs). After obtaining good results on this text, the other part of the text was presented without any vocal support. Its own reading of the text was a recognizable speech containing small mistakes.

The network consisted of three layers—input, hidden units, and output—totaling about 300 units (80 hidden units). The input layer reads a continuous text through a window of seven letters. The output layer compares the results produced by the hidden units to the discourse read by the child, and back-propagates the error signal to the input layer (using a learning algorithm). The output consists of a string of phonemes that are then passed through a speech synthesizer. Ten presentations of the whole text of 1,024 words were sufficient for the speech to be understandable; after 50 presentations, the network achieves a good speech level, with occasional mistakes (95% best guesses, and 55% perfect matches). Then on a novel portion of text, NETtalk keeps up a rather good performance (78% best guesses, 35% perfect matches). At the first stage it learns the distinction between vowels and consonants, and at a second stage word boundaries are recognized. The weights between input units and hidden units code for the letters, while the weights between hidden units and output units code for features. Note that the 309 units did instantiate roughly 19,000 weights.

5. Sejnowski & Rosenberg (1988), p. 663.

6. D. S. Levine & S. J. Leven (1995), Of mice and networks: Connectionist dynamics of intention versus action, in F. D. Abraham & A. R. Gilgen (Eds.), *Chaos theory in psychology,* Westport, CT: Praeger Publishers.

Learned helplessness may develop when a person has been through a situation in which he or she had no control whatsoever on events, no matter what his or her choices and behaviors. Its characteristics are a reduced capacity to escape from danger and to learn new tasks, as well as a reduction of motivation and sociability. Levine and Leven (1995) made use of a complex multilayered network (Grossberg's gated dipole network) to explain the depressive influence of learned helplessness. The network will lead to a diminished capacity to make choices and a reduced understanding of these choices.

Levine and Leven also showed that a back-propagation network (of the type: Adaptive Resonance Theory or ART network) will display other traits of learned helplessness—that is, a tendency to repeat its errors and to be unable to make a correct categorization.

7. In fact, changes instantiated internally have begun to be modeled through artificial neural nets. The ART network, conceived by Carpenter and Grossberg

(1987), shows a first level of features' detection and a higher level of category detection, called "attentional subsystem." In the category detection layer, each node stores a basic category pattern among those that keep being extracted by the network. This subsystem then acts as a mismatch-detecting device that sends internal feedback downward to the features layer. The ART network thus achieves more stability in the recognition of categories.

G. A. Carpenter & S. Grossberg (1987), A massively parallel architecture for a self-organizing neural pattern recognition machine. *Computer Vision, Graphics, and Image Processing, 37,* 54–115. See also Prueitt, Levine, Leven, Tryon, & Abraham (1995).

8. For example, the ACT model developed by Anderson (1983) blends a "localist network" (called a semantic network) with a production system. It permits parallel activations of the production system and thus competition between production units. Contrary to connectionist architecture, ACT integrates a control system that permits the selection of the most appropriate production unit. Each unit of the semantic network represents a concept, and a positive or negative weight is attributed to each connection beforehand (specifying the relationships between concepts). The competition between diverse constraints is equivalent to "supple constraints" (as opposed to deterministic rules): the network instantiates dynamical nonlinear interactions, looking for the solution that best satisfies all constraints.

J. R. Anderson (1983), *The architecture of cognition,* Cambridge, MA: MIT Press/Bradford Books.

9. M. J. Jordan (1986), An introduction to linear algebra in parallel distributed processing, in D. E. Rumelhart & J. L. McClelland, *Explorations in the microstructure of cognition: Vol. 1. Foundations* (Chapter 9), Cambridge, MA: MIT Press/Bradford Books.

10. P. Prueitt, D. Levine, S. Leven, W. Tryon, & F. Abraham (1995), Introduction to artificial neural networks, in F. D. Abraham & A. R. Gilgen (Eds.), *Chaos theory in psychology*, Westport, CT: Praeger Publishers.

11. Ibid, p.202. See also M. Peschl (1997), The representational relation between environmental structures and neural systems. *Nonlinear Dynamics, Psychology and Life Sciences, 1* (2).

12. L. Smith (1995), Stability and variability: The geometry of children's novel-word interpretations, in F. D. Abraham & A. R. Gilgen (Eds.), *Chaos theory in psychology,* Westport, CT: Praeger Publishers.

13. Here is an outline of the experiment: Several crude geometrical shapes would be presented to each child, each one having a distinct feature, such as a schematic eye, or a particular shape, color, brilliance, texture. An imaginary word is then associated to this set of shapes, presented as an adjective, a substantive, or a verb. Smith and her colleagues found that certain object properties (for example, presence of eye, or particular shape) did have a strong influence across subjects; equally influential was the type of word used (noun or adjective, and so forth.).

In this dynamical-system framework, the meaning of a new word is created according to the context, from multiple "forces" interacting in a nonlinear fashion. The nonlinearity is due to the existence of thresholds beyond which children's responses are radically different. When these responses are plotted into a diagram, the region of a dense grouping reveals the presence of an attractor in the state space, which means that the above-mentioned forces concur to the shaping of a patterned response among children. In some instances, the whole group's answers gather in a dense cluster (the performance region) and thus reveal one attractor; in other instances, most answers are shaped by one attractor while some others start gathering in a different region, thus revealing the existence of a second attractor.

14. Smith (1995), p. 71.

15. M. A. Wilson & B. L. McNaughton (1994), Reactivation of hippocampal ensemble memory during sleep, *Science, 265,* 676–79, July 29.

16. Wilson and McNaughton (1994) were able to monitor the behavior of groups of 100 to 150 neurons in the rat's hippocampus. They first gathered lots of data on the correlations between neural firings and the position of the rat in space; then, while analyzing just neural excitations, they were able to globally predict where the rat was. They also observed large "ripples" of coherent oscillations, implicating the total network of the hippocampus—a very interesting finding indeed.

17. This perspective is, of course, in agreement with network models, insofar as the latter accept that any concept, action, or proposition can be a node in the network. Nevertheless, it is a mind-boggling task to conceive of meta-networks linking all these various processes. Some hybrid systems, such as production systems, have been proposed connecting symbol-based knowledge and actions (chapter 3). See Baars (1988); Anderson (1983).

18. In this work I have not attempted to conceive of a dynamical network, in the abstract, and then find examples that demonstrate its validity; rather, I have sought to reflect on and formalize the mental dynamics encountered in complex situations. This approach led me to integrate dynamical and network perspectives only wherever this seemed relevant.

Insofar as I have been trying to analyze widely different types of SeCos, it is quite natural that a formalization adapted to propositional networks will not be adapted to a cooperative ensemble of processes (as in the "Drawing Skill" SeCo). A formalization satisfying all idiosyncrasies of cognitive networks is still way out of reach. Also, the integration of networks and dynamical systems may necessitate modifying some features of the classical network configuration. In this context, in order to treat processes and propositions in a similar way, I have adopted a shortcut: I use the term "Link" (with majuscule) to cover both the relator (the link specification, if any) and the node (the proposition, concept, or process).

19. A bifurcation in a dynamical system occurs when control parameters change, and the system's overall behavior and organization are modified—thus

instantiating a modification of the attractor. There are three main types of bifurcations:

• Catastrophic bifurcations: appearance or disappearance of an attractor;

• Subtle bifurcations: changes in the type of attractor (e.g., a fixed-point attractor bifurcates to a periodic attractor: a Hopf bifurcation); and

• Explosive and implosive bifurcations: a sudden change in the attractor's size (respectively augmenting or diminishing). See Abraham, Abraham, & Shaw (1990).

20. Let us recall Jordan's (1986) concept of network thresholds—beyond which the network displays nonlinear behaviors.

21. Prueitt, Levine, Leven, Tryon, & Abraham (1995).

PART II

MIND-IN-THE-WORLD

7

ENVIRONMENT, ENDO-CONTEXT, EXO-CONTEXT

Thus far, we have been dealing essentially with the mind's dynamic-network architecture—its self-organization and the processes of novel meaning-generation. I would now like to address the role and import of the environment in generative semantic processes.

The concept of "environment" refers to widely different things within different scientific domains: the space-time manifold, physical surfaces, objects and fields, a source of stimuli, the domain of interpersonal relationships, the social and cultural background, an ecological niche, nature at large, and so forth.

The semantic fields theory poses, as a basic premise, that everything a mind can perceive is, in principle, endowed with meaning; therefore, all physical systems, the environment at large, as well as other minds and society, are seen as nested semantic fields.

I thus propose that context, environment, and culture be viewed as interacting with the workings of the mind. No mind constitutes a separate system, independent of other minds and its surroundings; it is assumed the noo-fields of individuals interact with each other as well as with collective SeCos.

THE ENVIRONMENT IN THEORIES OF PERCEPTION

Contemporary cognitive models have mostly dealt with the environment indirectly, through different theories on the nature of perception. We will focus on three of these: the theory of mediated perception, ecological theory, and enaction theory.

The Theory of Mediated Perception

The *mediated theory* holds that perception is constructed, wholly internal to the brain, involving bottom-up processes. Physical stimuli (light, sound waves, etc.) are detected and translated into nerve impulses through the sense organs; these give rise to symbolic representations that are processed by the central nervous system (CNS) and then stored in some form of traces in the CNS.

Embedded within the symbolic paradigm, this theory considers that perception depends upon algorithmic procedures: the brain is like a computer that sequentially processes data and performs distinct sets of operations (data collection, data storage and retrieval, logical processing on propositions); it thus builds a propositional knowledge-system. Indeed, according to the functionalist perspective, analogous functions could be equally well performed, given equivalent rule sets, whatever the underlying hardware (or "wetware").

What, then, is the role of the environment in mediated theory? In this framework, all perceptual acts are restricted to a local interaction with the immediate sources of stimuli, which are stripped of their global coherence with the larger environment or cultural domain. As far as cognition is concerned, the outside world is little more than an input source, triggering internal symbolic representations and appropriate processing rules.[1]

Jerry Fodor stressed this point even further, stating that in purely computational theories of mind, the bearing of environmental information on mental processes is strictly formal.[2] In other words, the computer/mind just processes formal symbol-inputs without engaging in any semantic processes, such as attributing meaning or a truth value, or even knowing what the symbols are supposed to represent. However, even in Fodor's "representational theory of mind"—which does allow for semantic processes (e.g., the mind can assess its representations' truth value)—the mind still operates only upon representations; no real interaction with the environment is accepted.

Pushed to its logical extreme, the symbolic paradigm must remain essentially agnostic about the nature of the external world, treating it as the equivalent of a "bit-stream"—a linear sequence of stimuli with little intrinsic sense.

One must wonder whether such models have not gone too far in attempting to account for perception and cognition exclusively through internal brain structures and rule-bound symbolic processing. It seems that something essential, experienced in even the simplest perceptual acts, is lost. By focusing strictly on the sequential processing of internal information, mediated theories tend to ignore the rich self-organization of biological and ecological systems—and our own capacity, as self-organized systems, to interact with the world in a holistic and meaningful way.

Ecological Theory of Perception

Several neo-realist theories have sought to reinstate the apparent immediacy of perception—and to reintroduce the common-sense idea that, when perceiving, we interact with a real world, having its own structure and complexity. Thus, the *ecological theory* of James Gibson,[3] developed in the 1970s, links perception to the intrinsic structure of the stimulus flow, rather than to the brain's processing and interpretational activities. The perceptual system is activated in the presence of *stimulus information*; the process of perception is neither a construction nor the passive reception of stimuli, but rather a *picking up of information* in the environment. For example, in the case of vision the system responds to the information contained in invariant patterns in the ambient optic array. These invariants in the optic array point directly to the properties of the environment without any mediation through a "representation" of the world. Thus, Gibson stated perception is "an act of information pick-up,"[4] "an act of attention, not a triggered impression, an achievement, not a reflex"[5]; he added that his theory seeks "to exclude an extra process of inference or construction."

Gibson's theory nevertheless allows for learning through a refining of the perceptual process—stating, for example, that "the system has become sensitized. Differences are noticed that were previously not noticed. Features become distinctive that were formerly vague."[6] On the other hand, he affirmed that these learning processes "need not be thought of as depending on a memory, an image, an engram, or a trace."[7] Although he recognized the necessity of some abstraction, he viewed this process as wholly instantiated by the perceptual system itself.

Gibson sought to restore the "immediacy" of perception, and circum-vent what he rightly saw as a major drawback in mediated-perception theory—namely, its over-reliance upon past knowledge in dealing with present perceptual experience. In mediated theory, interpretation of sensory inputs depends entirely upon data stored in memory; perception of a particular stimulus would necessitate drawing from all previous knowledge of this stimulus—all the way back to the very first experience.

According to Gibson this is a major drawback in mediated theory: insofar as each perceptual act would be impossibly long, the mind *must* use shortcuts.[8]

This brings us to a fundamental concept of the ecological theory: that of *affordances*. Gibson posited that the environment of any species presents surfaces and substances that "afford" particular kinds of behavioral opportunities to that species. A path affords locomotion, while a brink "is a falling-off place" that "affords injury." A ground is certainly "stand-on-able," but it can also be "walk-on-able" or "run-over-able." Affordances are of course relative to the species and its physical characteristics—a space between trees affords a jump-through-able surface to a monkey, but is more of a "fall-off-able" one for its modern urban-dwelling human descendants.

The ecological theory has several interesting features. It seeks to circumvent symbolic representations and rule-bound processing. It also does justice to the informational complexity of the environment while stressing the interrelationship between organisms and environment during perceptual or motor acts. Yet, it seems to me that the cornerstone of Gibson's ideas—the concept of affordances—is not as useful as appears at first glance. Even from the perspective of a single member of a species, any given object certainly has numerous affordances suggested by its form: can the mind really review all conceivable—and competing—affordances of an object? When facing a landscape, does an organism go over all the possibilities afforded by each one of its surfaces—jumping, walking, sitting, lying down, climbing, and so forth? One would need a whole session of creative problem-solving just to sort out all the affordances of a single complex object like a tree. Should I climb it, hang a swing on it, sit on a branch, carve a stick, pluck the fruits, sit in its shadows? Yet, I was just looking for my hat, snatched by a gust of wind!

We must therefore question whether affordances are indeed the shortcuts Gibson was after, and whether we can really bypass all constructed process. Insofar as the extraction of affordances is bound to become more and more complex with experience, the processes of reflection, delayed action, strategy, choice, and so forth render cognition increasingly abstract and detached from a direct "picking-up" of information from the optic array. Furthermore, Gibson's theory has even greater difficulties explaining quasi-perceptual tasks that do not imply actual percepts in the optic array—such as visualization, imagination, or dreams.[9]

So, how does ecological theory view environment? Where does it leave us in terms of mind/environment interactions? Affordances do instantiate a rather intimate relationship between a species and its environmental niche. Note, however, that in Gibson's theory this interrelation does not allow for substantial modifications either in the cognitive subject or in the world: we do not have a form of mutual influence or interaction here. As the qualities of the world are given through invariants extracted from the optic array (e.g., affordances), the "refining of the perceptual system" has a rather small margin of operation. The cognitive subject is essentially reduced to a sensitive detector of external features and a clever opportunist exploiting predefined possibilities. Furthermore, no allowance is made for individuals to indulge in nonperceptual mental processes—such as reflection or intentions—and to experience their own mind.

So, as in the cognitivist paradigm, making sense of the world gives the person little possibility to influence the world. Cognition is still constrained by "invariants"—only now these are projected into features of the world, rather than internal concepts and representations.

If we wish to account for the full complexity of perception and for higher processes, such as reasoning and intentionality, then we cannot bypass the constructed facets of cognition; we cannot rely exclusively on Gibson's "refining of the perceptual system." Indeed, new findings in neuroscience show major contributions of central processing even at very basic levels of perception. Neurological research has revealed a dense bundle of fibers (around a hundred) stemming from the associative cortex and feeding into a single fiber that issues from the visual-cortex.[10] Such findings point to the enormous contribution of central (as opposed to peripheral/sensory) inputs, and underscore the interpretational or constructed nature of perception. While triggered by external stimuli and relayed by afferent pathways to the brain, sensory inputs must be thoroughly processed by diverse specialized brain areas before we can begin to experience a meaningful percept.

Enaction Theory

Gibson's essential insights—that cognition is coupled with experiencing the world and that the cognitive subject is primarily a perceiving/acting entity—have also been developed (albeit in a quite different framework) by Francisco Varela in his theory of *enaction*.

Varela held that, from the outset, perception develops through a strong "coupling" with motor skills; this allows the organism to interact with the world through "perceptually guided actions."[11] Thus perception and motor skills co-evolve and remain "co-dependent," a fact underscored by experimental data.[12] This forms the basis for "enacted cognition" or enaction, which Varela considered both a knowing and an acting. Furthermore, this learning process takes place through constant interactions with the world: "There is mutuality between animal and environment, in our terms . . . the two are structurally coupled."[13]

Varela firmly objected to the cognitivist conception of mind based on symbolic representations that just "mirror the world." He also opposed the idea of a rule-bound processing of these representations; for him, cognitive acts are not "instructed" as in a programming command, but rather "constructed" through experience.

In *Autopoiesis and Cognition*, Maturana and Varela's rejection of the computational and information-theory frameworks also led them to disallow information exchange and processing between coupled systems. Instead, they suggested, when one system is "perturbed" by another (its environment), it reorganizes itself internally through a self-created or "autopoietic" process.[14] Thus, in this work, the self-organization concept is rather reminiscent of the homeostasis concept (i.e., a continuous internal readjustment to maintain an optimal state, as when our body adjusts itself to keep a stable internal temperature).[15] However, in *The Embodied Mind*, Varela, Thomson, and Rosch stated: "These local situations constantly change as a result of the perceiver's activity," thus pointing to mutual subject/world influences.[16]

So, how is the environment viewed in enaction theory? Varela et al. remained adamant in refusing the primary cognitivist concept of an independent world with predetermined properties (which mental representations supposedly mirror): "The overall concern of an enactive approach to perception . . . is, rather, to determine the common principles or lawful linkages between sensory and motor systems that explain how action can be perceptually guided *in a perceiver-dependent world*"[17] (my emphasis).

The dynamical principle of coupling thus represents a very interesting new framework to understand cognitive processes, as these appear more and more clearly based on interactive, or "conversational" kinds of dynamics: "Knower and known, mind and world, stand in relation to each other through mutual specification or dependent co-origination."[18]

However, in my opinion, enaction theory has difficulties explaining higher cognitive processes, as well as collective semantic influences on individual cognition. The concept of enaction emphasizes a form of cognition that is "embodied" in sensorimotor couplings and instantiated in the subject's experience. However, not all cognition is linked to the sensorimotor system; concrete experiences with the environment will not necessarily help resolve a mathematical problem, or guide the mind in purely abstract thinking. While the enaction concept seems highly relevant, as far as sensorimotor experience is concerned, it does not clarify higher mental capacities.

The same critique applies to cultural influences: even though Varela often stated that these need to be taken into account, his theory does not yet seem to propose ways by which these influences can effectively interact with personally enacted cognition.

We are thus confronted with three models of perception, each having its own limitations. Perceptual models that are based on rule-bound processing of symbolic representations do not do justice to the complexity of the external world and its informational potential, nor even to the richness of the cognitive act of perception. Ecological models do stipulate a meaningful environment and a learning-process based on the experience of the environment, but they are severely limited by their one-sidedness in excluding mental constructs. Finally enaction theory, focusing on the coupling of cognition and sensorimotor experience, does not do justice to the complexity of higher-level mental processes.

It seems impossible to completely get rid of constructive processes, or of some kind of memorization process, while still accounting for abstract mental functioning and conative processes. To model even the simplest act of perception, we need to take into account the extreme complexity of both the mind, with its connective and logical processes, and the environment, with its multiple forces and structures.

ENDO- AND EXO-CONTEXTS

Disambiguating Meaning: The Role of Context

Studies in linguistics and artificial intelligence underscore the fact that the meaning of any declarative or narrative sentence depends heavily upon the context in which it is formulated. Thus, the immediate selection of a particular meaning among two or more possibilities (the disambiguation of meaning) is largely based on the context. For example, the selection of a particular signification for words that are homographic (identical spelling) or homophonic (identical pronunciation) is based on the contextual meanings surrounding the words. A lack of this informational context is largely what renders present-day computerized translation so awkward. Some hold that this is an intrinsic, irreducible shortcoming of artificial intelligence. As usual, however, things are less simple than they appear.

Let us first take a closer look at what we mean by "context." If we take a conversation as an example, then the context that disambiguates a given homophonic word encompasses many possibilities:

1) The grammatical structure of the sentence: choice between a substantive, adjective, or a verb, as in "He places the book on the table" versus "He has three places for. . . ."

2) Contiguity: the words or sentence(s) surrounding the homophonic word.

3) Language-set: words having specific meanings in a professional "jargon."

4) General nature of discourse: for example, symbolic or metaphoric versus literal contexts—implying specific vocabularies and expressions.

5) Mental-set or state: the shared feelings, sensations, ambiance, mind-state that highlight implicit meanings and intentions; for example, a humorous versus angry versus seductive exchange.

6) Interlocutors' shared background: for example, a shared past experience and the creation or usage of a term to refer to this experience.

7) The immediately surrounding scene: for example, a remark made "out of the blue," in the middle of a conversation, can be referring to the unfolding of a particular situation or a disruptive event occurring around the interlocutors.

8) The general setting or environment: for example, a social gathering, a functional building, or a structure, such as a sports complex, and so forth.

"Context," then, actually covers a wide range of different situations. Given sufficient data, intelligent computers could conceivably resolve the major meaning-ambiguities pertaining to some types of context (numbers 1, 2, 3 and 8 in the preceeding list). Most of type 4 could also be taken care of, insofar as these expressions are consensual and predefined. Context-types 5, 6 and 7 may remain opaque to computers, for the most part. However, we should not overlook the fact that human beings can also experience difficulties resolving meaning-ambiguities and choosing from among several competing contexts; errors occur quite frequently.

Looking at the above list, we may group the different types of significant contexts into two broad categories: the *exo-context* (external to the person) and the *endo-context* (within the person).[19]

The exo-context points to an ensemble of environmental and situational forces that are of paramount importance in an individual's interpretation of a given event.

If a person wakes up from a nap and beholds a gun in front of his nose, held by a big man wearing a hat, it will be crucial for him to know whether he fell asleep in a rough neighborhood or in a film studio. While the attentional object ("gun") is set within a *proximate exo-context* ("man holding gun," with all the associated implications), awareness of a still *broader exo-context* ("oh, of course, I am in a Hollywood studio") is vital to a correct interpretation of the situation and selection of the appropriate behavior. What we typically deal with, in other words, is neither objects nor just objects within an isolated context, but rather *levels of exo-context, nested in one another*.

Similarly, the endo-context involves several internal levels of context, reaching well beyond the strictly linguistic or conceptual dimension. In an exchange, for example, a person's particular choice of words, grammatical structures, linguistic expressions, cultural references, and so forth derive not only from the intended meaning, but also from immediately precedent cognitive acts and states—as well as her or his state of consciousness, psychophysiological state (e.g., stress level), past experience, knowledge- and language-sets, beliefs and values, feelings, sensations, the general psychological features of this period (in love, depressed, wild youth, etc.).

All these features—contained in the person's semantic lattice and noo-field—constitute an endo-context that shapes that person's meaningful interactions with the world. One of the main properties of the noo-field and the semantic lattice is to act as endo-contexts for any interpretation and attribution of meaning. At the lowest level, the organization and contents of the *lattice*—the accumulated experience, knowledge, and memory of the person—play the role of a broad and *remote endo-context*, a general background for the interpretation of meaning. The *noo-field*—the "primed" SeCos of a particular time period—acts as a more delimited and *proximate endo-context*, coloring and influencing the perception/interpretation of events and objects, and thus the creation of meaning. Finally, at the most immediate level, the *activated SeCo*, filling the flow of consciousness with its numerous Links, constitutes a *focused endo-context*.

To fully understand the attribution of meaning during the perception/interpretation process, we need to recognize the complexity of interactions between the multiple, nested levels of context—both the dynamics internal to the person, and those having to do with exo-contexts or eco-fields (see chapter 9).

Interaction of Endo- and Exo-contexts

Imagine that you find yourself in a quite novel situation—one in which you cannot rely entirely on past experience, but must rapidly generate new understandings, new meanings, to adapt to the situation. For example, imagine you have just arrived in a totally foreign and unknown culture and are invited to join in a feast, celebrating a wedding. You enter a large room. People are seated on mats, dressed in extravagantly luscious clothes. In front of each person lies a little mat, woven out of dried leaves. You are offered a place, sit cross-legged, engage in conversation. So far, so good. Somebody starts serving rice and vegetables directly on the leaf mat. Okay, looks like this is their plate. Oh-oh, no forks, no spoons! People are cheerfully dipping their hands in the food and somehow managing to bring packets of rice and vegetables to their mouths with astonishing grace.

All this is unheard of in your own past—and very awkward. Of course, you are no fool: you improvise, drawing on your little knowledge of foreign cultures and on all the clues available in the immediate situation. For example, before plunging both hands in the dish and driving your neighbors screaming out of the room, you remember to check out whether people are using both hands to eat their rice and veggies, or specifically their right hand.

In other words, you adjust and harmonize your behavior to the situation by reference both to your own past experiences—your lattice—and to this strange exo-context. Neither of these are sufficient, in and of themselves. Clearly, the adaptation process will be greatly facilitated by your previous knowledge of similar situations, or of foreign cultures in general. This knowledge, however, serves only as a guideline to quicken the interpretation of observations, to help draw inferences, to learn a new gesture or invent a new behavior—in short, to derive and choose the most appropriate way of responding to the novel situation.

In the present model, then, meaning-generation is neither driven by external stimuli nor strictly determined by internal processes; rather, it is influenced and modulated, in a totally relative manner, by the complex interaction of endo- and exo-contexts—indeed, by the whole network of interactions:

< endo-context / consciousness flow / object (or event) / exo-context >.

This network of interactions permits the perception/interpretation of an event or scene, and the buildup of an appropriate response or behavior (see Figure 7.1).

Figure 7.1
Endo- and Exo-contexts: Network of Interactions

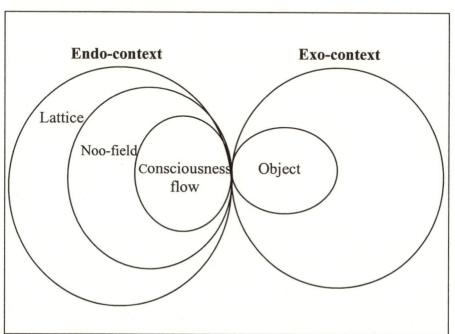

More precisely, the dynamics are as follows: the perception of an event or *situation-in-context* activates specific SeCos, and quickly generates spontaneous Links, modifying the SeCos or creating new ones—thus instantiating the creation of novel meanings related to the situation. This activation of internal SeCos during perception takes place, not in a tabula rasa but within the *remote endo-context*, that is, the person's lattice, which includes his or her past experience with, and understanding of, the exo-contexts he or she is facing.

Spontaneous linkages—hence, meaning-generation—will also be strongly influenced by the *proximate endo-context*, the state of the noo-field, or network of already organized and "primed" SeCos. For example, the person's mind-set just prior to interacting with someone (joyful or sad, focused or dispersed, interested or fed up) will affect the exchange; and, of course, the associated neural and physiological processes which were already activated, as well as those activated through the chain-linkage process, will also influence subsequent cognitive processes.

The above analysis suggests that just about any experience is necessarily novel and unique. Given the extreme complexity of the network of interactions, something is bound to be different, either in the semantic state, in the activated SeCos, or in one of the levels of the exo-context. The richness and diversity of combined exo- and endo- contexts, permits the experience to be memorized in the lattice as a complex and idiosyncratic cluster of Links; when the SeCo is reactivated, we can thus readily distinguish between an actual scene, an imagined scene, and a remembered scene.

While it seems we should never have exactly the same perception of anything, practically speaking, our repeated encounters with highly similar situations, events, places, objects, or persons lead us to ignore or "flatten" the small differences. The accumulation of experience within globally similar endo- and exo-contexts tends to render a particular perception/interpretation quasi-automatic: as long as these contexts remain relatively unchanged, the familiar interpretation will be re-evoked "as is." This is particularly apparent in procedural-type processing (see chapter 4) in which we seek out and value a reliable repetition of perceptions and activities. Nevertheless, it is important to recognize that, in general, the interpretative process situates the object in both an endo- and an exo-context, on the basis of a continuous connective dynamic: this dynamic modifies existing semantic structures, until contextually obsolete knowledge evolves into novel, contextually adapted knowledge. Seen from this perspective, perceptual or interpretational aberrations can be understood as imbalances in the endo-context/exo-context dynamic. An endo-context might predominate to the point of pronounced misinterpretations, or even hallucinations—a perception/interpretation contradicting consensual reality. Conversely, an exo-context might be at the forefront, eliciting particular interpretations and behaviors despite one's efforts to view things differently (optical illusions are a good example).

Constructing an Exo-context

In our modern societies, much of what surrounds us is not so much the natural environment, as it is *culturally constructed exo-contexts*: collective settings, structures, events, or activities that are planned and organized with particular meanings and objectives in mind. Whether designing a hospital, organizing a political rally, or planning a scientific conference, we seek to construct contexts and situations that will explicitly or tacitly influence those who participate. In other words, we intentionally set up exo-contexts to induce specific mental states upon the individuals present, and confer certain meanings upon the experienced events. A brief example will clarify the matter.

The Creativity Workshop. Patricia is a somewhat stiff executive with a touchy character, anxious about her self-image and very much identified with her social roles. In order to stay "upwardly mobile" in her company, she decides to take a summer workshop on creativity. In one particularly powerful session, participants are focusing on their social roles and public image. Each of them is supposed to take turns on the "hot seat," becoming the focus of others' observations and feedback. When it is Patricia's turn, she quickly discovers that participants see her as a closed, self-absorbed individual who wears a terribly self-serious mask. Initially, she reacts to the comments defensively—or, rather, pretty aggressively. Suddenly, she goes silent, and then begins to laugh. With each new, excruciating revelation, she laughs harder. A few months earlier, when everything seemed just fine to her, Patricia would have jumped on anyone so insolent as to judge her like this. Now, the exercise unleashes an unprecedented catharsis in Patricia's psyche, essentially liberating her from her tight identification with her social and professional role.

It is obvious that Patricia's cathartic reaction can only take place in the experiential and intentional context of the hot-seat session—which itself draws part of its meaning from the overall goals and scheduled activities of the creativity workshop. The workshop thus acts as an intentionally set-up exo-context—a semantic context mainly defined by the intentions and objectives of the organizers, as well as by their general knowledge and experience with creativity workshops. The group of participants also contributes, however, as do the physical setting and surroundings—meaning that several different types of exo-contexts are simultaneously at play. This complex exo-context orients and influences Patricia's attribution of meanings to events and interactions, and thus casts the hot-seat session in a certain semantic light.

Of course, not everybody in the workshop experiences such a catharsis; Patricia's reaction crucially depends on her own semantic organization, as well. Her lattice and noo-field act as endo-contexts in several ways: in the fact that she previously had rigid value-concepts and self-image; in her decision to take the workshop; in her expectations and tacit hopes as to what she would get out of it, and so forth.

Following the hot-seat session, the catharsis radically changes her internal relation (or links) with her own rigid value-concepts, which in turn begins to alter her lattice organization. We thus have a good example of connective logic. The interaction of endo- and exo-contexts and the process of generating meaning are based not so much on causal relations, as upon a complex, continuous connective interrelation in which each set of contextual parameters influences the other.

Once seen in this manner, it becomes obvious that

1. People are constantly interacting with exo-contexts (settings, events, situations, other people, and so forth.) that are imbued with meaning.[20]
2. In these interactions, each individual perceives the external context through her or his own endo-context.
3. Mutual influences between exo-contexts (imbued with meaning) and individuals (having their own flexible semantic organization) can result in the generation of truly unique or novel meanings.

COLLECTIVE SEMANTIC CONSTELLATIONS

As mentioned, intentionally constructed exo-contexts—such as the creativity workshop—are typical of our social environment and interactions. From ski resorts to libraries, from highways to restaurants, from churches to courts, we are literally surrounded by settings, structures, and institutions explicitly conceived to encourage certain behaviors or mind-sets, while excluding other ones.

Though they generally do not compel, such exo-contexts do predispose people to act in a certain way, that is, to follow rules tacitly built into that particular setting, institution, or group. For example, Linda Dennard showed how norms, beliefs, training, and the knowledge system of social workers shape their work-related activities: they tend to perceive people on the basis of predefined categories, to diagnose problems according to existing schemas, and to propose the corresponding prefabricated solutions.[21]

Insofar as it is based upon shared values, assumptions, behavioral codes, and so forth, the influence of such exo-contexts on individuals is largely *semantic* in nature. Though reified in the physical world (e.g., in buildings such as a courthouse, artifacts such as books, communication networks, instruments, and so forth), they are organized by and reflect the meaning-generative activities of individuals and groups.

I suggest, then, that we view these exo-contexts as *collective semantic constellations* (collective SeCos) that influence people by channeling mind-sets, behaviors, exchanges, even linguistic expressions according to a predefined set of conventions.

Dynamical Evolution of Collective SeCos

Whenever a group of individuals share a particular framework or worldview, they partake of and nurture a collective SeCo. Thus, from a semantic fields perspective, any major school of thought, whether religious, philosophical, scientific or political, constitutes a huge collective SeCo. The core organization of any such SeCo will be rooted in the original inputs of its founder (or co-founders); but the collective SeCo may evolve in several different ways, depending upon the multiple inputs of that school's proponents.

Let us take the example of a new science. Its fundamental organization will derive from the initial axioms, laws, and methodologies specified by those who established that science. Subsequently, the growth, expansion, and complexification of this domain will, to different degrees, reflect the generative semantic processes of all researchers connected to it. Specialization will eventually lead to multiple research subdomains; these may be seen as sub-SeCos, the organization and contents of which evolve as a function of researchers' activities.

Now, as suggested above, the collective SeCo—the scientific domain—channels and influences the organization of any new contributions, so that they remain coherent with its foundational principles. In this sense, *the collective SeCo acts as an attractor* that dynamically specifies how this domain is organized, and influences its evolution. As Frederick Abraham expressed it: "Dynamical systems theory . . . itself constitutes an attractor."[22] In other words, just as a personal SeCo acts as an attractor, shaping one's perceptions and behaviors (see chapter 6), in the same manner a collective SeCo, such as a scientific field, constitutes a powerful attractor, influencing the activities and perceptions of all who partake of it.

Insofar as it is a complex dynamical system, the collective SeCo will evolve in nonlinear ways. As more and more scientists contribute to the research, they will greatly enlarge the collective SeCo or modify its organization, and they may instantiate a number of different bifurcations.

1. *An explosive or implosive bifurcation*, respectively enlarging or decreasing the attractor—that is, changing the size and strength of the SeCo itself: as a rule, sciences keep expanding, insofar as the number of researchers, the volume of publications, as well as the technological inventions they trigger keep increasing. However, domains can also gradually become outdated and show a downward curve in size; this could be the case if the methodology or the technology they support is

slowly becoming obsolete.

2. *A catastrophic bifurcation*, that is, the appearance or disappearance of an attractor: for example, as a result of a new discovery or invention of major import, a new domain is created, thus instantiating the appearance of a novel attractor (e.g., the invention of the magnetometer and its use in brain research).

Another possibility here would be that two distinct attractors (fixed point, spiral point) merge into a unique complex one (chaotic): two separate domains may gradually merge into a single field displaying a more complex organization (as with electromagnetic theory). Inversely, a unique attractor may split into two distinct ones. For example, the SeCo may split into two or more competing SeCos, that is, competing interpretations or paradigms (e.g., the wave versus particle theories of light, which were mutually exclusive prior to the work of Louis de Broglie and others).[23]

3. *A subtle bifurcation*, or modification of the attractor's type (e.g., from a static attractor to a periodic or a chaotic one); this means a drastic change in the SeCo's organization.

A domain may reorganize itself around a novel attractor, entirely discarding the old one—what Thomas Kuhn called a paradigm shift (e.g., from the geocentric to the heliocentric model of the solar system).[24] In periods of paradigm shift, scientists may explore many different avenues of research and junctions between diverse domains. The system then will begin to oscillate and display chaotic behavior: an "excitation of chaos" occurs, as the previous attractor shifts to a chaotic attractor.

This may be what is actually happening in psychology, with the integration of systems theory, sciences of complexity, neural nets, and dynamical systems theory. Referring to the integration of dynamical systems theory in psychology, Frederick Abraham stated: "We conjecture that dynamical systems theory is that sought after mathematics for psychology, or the beginning of such a mathematics. . . . Its appearance within psychology represents a metabifurcation (paradigm shift . . .) to a new level . . . of this science."[25]

ORGANIZATIONAL CLOSURE OF THE LATTICE

Given our extensive semantic interactions with shared exo-contexts (people, situations, settings, or institutions), it might seem surprising that we manage to retain any sense of individuality at all. How does an individual mind protect itself from an overload of semantic linkages with the environment? What dynamics allow for the specificity and uniqueness of an individual psyche despite immersion in cultural and social networks?

This brings us to the concept of *organizational closure*—a modified version of the "operational closure" first developed by Maturana and Varela.[26] According to Varela,[27] operational closure is produced by the entity itself: it constitutes the entity's individuality by rendering it distinct from the background or ambient milieu. Taking the cell as an example, he showed that the primary elements of the cell membrane are produced by the organelles of the cell itself; these elements both constitute and specify the individual cell. The membrane is an excellent example, because it is both the frontier of exchanges between the cell and its milieu, and the locus of control for these exchanges. Not only does it specify the individualized entity, it also determines that entity's interaction with its environment.

A person's semantic lattice also has the two features spelled out by Maturana and Varela: it is individualized by organizational closure, and it is also a system regulating its exchanges with its semantic environment. However, there are some significant differences. Varela's concept of self-organization is largely based on the processes by which a biological entity (whether a cell, organ or body) tends to reorganize itself after any perturbation. It seems to me that this is not an adequate representation of our semantic activities. What truly distinguishes the mind from biological processes is its capacity to continuously generate new meanings and expressions. The healthy mind is prone not so much to reconstruct its past states as to explore new states and new ideas.

In the semantic fields model, the lattice tends to continually increase and modify its organization; it hardly ever returns to an earlier state. We can go so far as to say that the reliving of an exactly identical previous state is an impossibility for the mind. As William James puts it (following Heraclitus): you can never swim in the same river twice. That is probably true for any complex biosystem; but the mind is truly alive and healthy when in constant evolution, acquiring new knowledge or wisdom along the way. This ideal has been proposed in most knowledge systems, whether scientific, traditional, clinical, or spiritual.

This is why I prefer the concept of *organizational closure*, employed by von Lucadou and Kornwachs,[28] who underline that a cognitive system's individuality is based on its organization of meaningful information. So, in the present model organizational closure is based on semantic fields, and refers to the internal coherence of the lattice; it is on the basis of this coherence that individuals create their own unique semantic links to collective constellations.

We integrate only a small subset of the mass of potential information with which we are confronted—perceiving and processing that which makes sense to us, that which activates significations that concern us. In other words, only the information that "speaks" to us—that is, information that can generate links with existing constellations—will be integrated into the organizational closure of our semantic lattice. This is what protects us, so to speak, from losing ourselves in collective semantic networks (an exception being pathological cases).

Of course, all this is relative. As we will be seeing in coming chapters, we are far more "plugged into," and influenced by, environmental and collective networks than we imagine.

NOTES

1. The totally unexplained pre-existence of these processing rules (who is the programmer?) has been of course viewed as a major drawback of the theory.

2. J. A. Fodor (1981), Methodological solipsism considered as a research strategy in cognitive psychology, in J. Haugeland (Ed.), *Mind design,* Cambridge, MA: MIT Press.

3. Gibson (1986).

4. Ibid., p. 57.

5. Ibid., p. 149.

6. Ibid., p. 254.

7. Ibid., p. 254.

8. I addressed this problem of necessary shortcuts in chapter 5 (on Learning). As I suggested, under normal conditions it is the latest state of a SeCo that is activated, linking the more recent heuristic propositions and behaviors.

9. Gibson (1986) is on even slippier ground when he seeks to account for "nonperceptual awareness," as in remembering, anticipating, or daydreaming. He seeks to explain these activities as an awareness of surfaces or events that have ceased to exist or that do not exist at all (1986, p. 255). We thus definitely come to the idea of a perceptual system able to activate, reproduce, or create partial states of itself—while the ambient optic array and all environment's affordances have ceased to be the prime object of the interaction—all of which seems to contradict the theory's premises.

10. Changeux (1997).

11. Varela, Thompson, & Rosch (1991), p. 173.

12. F. Varela (1989), *Autonomie et connaissance,* Paris: Seuil.

Varela (1989) cited the Held and Hein experiment. Kittens were prevented from actively exploring the world and were just moved around by the experimenters. When finally left free, they would behave like blind animals, bumping into objects and falling. Thus motor skills act as a kind of feedback mechanism for the development of perceptual skills in young animals. See Held & Hein (1958).

13. Varela, Thompson, & Rosch (1991), p. 204.

14. Maturana & Varela (1980).

15. Here, self-organization (or autopoiesis) is not viewed in Prigogine's sense—as the emergence of new global orders in the history of a dynamical system. See Prigogine & Stengers (1984).

16. Varela, Thompson, & Rosch (1991), p. 173.

17. Ibid., p. 173.

18. Ibid., p. 150.

19. I owe the endo/exo distinction to system theorist Walter von Lucadou, who distinguished between endo- and exo-perspectives in the study of nonlocal phenomena and psi (von Lucadou himself borrowed this term from physicist Hans Primas).

W. von Lucadou (1994), The endo- exo- perspective—heaven and hell of parapsychology. *Proceedings of the 37th Annual Convention of the PA,* Amsterdam, Netherlands: University of Amsterdam.

20. In the case of two interacting individuals, the noo-field of one (his endo-context), acts as an exo-context for his/her interlocutor—and vice versa.

21. L. Dennard (1996), The new paradigm in science and public administration, *Public Administration Review, 56* (15), 495–99.

Dennard (1996) emphasized that the very paradigm adopted by such institutions needs to shift to a dynamical systems framework that underscores more democratic and synergistic interactions. Instead of working on the basis of fixed diagnoses and solutions, she suggests emphasizing spontaneous mutual exchanges that lead to the co-discovery of pertinent and workable solutions.

22. F. Abraham, R. Abraham, & C. Shaw (1990), *A visual introduction to dynamical systems theory for psychology,* Santa Cruz, CA: Aerial Press, p. (III) 21.

23. L. de Broglie (1947), *Physique et microphysique,* Paris: Albin Michel.

24. T. Kuhn (1970), *The structure of scientific revolutions,* Chicago: University of Chicago Press.

25. Abraham, Abraham, & Shaw (1990), p. (III) 21. See also W. Freeman (1995a). The kiss of beauty and the sleeping beauty of psychology, in F. D. Abraham & A. R. Gilgen (Eds.), *Chaos theory in psychology,* Westport, CT: Praeger Publishers.

26. Maturana & Varela (1980).

27. Varela (1989).

28. W. von Lucadou & K. Kornwachs (1980), Development of the system-theoretic approach to psychokinesis, *European Journal of Parapsychology, 3* (3), 297–314.

8

MIND, MATTER, AND QUANTUM MECHANICS

The worldview developed by quantum mechanics (QM) constitutes a major paradigm shift for the 20th century. It introduced paradoxical new concepts such as indeterminacy, antiparticles, nonlocality, and retrocausality into the previously Laplacian, clockwork views of the universe. In the cognitive sciences, a number of researchers have shown special interest in QM's challenge to the primary assumption of mechanistic science—namely, that all interactions are based on proximate, local causes.

The discovery of nonlocality in physics, as we will see, may indeed turn out to be highly relevant to neural and mental processes. Thus, a new set of cognitive theories seeks to study and model quantum events in the brain's functioning.

QUANTUM PARADOXES

Nonlocality

According to QM, the basic nature of microphysical reality is probabilistic. QM states that quantum systems are intrinsically random, that there is a fundamental indeterminacy concerning the exact state the system is going to be in at the moment of measurement. Einstein's famous "God does not play dice" expressed the frustration of many theoretical physicists with this emphasis on indeterminacy. The thought-experiment proposed by Einstein, Podolsky, and Rosen, known as the *EPR Paradox*, sought to demonstrate that QM could not be considered, as

Niels Bohr claimed, "complete"; there must be additional underlying forces locally determining micro-events. However, theoretical developments in the 1950s (by mathematician John Bell), coupled with extremely fine measurements in the 1970s and early 1980s, established the existence of nonlocal correlations between remote particles—in full violation of the local-realistic assumptions of relativity and classical mechanics. A series of experiments involving paired particles demonstrated that if we interfere with one particle the other one instantaneously adopts a state complementary to that of the first one. These correlations are described as "nonlocal" because they are independent of the distance between the two particles, precluding any explanation based on classical signal transmission. The EPR Paradox has thus been central in establishing that the "weirdness" of quantum mechanics is real, and not just apparent.

The Measurement Problem

The measurement problem points to an equally striking paradox. In QM, the central, deterministic Schrödinger equation poses that the wave function describing any microphysical system is the superposition of all possible states of that system. Yet, when a measurement is made, the system is found to be in one fixed state (e.g., a particle with a certain speed or position). How does this abrupt shift occur? Traditionally, it is supposed that, following measurement, the superposed possibilities "collapse" and the system settles into one of its possible states, in a purely probabilistic fashion. In so doing, the system has shifted from a mathematical construct (the wave function) to a particle in space-time with specific properties.

According to this orthodox interpretation of QM, then, the collapse of the wave function occurs at the moment of measurement. However, "measurement" can be understood in several different ways. For some physicists, it is the moment of interference between the microscopic system and a measuring device. Others have proposed that the observer—or the act of perception—is the crucial element in the collapse.

Actually, the idea that *the observer influences observed reality* was introduced early on by some of the central figures of QM—Werner Heisenberg for one. With analyses of the measurement problem, this notion was reinforced and extended. In particular, mathematician John von Neumann and physicist Eugene Wigner explicitly implicated consciousness in the collapse of the wave function—without going so far as to imply that consciousness actually *determines* the observed state of the system.[1]

However, the observational theories (OT) do suggest that observation involves a "biasing" of measurement outcomes. Physicist Evan Harris Walker, one of the most influential OT theorists, proposes that quantum processes play an important role in brain functioning[2]; he also argued that the act of observation creates a nonlocal coupling between these internal brain processes and external quantum events. From this it follows that consciousness can occasionally influence the outcome of external micro-events: to the extent to which it can direct its own brain processes (e.g., willing a certain gesture), consciousness can also affect coupled, external micro-events.[3]

German physicist Walter von Lucadou extended the OT approach beyond microphysical events, suggesting that nonlocal coupling can directly implicate macrophysical systems. Adopting a systems-theoretical approach, von Lucadou postulated that, under certain circumstances, individuals and physical systems can form a metasystem, a more inclusive whole having its own individuality or "organizational closure."[4] At this point, nonlocal correlations will briefly link the person's mental state with the external system and produce temporary "mind-over-matter" effects.

In a typical physics experiment, it would be difficult to assess whether the collapse is provoked by measurement devices or the act of observation. However, if the observer were to shift mental states (e.g., intentions or expectations) and noted a corresponding shift in the statistical pattern of outcomes, then this would strongly support the idea that consciousness is indeed implied in the collapse. Parapsychologists' investigations of micro-psychokinesis (microPK) are highly pertinent in this context: a massive experimental database involving hardware Random Number Generators (RNGs)[5] now provides evidence that individuals can intentionally bias probabilistic microphysical events. In particular, it is found that the normally random output of RNGs is slightly, but consistently skewed, in accordance with the intentions and mental state of subject-observers.[6]

Let us then assume, for the moment, an active role for the observer, as described by Heisenberg, von Neumann, and others. Before the advent of the observer and his measurement activities, the microphysical system was said to be in an indeterminate state, a set of superposed probabilities —that is, the wave function. At this point, apart from the observation/ measurement event, no other force can provoke its collapse into a specific state. Then, following the *cognitive act of observation,* the system is fixed into a single macroscopic state with specific properties.

What interests me here is the presumed nature of the influence of the observer on the system: just what *kind* of cognitive processes are implied? Is it simply the perception of the result that leads to collapse? I suggest that, in focusing on observation, we are overlooking some major mental events that logically and temporally are prior to perception.

Part of the answer, I believe, may be found in Heisenberg's *Uncertainty Principle*. A quantum entity can be represented through three dimensions of position (a particle measure), and three dimensions of momentum (a wave measure). According to the Uncertainty Principle, choosing to precisely measure the particle's position excludes simultaneous and precise measurement of its momentum (and vice versa). In fact, the Uncertainty Principle indicates that, prior to the act of measurement and observation, the experimenter has to first *choose* what to measure— and, accordingly, what kind of measuring device to use (e.g., one yielding knowledge about position versus one focusing on momentum). Insofar as no extraneous force is supposed to lead the observer to a particular decision, the experimenter-observer's pre-measurement choices must be equated to acts of free will. In other words, the experimenter freely decides upon the kind of information he or she wants to "extract" from the quantum system, and defines the measurement procedure accordingly.

Therefore, on the basis of the Uncertainty Principle, we are grounded in posing—from within this QM framework—a conative agency leading to the choice of a measuring mode, and consequently constraining measurement in specific ways. Thus, the observer interacts with the quantum system via conative acts, that is, intentions, choices, and decisions. This may imply a series of decisions and actions until the measurement is made, as well as the involvement of several experimenters. Therefore, the experimenter's (or experimenters') influence on the quantum system does not occur only at the moment of perception/observation, but is *distributed all along the conative process,* up through the moment of measurement and observation of results.

As we will see in the next chapters, analyzing mind-object and mind-event interactions strictly through the semantic fields framework has led me to an analogous conclusion. From a semantic perspective, it is not observation or perception per se that interferes with events, but rather *the act of purposeful thinking*, even before the event's advent in macroscopic reality. In other words, the fundamental cognitive agency interacting with and influencing macroscopic reality is not the perceiving subject, nor even the perceiving/acting subject; rather, it is the conative agent, able to consider alternatives, nourish intentions, and make decisions.

An Alternative Interpretation: Hidden Variables

Many physicists, following Einstein's lead, are still uncomfortable with the ideas of an intrinsic microphysical indeterminacy and a mysterious collapse associated with measurement. Several alternative models have thus been proposed, involving no collapse of the wave function.

Certain of these models posit the existence of "hidden variables" that underlie the known, measurable level dealt with by QM, and that would fully determine the state of microphysical events in a local manner. Most of these theories are not part of mainstream physics today. As mentioned above, nonlocality or nonseparability is now solidly established; local hidden-variable theories are simply inconsistent with the known facts.

However, *nonlocal* variants of these theories are still very much alive and well, and are consistent with the known experimental facts. First elaborated by physicist David Bohm, this kind of model proposes the existence of an underlying quantum field that is fully deterministic, though nonlocal in nature. Bohm referred to this field as the *implicate order*: a level of interconnectedness, or nonseparability, that lies at the very foundations of the universe.[7] His theory poses that the macroscopic world (or explicate order) is an "unfolding" of this deep, implicate order.

Generally, Bohm did not fully develop his ideas to specify just how this subtle level of reality interacts with the macroscopic level—including, in particular, the human brain and mental events. This issue has been dealt with more explicitly by brain scientist Karl Pribram. In Pribram's *holonomic model*, there is no absolute gap between the "frequency domain," consisting of electromagnetic and quantum waves, and the brain, which is a three-dimensional structure in the "space-time domain."[8] Sensory receptors translate wave-patterns into space-time neural patterns; inversely, patterns in the space-time domain are translated to the frequency domain. These dynamics, Pribram proposed, are based on processes analogous to Fourier and Gabor transforms. The dendritic neural network—with its dense lattice of vertical and lateral pathways and its immense connectivity potential—would be the locus of quantum interference processes. Pribram's model posits a continuous exchange between the frequency domain (loaded with information) and the space-time domain (the macrophysical world). Thus, information of the whole world is stored in holographic-like interference patterns; under certain conditions, individuals may access this information.

Extending Bohm's implicate order and Pribram's holonomic theory, Ervin Laszlo viewed interference patterns as an information field, or *psi-*

field.[9] He proposed that the foundation of this interconnection (through space *and* time) is the quantum vacuum field, acting as the "universe's holographically interconnecting field."[10] The vacuum field also acts as a "memory," a psi-field with contents accessible from any system in the universe.

Laszlo avoided both the strictly deterministic framework of Bohm and the strict indeterminism of orthodox QM; the latter, in his view, would lead us to expect only more and more divergence and, hence, an absence of regularities across phenomena. Instead, Laszlo suggested, the coherence we observe in the evolution of physical and biological systems points to a "dynamics of convergence" that would account for macrodetermination in large ensembles of systems. As he stated, "The conceptual basis for that dynamics (of convergence) is furnished by the constant interconnection of the nonequilibrium system with its environment."[11] Thus, Laszlo saw the interaction with the environment as providing constrained feedback, which acts as a convergent force: "With such interconnection, the conceptual requirements of an evolutionary process capable of generating divergence as well as convergence are met."[12]

It is interesting to note that some of the main proponents of models based on a subquantum field go beyond physical implications to emphasize transpersonal dimensions. Bohm extended his ideas well beyond the realm of particle physics, suggesting that natural macroscopic systems in general are rooted in the underlying interconnectedness. As such, any system "enfolds" information about the whole. Moreover, the implicate order supersedes distinctions based upon spatial or temporal distances, between mental and physical events, between self and not-self. Bohm thus explicitly allowed for nonlocal or transpersonal exchanges, such as psi phenomena, viewing these as natural expressions of the underlying interconnectedness: "The main unusual feature of parapsychological phenomena is that they generally involve what may be called a nonlocal connection between the consciousness of a person who is in one place and an object, event or person in some distant place."[13]

Pribram similarly suggested that an individual is in constant exchange with the information of the whole world, encoded in holographic-like interference patterns. Although our sensory system normally filters out all but a tiny portion of this information, under certain circumstances the "lens" through which we interpret reality recedes. To the extent to which we get in touch with the frequency domain itself, we might perceive spatiotemporally distant events or have experiences of interconnectedness.[14]

Like Bohm and Pribram, Ervin Laszlo also saw transpersonal and psychic phenomena as an emergence of relations and connections that are part of a hidden order. He has proposed that the quantum vacuum is the carrier of psi information[15]; it is the tissue upon which all movement and all thought is inscribed. The brain, immersed in this psi-field, is naturally sensitive to its movements and can thus capture subtle information encoded therein.

QUANTUM EVENTS IN THE BRAIN

It seems clear that the paradoxes of the particle world, such as nonlocality, are no longer seen as the exclusivity of quantum physics; they probably also touch on the macroscopic world of human activity and thought. The brain, the most complex known system in the universe, is a plausible meeting place for the micro- and macro-domains, and a growing number of scientists are now advocating the possible role of quantum events in brain processes.

Such views are encouraged by recent neurophysiological findings, such as the discovery of synchronous firing of widely separate neurons in response to perception of a single long object. What kind of process would support such finely tuned correlations at a distance between oscillating neurons? Quantum phenomena seem to offer the only sound explanation, insofar as nonlocal quantum correlations are already well established.

The newly proposed quantum models of cognition mainly have sought to establish the possibility of quantum brain processes—by proposing and assessing different possible neurophysiological substrates (microtubules, synapto-dendritic networks, etc.) or different types of quantum dynamics (interference patterns, coherent quantum processes, etc.).

Several theories propose that the brain involves *coherent quantum processes*, such as those found in lasers, superconductors, superfluids, and so forth, and generally referred to as "Bose-Einstein condensates." The major issue confronting such theories is that coherent quantum processes occur either at very low temperatures or very high energy states. So how can such quantum processes occur in a macroscopic structure like the brain, specifically at a high body temperature and relatively low energy states?

Whatever the conceptual difficulties here, some research does support the possibility of quantum processes in organisms. According to Danah Zohar, experiments done to test Herbert Fröhlich's predictions that quantum processes could occur at body temperature showed coherent quantum phenomena in living tissues, notably in yeast cells and in the DNA molecule.[16] Fritz Popp, in Germany, discovered a weak "glow" emitted by living tissues—a finding independently corroborated by Japanese scientists; Popp interpreted this weak glow as photon emission from a coherent biophoton field.

In the Hameroff-Penrose *quantum correlates theory*, consciousness emerges from quantum coherence fields in the brain—Bose-Einstein condensates processes that, according to Hameroff, are generated in the microtubules of the neuron's cytoskeleton.[17] Conscious experience in its qualitative aspect (e.g., qualia) would thus be correlated with specific frequencies of these quantum coherence processes.

Proposing a model of the brain based on both quantum collapse and "biomolecular computing," Michael Conrad developed the fascinating concept of a *quantum computer*.[18] He proposed a continual collapse of micro-events in the brain; at each level, only one state is selected through the collapse, and this process (which he calls "percolation") moves up the scale from enzymes, to cells, to the organism. Thus, choices and decisions are made at all levels by the system, while, from a first-person perspective, the individual enjoys a "sense of" freedom and free will.

Roger Penrose also advocated the concept of the brain behaving as a quantum computer: the superposed wave function would permit the brain to try out and assess different possibilities or solutions. Following the collapse, one of these possibilities would then be selected, thus instantiating preconscious choices.[19] In proposing this, Penrose essentially granted the brain an ability to trigger the collapse internally or self-collapse. Note, of course, that this does not preclude a brain wave function collapse triggered by an external measurement agency.[20] In fact, Penrose predicted that collapsing a brain wave function (through EEG measurement, for example) should affect the cognitive abilities specifically related to the brain area in which measurement is done. A recent experiment indeed showed that measuring the brain waves of a subject through an EEG affected the subject's cognitive abilities—in particular, those related to the measured area.[21] This, of course, strongly supports the possibility that quantum processes play a role in the brain; in the absence of a brain wave function, we would expect no alteration of cognitive processes with measurement.

In general, supportive evidence on quantum brain processes has already been found, and will continue, in my opinion, to accumulate. Although this field is still in its early stages, we should not overlook its enormous potential. Indeed, if QM is a fundamental formalization of the stuff of reality, which all scientists agree it is, it would be quite surprising if quantum processes played no role whatsoever in brain activities. On the other hand, we should not expect that quantum processes, at least as presently formalized, will give an adequate description of cognitive processes. The latter have to be understood and modeled through phenomenological and epistemological grids as well. Irrespective of the debate whether QM is a "complete" model of microphysical reality,[22] it seems highly questionable to consider it a complete description of reality *in general.* For example, the formalisms of QM currently exclude the possibility of using nonlocal correlations for information transmission; but, as Nobel laureate Brian Josephson and physicist Fotini Pallikari-Viras stated, this may have more to do with the limitations of QM formalism than reality per se.[23] Josephson and Pallikari-Viras argue that, even if we are unable to formally "map them out," patterns of quantum interconnectedness may be detectable by living organisms, which have evolved complex pattern-recognition systems over millions of years. In other words, living systems have evolved mental processes to pick up nonlocal information pertinent to their survival.

QM formalizes only microphysical processes and, at best, their interaction with consciousness; it ignores the complex forces of the macrophysical world. From a psychosocial and semantic perspective, it seems clear that a complete description of reality must necessarily take into account the cognitive agent and the forces that interact with cognitive processes: the endo-context as well as environmental, social, and contextual forces.

NOTES

1. J. Casti (1989), *Lost paradigms,* New York: William Morrow.

2. See the discussion on quantum events in the brain, below in this chapter.

3. E. H. Walker (1975), Foundations of paraphysical and parapsychological phenomena, in L. Oteri (Ed.), *Quantum physics and parapsychology.* New York: *Parapsychology Foundation.*

E. H. Walker (1984), A review of criticisms of the quantum mechanical theory of psi phenomena, *Journal of Parapsychology, 48,* 277–332.

4. W. von Lucadou (1983), On the limitations of psi: A system-theoretic approach, in W. Roll, J. Beloff & R. White (Eds.), *Research In Parapsychology 1982.* Metuchen, NJ: Scarecrow Press. See also W. von Lucadou (1987), The model of pragmatic information (MPI), *Proceedings of the 30th Annual Convention of the Parapsychological Association.* Edinburgh, Scotland: Edinburgh University.

5. Random Number Generators (RNG), or Random Event Generators, are

based on microphysical processes such as electronic noise or radioactive decay.

6. Dean Radin and Roger Nelson report a meta-analysis of research specifi-cally exploring correlations between subject intentions and RNG outputs. They located 597 experimental and 235 control studies, involving a total of 68 investigators—the bulk of this has been conducted over the past 25 years. Control studies showed a zero effect size, confirming the randomness of the RNGs. The experimental studies yielded a small effect size, which is, however, significantly superior to that of the control studies ($z = 4.1$). The combined result of all experimental studies ($z = 15.58$, $p = 1.8 \times 10^{-35}$), clearly establishes the genuineness of these anomalous phenomena.

The interpretation of these results is still hotly debated within the field. Proponents of the ESP model hold that the observed deviations from randomness are based on some form of "anomalous cognition," such as precognition; they represent a kind of selective sampling, the subject somehow sensing when to sample the RNG and thus picking favorable numbers out of an unperturbed distribution. This model, developed by Edwin May and his collaborators (1995) and known as "decision augmentation theory" (DAT), suggests that incoming psi information contributes to the decision-making process, along with other "normal" sources of data (from the environment or from memory). The authors consider this anomalous form of cognition to be mostly precognitive in nature, that is, involving a transfer of information from the future to the present.

In the DAT model, then, the random distribution is unperturbed, while the sampling is biased. By contrast, proponents of the "psychokinesis" model hold that RNG functioning is itself perturbed by subjects' psi. The random distribu-tion becomes biased or skewed, and the observed samples reflect these shifts in the distribution. In the words of May et al., in this "anomalous perturbation" model, the sampling is unbiased, while the distribution is perturbed.

Whatever the model, it is agreed, on the basis of the huge experimental database produced by different laboratories, that the *observed* RNG outputs—the outcomes of measurement, so to speak—deviate significantly from pure ran-domness in accordance with subjects' intentions.

D. Radin & R. Nelson (1989), Evidence for consciousness-related anoma-lies in random physical systems, *Foundations of Physics, 19,* (12), 1499–514.

E. C. May, J. M. Utts, & S. J. P. Spottiswoode (1995), Decision augmenta-tion theory: Toward a model of anomalous mental phenomena, *Journal of Parapsychology, 59* (3), 195–220.

7. D. Bohm (1980), *Wholeness and the implicate order,* London: Routledge & Kegan Paul.

8. K.H. Pribram (1991), *Brain and perception: Holonomy and structure in figural processing,* Hillsdale, NJ: Lawrence Erlbaum.

9. E. Laszlo (1995), *The interconnected universe,* River Edge, NJ: World Scientific.

10. Ibid.

11. Ibid., p. 8.

12. Ibid., p. 9.

13. D. Bohm (1986), A new theory of the relationship of mind and matter, *Journal of the American Society for Psychical Research, 80,* 113–36.

14. K. H. Pribram (1979), A progress report on the scientific understanding of paranormal phenomena, in B. Shapin & L. Coly (Eds.), *Brain/mind and parapsychology,* New York: Parapsychology Foundation.

15. Laszlo (1995).

16. For a review of experimental data, see D. Zohar, & I. Marshall (1994), *The Quantum Society,* New York: William Morrow.

In *The Quantum Self,* Danah Zohar had proposed Fröhlich-type quantum brain processes, occurring at the cell level (where frequencies are extremely high). She now infers that a better candidate-process should be oscillating around the EEG frequencies. See D. Zohar (1990), *The Quantum Self,* New York: Quill/William Morrow.

17. S. R. Hameroff (1994), Quantum coherence in microtubules: A neural basis for emergent consciousness? *Journal of Consciousness Studies, 1* (1), Thorverton, UK.

18. M. Conrad (1996), Percolation and collapse of quantum parallelism: A model of qualia and choice, in S. R. Hameroff, A. W. Kaszniak, & A. C. Scott (Eds.), *Toward a science of consciousness,* Cambridge, MA: MIT Press/Bradford Books.

Michael Conrad (1996) proposed a "percolation network" model of the mind-brain. This network extends from the vacuum level (where pairs of manifest and unmanifest particles form "fluctuon chains") to the level of subjective experience. The continual collapse of micro-events in the brain is viewed as the biophysical system aspect of what subjects experience as choice and decision making; while the dynamics engendered by the quantum superposition is the system aspect of subjects' qualitative experience (qualia). The percolation network, Conrad (1996) stated, "emphasizes the interweaving of processes at many different scales"; influences from the environment percolate down-scale through the network, while "decisions" made by enzymes, and then macromolecules and cells percolate up-scale. See also Conrad (1992).

19. R. Penrose (1989), *The emperor's new mind,* Oxford, UK: Oxford University Press.

S. R. Hameroff & R. Penrose (1996), Orchestrated reduction of Quantum Coherence, in S. R. Hameroff, A. W. Kaszniak, & A. C. Scott (Eds.), *Toward a science of consciousness,* Cambridge, MA: MIT Press/Bradford Books. In this joint article, Hameroff and Penrose distinguish between two types of computing in the brain. The first is digital, based on the two basic shapes (or states) of microtubules; this instantiates autonomic unconscious processes. The second one is the "self-collapse" of wave functions within microtubules, which instantiates pre- and subconscious processes.

It is also worth quoting Hameroff and Penrose (1996) on time: "The coherent superposition phase may exhibit puzzling bi-directional time flow prior to self-collapse. . . . This could explain the puzzling 'backwards time referral' aspects of preconscious processing observed by Libet et al. (1979)."

20. Penrose (1989) maintained that the "act of measurement" is responsible for the collapse of wave functions, as in orthodox QM. However, he has proposed an additional mechanism: collapse depends on the gravitational field.

21. C. H. M. Nunn, C. J. S. Clarke, & B. H. Blott (1994), Collapse of a quantum field may affect brain function, *Journal of Consciousness Studies, 1* (1), Thorverton, UK.

22. See Laszlo (1995), and also H. Stapp (1993), *Mind, matter and quantum mechanics,* Berlin: Springer-Verlag.

23. B. D. Josephson & F. Pallikari-Viras (1991), Biological utilisation of quantum nonlocality, *Foundations of Physics, 21,* 197–207.

9

ECO-SEMANTIC FIELDS

As far as our mental world is concerned, objects are rarely, if ever, isolated semantic units; rather, they are imbued with a set of context-dependent meanings. Embedded in nested exo-contexts, they are organized by the current situation, the surrounding people, and the environment. The current theory therefore views objects, as well as artificial and natural environments, as contextual semantic fields, or *eco-semantic fields (eco-fields)*.[1] The nested levels of exo-contexts show that diverse eco-semantic fields interact with each other, thus forming a complex semantic environment for a cognitive subject. In this chapter, we will see how the mind informs and organizes the surrounding eco-fields, and inversely how it is itself influenced and shaped by environmental semantic fields. We will also touch upon the collective dimension of eco-fields, using renowned art objects as examples.

MIND/ENVIRONMENT INTERACTIONS: A DYNAMICAL VIEW

Complex dynamical systems theory introduces a sophisticated view of the environment and our interactions with it. It suggests that, as individuals, we interact not with isolated, discrete energies but with whole integrated systems, having their own coherence and internal dynamics. In this approach, other living beings and people are seen as coherent self-organizing systems, evolving along their own trajectories, yet in constant interaction with each other. It is an approach that implies a far more respectful outlook on people and on life in general than does computational theory. Apart from its ethical value, dynamical systems theory also constitutes a much richer framework for understanding our interactions with the environment and the world at large. In particular, it changes our understanding of the environment in two major ways.

First of all, the *coupling* of an organism's internal forces with specific environmental forces may be understood, and formalized, as a dynamical metasystem—provided these internal and external forces are interrelated through feedback-loops. This is the powerful framework proposed by Varela, who underscored the "circularity" of such metasystems: a system reorganizes itself after being perturbed by the system it is coupled with.[2] One example here is homeostasis, for example, the organism's ability to maintain a relatively constant body temperature despite wide variations in external temperature.

As a more interesting example, let us consider the synergistic interrelation between two populations, for example, an animal (A) and its food (B)—a classic dynamic ecological system.[3] If there are too many As eating Bs, then the B population decreases, which leads to food shortages for A, and hence provokes a decrease in the A population. Less Bs are eaten, which in turn permits the B population to increase, which means As can eat more Bs, leading to an increase in the A population, a corresponding decrease in the B population, and so forth.

What we have here is an example of a metasystem, consisting of two "coupled" biosystems—the animals and their food, situated in their immediate environment. Clearly, the food aspect of the environment is not purely "external" and distinct from the animal population (as would be seen in a mechanistic framework). The food is tightly coupled with the animal population, reaching deeply into its dynamics. Insofar as the coupled environmental system contains some of the control parameters of the animal population, it is a "proximate environment"—most aptly defined as an "ecological niche." The animal-food metasystem thus underscores the existence of qualitatively differentiated structures in the experienced environment.

Of course, the organism itself is the locus of an enormous number of coupled subsystems. In *Autonomie et Connaissance*, Varela gave the example of the cell's membrane specifying the organization of the whole cell, which in its turn produces the membrane[4]; as he emphasized, the coupling dynamic modifies the distinction between internal and external. Varela employed a most revealing metaphor for this concept of circularity: Escher's *The Art Gallery*. In this painting, we see an observer standing inside a gallery that "opens" right onto the street and town; the observer is looking at a painting representing a street in which stands the very art gallery the observer himself is in. The space dimension of the whole street (including the gallery) shrinks, while rotating upward and toward the left, where it literally sinks into the tiny space of the painting; from there it starts expanding, while moving to the right, to finally become the whole street. Thus *The Art Gallery* is drawn on the model of a Klein bottle—in which the inside becomes the outside, which becomes its inside, in a circular loop.

The complex dynamical systems approach changes our understanding of the environment in a second manner: it suggests that we may be naturally attuned to external systems' global structure—their organization, their dynamics, and even their developmental trends. In dynamical terms, this means that we quite easily learn to grasp the possible states of the system (its state space), its minute changes (its trajectories), and the forces that influence it (the control parameters). From this perspective, we do not just register the discrete energetic patterns of the external system, processing these according to past knowledge (as in the cognitivist framework); nor do we simply perceive the invariant features or affordances of the environmental system (as in the ecological theory). Rather, with experience we build up a refined understanding of the global organization of external systems, their control parameters, their possible states, and their dynamical evolution.

In fact, experiments have been done to assess if humans can learn to grasp chaotic patterns and predict either the next point in a graph or the next digit produced by a chaotic function; the difference between their prediction and the real values decreased rapidly with experience, showing learning was taking place.[5]

It seems entirely plausible that we should be particularly sensitive to the global characteristics of external systems. A holistic grasp of other systems' dynamics would be a highly efficient means for making sense of the world. The ability to understand the complex and chaotic systems constituting the environment would clearly provide an adaptation advantage and have enormous survival value. Self-organizing systems are systems that fundamentally change and evolve. Interactions between such systems necessarily are constantly shifting and changing: a previously edible mushroom at some point becomes poisonous, a prairie is suddenly flooded, what was once a shelter becomes a dangerous spot, and so forth. For any cognitive system it is imperative to be able to distinguish the current, possibly modified state of an environmental system, to infer its probable interaction with oneself, and to predict its next state or behavior. As Ben Goertzel put it: "Given the assumption that some past patterns will persist, a mind must always explore several different hypotheses as to which ones will persist. . . . Therefore intelligence requires the prediction of the future behavior of partially unpredictable systems."[6]

Thus, the ability to perceive emergent global orders or patterns of evolution—one of the properties exhibited by complex systems—may afford us an extreme sensitivity to the dynamics of our surrounding self-organizing environment. A farmer somehow learns to diagnose subtle ecological events with minute accuracy and predict the effects of the weather on crops. Surfers use holistic understanding of complex chaotic systems like waves and wind, making continual adjustments so as to achieve a very fine body balance in sync with shifting natural elements. Even very young children quickly and intuitively pick up and fine-tune sophisticated strategies to get their way with those highly complex systems: human parents.

The point is that self-organized systems may be sufficiently flexible and internally coherent to grasp the systemic organization and evolution of other complex systems, as well as their own and they continually shift their interactions with these systems.

The viewing of the individual/environment interaction as an instance of mutual interaction between complex systems is especially interesting when it comes to understanding our interpersonal relationships and the cultural influences that bear upon our experience. Indeed, this approach may be applied to relationships between individuals, or between an individual and a group of any size, or in general to most interactions belonging to the semantic, cultural, and social domain.

It seems quite evident that every cultural group has a kind of self-created global coherency that will influence the individual members of that same group. Conversely, all individuals contribute to the building up of culture, some of them being major forces in this process (e.g., the founders of a new science, or art style, or political movement). Thus, neither the influence of individuals on society nor the influence of society on individuals can be ignored: individuals are co-creating culture and social systems while cultural forces, along with internal forces, build up individuals' cognitive systems and personalities. So the individuals/society metasystem consists of two interacting systems that both self-organize and exert a mutual influence upon each other. In other words, neither system is controlling or directing the other one: rather, each is *influenced* both by its own internal organization *and* by the other's organization. To put this in a more affirmative way: each system actively influences both its own internal organization and the coupled system's organization.

The dynamical systems framework may allow us to move a step

further. If we consider biological and complex physical systems as self-organizing, then we should view our interaction with them not in terms of linear, one-way causality, but rather in terms of *complex nonlinear interactions of mutual influence.* As it is, when we try to model the interaction of forces within a complex system, linear, one-way causality is wholly inadequate. It presumes a very improbable situation in such systems: that is, a force acting upon an isolated simple system, and the system always responding in the same linear manner. When it comes to dealing with an individual's cognitive and semantic interactions with external biological and physical systems, it seems all the more appropriate to formalize these in terms of complex, nonlinear, mutual-influence exchanges. This is what I will focus on in the present and following chapters, analyzing in more detail the interaction of individuals with objects, events, and other people.

SUBJECT/OBJECT SYNERGY

Injecting Meaning into the World

In our earlier discussion of theories of perception, we focused exclusively on the way in which the external world activates internal SeCos and influences the workings of the mind. Yet, to the extent to which we view both mind and environment in terms of complex, self-organized systems and network dynamics, it seems artificial to consider perception as simply an internal, interpretative process, riding a one-way causal flow (from environment to sensory system to brain). If we accept that perception and the attribution of meaning influence behavior, then we must recognize that these *cognitive acts are also organizing forces;* they are factors that change not only our internal world, but also the environment.

Cognitive frameworks like Gibson's or Varela's make room for the coupled development of motor skills with perceptual and cognitive processes; they also allow for a broad coupling of cognition/action with the environment. However, this is viewed as a "pick-up" of information in Gibson's ecological theory, or as an internal reorganization, due to perturbations, in Varela's enaction model. In the semantic fields framework, I propose that, while attributing meaning to the environment, consciousness actively contributes to its organization. Even if often too subtle to be immediately noticed, consciousness interferes with and modifies the self-organizing processes at work in nature.

This reality-shaping dynamic is obvious, of course, in the artifacts we produce. We create these on the basis of our needs, objectives, desires—all of which are clearly influenced by our perception and interpretation of the world we live in. These man-made objects have encoded in them the intended functions, or meanings projected by a given artist, inventor, manufacturer, or culture. Even a discarded object still bears such meaning—which is why we can learn so much about people long gone (say, of the Neolithic age) solely on the basis of their artifacts. Our objects are cultural objects ("World-3 objects," in Popper's terms[7]) that reflect entire knowledge and value systems; consequently our world is shaped largely by our perception and interpretation of the world.

Beyond such artifacts, our mental world alters the manner in which we interact with our environment as a whole. Our actions are based on the signification we attribute to situations; they are influenced by our worldview, our values, and our priorities. For example, we modify our environment—through urbanization, deforestation, industrialization and agriculture—according to our social and individual priorities.

Take the status of a tree in three different cultures. In an animist culture, it is a tree-spirit, worshiped, feared, and protected. In another, it is simply a source of firewood—entirely ignored as a "being," unhesitatingly exploited and harmed. In yet another culture or epoch, the tree regains some of its "specialness" as it is valued for its beauty and ecological import; it is attended to, protected, perceived aesthetically in the context of a broader setting. So, by the very nature of the diverse meanings projected onto these three trees, human beings will interact with them in very different ways, and each tree's destiny will be different. Humans obviously change the actual state of trees, as well as the trees' evolution, based on the meanings they project onto them.

This gradual modification of objects and of our environment through meaning-based actions and behaviors is hardly debatable. However, what I propose is the existence of another type of process—one that involves a subtler "real-time" injection of meaning into the world at the very instant of meaning-attribution. Although the effects are rarely observable, the environment—a tree, a man-made artifact—is modified not just via our actions but also more directly, by our interpretations of it. The semantic fields model suggests a subtle, but constant, influence of consciousness upon the external world; meaning-generation organizes physical reality in a way that reflects the mental dynamics of the imprinting individual or group.

In other words, the mere elaboration of new meanings vis-à-vis an object or event affects that system and modifies its semantic state. The instant of internal meaning-attribution is complemented by an externally oriented projection of meaning that modifies the eco-field of the object; it thus modifies the object itself, that is, its status in consensual reality.

It is postulated, then, that this projective dynamic influences the semantic organizational level in objects themselves—the eco-field. Thus, an object cannot be dissociated from the meaning we project unto it; an object whose semantic field is modified is a different object.

A circular dynamic of inter-influences takes place between the subject's mind and the object of attention (see Figure 9.1).

Figure 9.1
Subject/Object Synergy

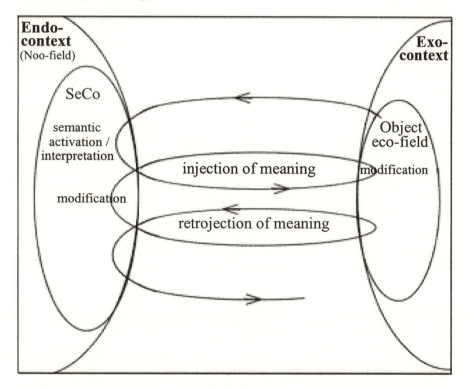

First, the perception of the object activates in the subject the internal object's SeCo. This activation spreads to related clusters through a spontaneous linkage process, generating new meanings and modifying the internal object's SeCo. Second, these newly elaborated meaning clusters are injected into the eco-field of the object itself; it is this projective process that modifies the eco-field. Finally, the modified eco-field is retrojected back into the subject's noo-field, triggering a new injection-retrojection process. This dynamic loop continues until no new meaning is generated and the subject-object synergy stabilizes.

We may thus view meaning-generation as a complex synergistic process of meaning injection-retrojection between the mind and the object, introducing constant subtle influences on consensual reality. Such generative interactions with the environment can be described as synergistic processes evolving in a time frame: the mutual influence will last until no new meaning is generated. Initially, the creation of novel meanings introduces a reorganization of both the associated SeCos (new Links being added) and the object's eco-field; then, as we habituate to a particular object, environment, or situation, and we lose intensity and focus in our interaction, the injection-retrojection synergy will tend to diminish. Thus, I would expect meaning-injection to remain latent (or subsist at a very low level) during the many human behaviors involving overlearned or rote activities and quasi-automatic actions.

At this stage in my analysis, I distinguish three major parameters influencing objects' eco-fields:

1. The *intensity* of meaning-generation—linked to emotions, felt-importance, mind-set, and so forth;

2. The frequency or *recurrence* of thoughts of similar quality (or meaning); and

3. The global *coherency* of our thought processes vis-à-vis the object (conflicting or dissonant meanings toward the same object compromise, blur, or annul the effect of a specific semantic injection).

These parameters interact according to the following rule: the more coherent, recurrent, and intensely meaningful the semantic interaction with an object, the greater the injection of meaning, and the greater the influence on the object's eco-field.

Note that this dynamic is not limited to intentional or conscious semantic effects. A very intense unconscious psychic cluster may well override consciously stated intentions and assumptions, and thus produce an observable effect in reality, in accordance with its own semantic content and dynamics. In fact, clinical and psychoanalytical observations point to very basic inter-influences between a person's psychic organization, objects that are psychically "charged" or meaningful, and situations implicating the person and these objects. For example, the psychiatrist Djohar Si Ahmed cited the case of a patient who transferred onto his brand new car some of his relational problems; his car repeatedly showed unexplained damage and decay.[8] A self-defeating neurosis may thus produce adverse, destructive effects on the person's physical environment or material belongings.

Conversely, a major growth-oriented process, such as individuation (as described by Jung), may generate positive synchronicities or meaningful coincidences between an inner mind state and an environmental situation. Series of such positive synchronicities often nurture and further the growth process itself. (We will be dealing with synchronicity in more detail in chapter 11.)

Eco-fields' Influence on the Mind

If objects' eco-fields store meaning, we must infer that they necessarily modify or influence their semantic environment—for example, the noo-fields of individuals. The semantic fields model addresses not only the influence of individuals on the environment but also the influence of meaning-loaded objects and environments upon individuals' consciousness.

To consider an object as a complex eco-semantic field, fluctuating as a function of meanings projected onto it, permits us to account for the qualitative relations we sustain with objects—emotional, metaphorical, or symbolic. It also captures its dynamical aspect, the vividness and vitality of our relations with objects—at both personal and collective levels. Let us first focus on the individual.

One's use of an object, particularly in a focused (as opposed to incidental or quasi-automatic) way, tends to activate various linked semantic constellations. This internal processing, which involves affective as well as mental facets, will be injected and thus "imprinted" in the eco-field of the object. The eco-field, in turn, will influence individuals' cognitive processes through its semantic imprints, reinforcing similarly patterned elements in the person.

"Lawn Mower" SeCo. For example, say Mr. Y's mother-in-law is visiting for the weekend, and loudly complains about the untidiness of the backyard. Soon afterward, Y's wife produces a brand new lawn mower, with compliments from her mother. Y, definitely unhappy with the criticisms in the first place, now feels like insult has been added to injury. He begrudgingly starts to use the lawn mower, but given his feelings, he is prone to find fault with it, perceiving it as impractical, badly conceived, and so forth; he also tends to be nervous and clumsy in his handling of the machine. As a result, his negative perception of the machine will constantly be feeding the machine's eco-field. These negative attributions will, of course, be retrojected toward Y with increasing intensity, further reinforcing Y's biases and thus strengthening the negative loop—until the

mowing machine indeed begins to malfunction and finally breaks down.

This unhappy situation may still be salvaged. Major bifurcations could occur with the introduction and adoption of novel meanings, a novel perspective on the machine. Say that the repair shop sends out a very professional, authoritative-looking repairman to fix the machine. While he is working on it, the repairman repeatedly sings the praises of this lawn mower—it has incredible new features, it is really top of the line, few people can even afford it, and so forth—and tops it all off by guaranteeing that it will work perfectly from now on. Awestruck, Y believes every word. A major modification takes place in Y's internal "Lawn Mower" SeCo, and his new positive attitude has positive effects on the machine's eco-field, which tends to enhance its functioning, which reinforces X's newfound mind-set, and so forth. A happy ending and everyone is smiling—especially the mother-in-law.

We must not over-generalize from such cases, however. In the above example, Y is the original owner and only user of the lawn mower. Its eco-field will thus largely reflect the corresponding internal SeCo (i.e., the "Lawn Mower" SeCo in the owner's psyche). Given a "tightly coupled" injection/retrojection process, the two semantic fields will tend to reinforce each other and co-fluctuate. On the other hand, in many, if not most, cases, things are less clear-cut.

First, the object may be imprinted by an earlier history. An object may reflect the semantic imprint of previous owners, as well as the meaning-projections (social, cultural, and personal) that led to its creation in the first place. The eco-field of an object is thus constituted by, and retains, the semantic projections of people who have interacted with it. I hypothesize, in other words, that the "imprinting" process may be cumulative: more recent or intense meanings do not necessarily wipe out older ones, but are simply added on to them.[9]

Second, insofar as an object is used or perceived by other people, it could subtly be imprinted by them as well. Whereas the eco-field of a highly personal object is presumably tightly "coupled" to its owner's noo-field, a more public object, being the focus of meaningful projections by large numbers of individuals, will acquire transpersonal or cultural semantic qualities. The subject/object synergy—the two-way semantic influences going on incessantly between individuals and objects—must therefore be viewed within a much broader network of interactions, including a range of collective and cultural influences.

While most people may not consciously perceive subtle imprints in the eco-field of objects, some individuals seem able to pick up certain information from it. In what is known as psychometry, a "sensitive" or "psychic" can sometimes sense an object's origins, or describe its current or past owners. One of the most extensive series of psychometry experiments was conducted in the 1920s by Gustav Pagenstecher, a German physician.[10] He worked extensively with a female subject who, while hypnotized, provided very precise information about the owners of objects she held in her hand. Clearly, clinical and experimental studies of this phenomenon would constitute a fecund means for evaluating the existence and nature of eco-semantic fields.

The Local Universe

It is a common experience to visit someone's home for the first time and feel that it reveals something about that person. By carefully studying the organization of the whole place, its furniture, the decoration, the objects and works of arts, and so forth, we feel we can infer a number of things about the person (habits, general outlook and interests, whether she or he tends to be artistic, intellectual, pragmatic and down to earth, a workaholic, etc.). Beyond this inferential "decoding" of a person's surroundings, however, certain visitors might sense subtler facets of the homeowner's psyche—for example, memories of important events that took place in that house, or the person's current mental state.

Given the above discussion of eco-fields, we would expect a person's immediate, day-to-day surroundings to be particularly imbued with his or her semantic "print." The global organization and qualities of the eco-fields that, in their totality, constitute the semantic dimension of this home, will reflect the feelings, mental dynamics, and values of the person who has been living there.

I propose using the term *local universe* to denote that aspect of the environment that tends to be shaped by a person's thoughts, values, and feelings; this specific environment's semantic organization reflects people's internal semantic organization.[11] The local universe is that part of phenomenal reality that is in semantic proximity to a person (or group) and that is subject to a strong and recurrent semantic influence from that person (or group).

Of course, the boundaries and specificity of each person's (or each group's) local universe cannot be rigidly defined—it is more a matter of degree. To the extent to which a person lives alone in a place, we would expect his or her print on it to be specific to that person—in terms of its intensity (how strongly the person relates to surrounding objects) and its qualities (the particular significations projected onto those objects) (see Figure 9.2). On the other hand, we live in an intensely social world, and places tend to be inhabited by more than one person. In a typical family situation, the house as a whole is a *shared local universe*, showing a blend of semantic influences from all the family members. The house, however, is part of yet a larger, shared local universe. In a community, such as a town or village, each family's local universe crisscrosses and intersects with that of others', creating a unique semantic blend. The town as a whole must then be seen as a larger shared local universe.

Figure 9.2
Person/Local Universe Synergy

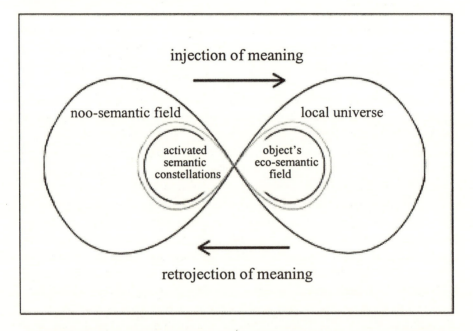

It should be emphasized that the local universe is not necessarily the physical surroundings of a person. "Local," in this context, refers to *semantically local* or *proximate*, that is, objects, events, or people closely linked to the person on a psychological or mental level. Of course, it so happens that semantic proximity often overlaps with spatial proximity; for most people, one's workplace, house, or town also happens to be the place where recurrent psychological interactions of significance take place. Nevertheless, the psyche could be just as intensely focused on faraway places, persons, or objects—rendering these semantically more proximate than those of our immediate surroundings. A painter may have her main studio in New York and a summer studio on a Greek island; the painter's local universe then includes both studios, as well as aspects of their respective surroundings. Semantically speaking she may sometimes be more tightly coupled to the distant studio, even though it is thousands of miles away. For example, while in New York, she may intensely daydream about her island, instantly introducing a synergistic loop that activates the internal "Island-Studio" SeCo and directly imprints the island-studio's eco-field.

Let me summarize the basic points concerning subject/object synergy:

- Perception/interpretation is not only an internal generation of meaning but simultaneously an act of semantic influence on whatever is perceived. This injection of meaning in the environment is in itself an organizing force, transforming the eco-fields of objects and events.

- The perceived object retrojects back into the psyche the meanings previously projected on it, as modified by its own eco-field; thus a circular semantic synergy takes place between the internal SeCo and the eco-field of the object.

- In a deeper sense, a person's noo-field tends to organize that portion of the world with which it is in constant interaction or semantic proximity, creating a kind of semantic singularity within physical reality, or local universe.

ECO-FIELDS: THE CULTURAL DIMENSION

The artifacts we produce—Popper's World-3 objects—strongly influence our culture, our collective intelligence. This is especially obvious for all kinds of informational supports—books, tapes, films, computer programs. French sociologist Pierre Lévy pointed out that such "mind technologies" ("les technologies de l'intelligence") should be seen as cognitive "agents" rather than just passive artifacts.[12] Along with human minds, they participate in a vast collective dimension of mental functioning, which he refers to as a "human/machine thinking collective."[13] In his terms, this community is equivalent to a transpersonal cognitive network.

Actually, any cultural object may also participate in the transpersonal cognitive network. Take, for example, the first chair without legs—something that was truly astonishing, when originally introduced. The new design may have been a witty and innovative mix of diverse structural and functional constructs such as "chair," "sitting," "esthetics," "decoration," "marketing," and so forth. When the new chair began to meet commercial success, and the new design became an accepted fact, the collective constellation of the concept "chair" evolved; it now integrated the possibility of "chair without legs." At that point, something shifted in the culture as a whole, insofar as the consensual definition and conception of chairs was no longer exactly the same.

It follows, then, that the creation of new meaningful objects by innovative thinkers, artists, designers, scientists, or inventors influences their whole culture. Embodied in the object—a work of art, an influential book, a new technology, an innovative architectural design—the new meanings will generate a collective semantic process, as people adopt and modify these meanings, integrating them into their own semantic lattices. In their creative interpretation of novel works, individuals tacitly penetrate the collective semantic dimension, participating in the generation and stabilization of shared meanings.

The eco-field of any work, of course, retains, as its nucleus, what has been embedded into it by its creator. To the extent to which it becomes renown, it acquires an added semantic energy; the more individuals relate to it, and the greater its impact on their minds and imagination, the more intense the object's eco-field. Art books, reprints, and references to the work will all enrich the work's eco-field: eventually, it belongs as much to the culture as a whole, as it does to its creator.

Prestigious cultural objects may exert a profound influence on a culture. Through its eco-field, for example, a historical monument may organize the semantic space of a town's quarter and influence the mood and behaviors of its inhabitants. To take a concrete example, think about Leonardo Da Vinci's *La Joconde* (Mona Lisa)—a vital part of the eco-field of Le Louvre museum. Over the course of several centuries, *La Joconde* has inspired meaning-generating activities worldwide—thus forming a huge collective SeCo. What I am suggesting is that the painting's eco-field itself bears the imprints of these collective significations; it is modified by the continuous projection of meaning into it. As a renowned work of art, *La Joconde* is a different object from what it would have been were it simply an unknown painting tucked away in someone's attic.

The painting itself (the object) is the embodied portion of this vast collective SeCo—a focal point through which intense semantic synergies are channeled. If the object is destroyed, the collective SeCo still lingers in the culture, but its focal point has become virtual. In this perspective, even if a perfect copy were made to replace the real work—so perfect that it would fool the best art critics—this copy's eco-field would not be the same as that of the original. It would lack major semantic inscriptions, not only from *La Joconde*'s creator, but also from all those who have seen and discussed and admired this work down the centuries. It follows that the copy's influence on new observers and even upon its surroundings would be different. Destruction of the painting would modify not only the organization of the collective constellation *La Joconde*, but also that of Le Louvre: Le Louvre without *La Joconde* would not be the same museum.

NOTES

1. I am excluding evolved living systems (such as higher animals and humans) from this discussion, as they display quite distinct dynamics. In particular, the organizational closure of their noo-fields and their generative semantic dynamics preclude a passive semantic influence. We will be treating interactions between such systems in chapter 10.

2. Varela, Thompson, & Rosch (1991).

3. The application of dynamics to the interaction of two animal populations (in particular, to the prey-predator relationship) was first developed by Lotka and Volterra; see the well known Lotka-Volterra vectorfield in Abraham, Abraham, & Shaw, C. (1990), p. (II)32.

4. Varela (1989).

5. S. Guastello (1995), *Chaos, catastrophe, and human affairs,* Mahwah, NJ: Lawrence Erlbaum Associates, p. 121.

6. Goertzel (1994), p. 37.

7. Popper & Eccles (1977).

8. D. Si Ahmed (1990), *Parapsychologie et psychanalyse,* Paris: Dunod.

9. I have already suggested that, in the mind, earlier experiences with a particular situation are not wiped out by more recent ones, but are rather more deeply "enfolded," or fractalized in several linked SeCos. A similar dynamic might exist in eco-fields: earlier semantic influences on an object remain deeply "enfolded" in its eco-field.

10. W. Roll (1967), Pagenstecher's contribution to parapsychology, *Journal of the American Society for Psychical Research, 61,* 219–40.

11. C. Hardy (1997a), Semantic fields and meaning: A bridge between mind and matter, *World Futures, 48,* 161–70, Newark: Gordon & Breach.

12. Lévy (1990).

13. Ibid., p. 11.

10

EVENTS-IN-MAKING

A significant part of our interactions with the environment involves what we generically call "events." That term covers a lot of ground, of course: from microscopic quantum events, to insignificant human-scale events (like dropping a pencil), to international or global events affecting our species or our planet, all the way up to cosmic-scale events that occurred billions of light years in our past.

My focus here is on human-scale events that have significant consequences, whether on a personal or a collective scale. My approach will be to treat these as highly complex and multifaceted systems, spread out in time and space, and characterized by a kind of fluid, evolving quality. Given this fluidity, we could think of events as vortex forces in a historical or biographical flow that become somewhat more fixed and defined once a stable, consensual interpretation has been reached. As we will be seeing, the meaning we attribute to these complex systems is a prominent aspect of their reality, and of their influence; they are therefore of major import for any semantic model.

DYNAMIC UNFOLDING OF AN EVENT

The interpretation of a social, collective event is a holistic process. We simultaneously perceive a whole network of forces and activities: major players, circumstances, emotions, the setting and background, the interests at play. We are also often aware of the evolution of the event in time and its subtlest developments.

When individuals first perceive an event, this generates an internal semantic constellation or SeCo that will be integrated in their semantic lattice. If a similar event is observed later on, this SeCo will be reactivated, serving as an interpretational background. Nevertheless, given that no two events are likely to be identical, the perception of the new event will tend to trigger some new linkages and generate a novel meaning-cluster that, of course, ends up modifying the original SeCo.

The event itself is a semantic constellation—or event-SeCo—that groups clusters of meanings, projected by the people who observe and participate in it. Event-SeCos are thus quite analogous to object-SeCos or eco-fields and manifest synergistic dynamics analogous to those we have seen for eco-fields. I suggest, in other words, that the semantic dynamic of mind/event interactions is similar to that of mind/object interactions: people inject meaning into the event-SeCo that, thus modified, will then be retrojected back into each observer's noo-field. Thus, while perceiving/interpreting the event, each person's noo-field is not only affected by it, but also interferes with it, modifying its unfolding to some degree or another. As with eco-fields, each of the participants in a given event influence it in their own, particular manner.

The Event as a Semantic Dynamical System

What we commonly refer to as "an event" is in fact a complex, multi-faceted system, spread-out in time and space, and involving dozens, perhaps hundreds of sub-events. These sub-events are all products of interactions between numerous forces, as the whole system evolves in a given time period and context.

Let us consider the evolution of a complex social event—for example, a strike. In attempting to explain any strike, a multiplicity of factors is generally brought up by experts, the media, politicians, and so forth; this leads us to interpret the event within a multicausal framework. However, it is clear that, depending upon the experts' background (e.g., sociology, macro-economics, psychology) and the organization calling on them (e.g., government versus media), they are bound to come up with quite divergent views on the relative import of different factors, the ways in which these factors interact, and so forth.

There is nothing new, here. This is the kind of interpretational combat we witness all the time as each opinion-group seeks to rally the consensus to its own particular viewpoint. What *is* important, though, is to note that the interpretations that predominate will largely determine the unfolding of the event itself. For example, from the very outset of the strike, the strikers' interpretation-in-the-making of others' reactions to the strike will influence their own subsequent behaviors and the strike's evolution. Indeed, all the different or opposing social groups will be pursuing such semantic strategies of interpretation/action, analyzing feedback from the larger social context. Glued to their TV and the media reports, they will be interpreting and re-interpreting the statements of the government, the general public, corporations, and so forth and adjusting their own subsequent decisions and actions accordingly.

Whenever one particular interpretational framework concerning an event (the strike) predominates, it stabilizes a cluster of concepts concerning factors, meanings, and consequences. This framework will involve inferences and implications not only about the present event, but also about future ones as well: from now on, the interpreted event will itself act as a precedent, a determining factor for future similar events and their associated contexts.

The point is that social events are predominantly semantic events. They are woven by, and weave themselves into, networks of meanings—complex, ever-shifting blends of individual and collective SeCos. Any significant analysis of social events implicitly recognizes their semantic nature, insofar as it necessarily refers to psychological—as opposed to merely physical—factors: the overall social "climate," the stress, tensions, frustrations and anger, the symbolic import of the event, the political context, the priorities, values and demands of those involved, the profiles of leaders and speakers, public opinion polls, media coverage and interpretations, and so forth. Indeed, negotiating a settlement in an event such as a strike has more to do with finding a common semantic ground than figuring out the numbers.

An event, then, is produced by a whole system of forces, interacting with a given context. A dynamical system framework is ideally adapted to formalize the evolution and probable outcomes of such a complex system.

A good example of dynamical formalization was given by Stephen Guastello when analyzing accidents in the workplace. He highlighted a basic "circular causation": stress gives rise to anxiety, leading to error and accidents—which then leads to subsequent increases in stress.[1] Guastello presented two additional loops. In one, the ratio of environmental hazards in the workplace and the witnessing of actual accidents increase workers' sense of danger, leading to heightened stress, and increasing the probability of future accidents. In the second loop, workers' beliefs concerning the cause of accidents—due to their own behaviors versus being beyond their own control—also influences stress levels. For example, the belief that the company has taken "strict safety measures" decreases the probability of future accidents, simply by changing workers' beliefs about the likelihood of accidents.

In this dynamical system formalization, then, we see how mechanistic forces (environmental hazards) can interact with psychological ones (beliefs), as well as psychophysiological states (anxiety). Clearly, a linear reconstruction of such sociopsychological events cannot possibly account for the complexity of what is really involved. The sheer number and complexity of interacting variables (or, high dimensionality) render the event-system nonlinear; its pronounced instability highlights the presence of chaos.

In order to understand such systems, we need to take into account both the immediate and the more remote contextual forces that bear on an event's unfolding, as well as the fundamental acts of attributing and creating meaning. Most important, we cannot treat events as simply occurring at a given point in time; rather, we must view them as dynamical systems of interacting forces, evolving in a time frame.

In the semantic framework, then, an event is the end product of an entire system of interacting forces, evolving nonlinearly in a given context and time frame. To understand an event, we need to understand the *event-in-making*, the process of an event being informed by an ensemble of forces.

THE EVENT-IN-MAKING

Let us then focus on the processes leading up to and informing an event prior to its actual occurrence. The event-in-making can be viewed as a SeCo, a constellation consisting of numerous forces, the interaction of which in time leads to a specific outcome (the event).

Say, for example, that the potential future event is the outbreak of a serious back problem in person P. The possible outcomes range from P developing an acute lumbago, to his having a mild, transitory back pain—and all shades in between. The event-in-making-SeCo is shaped by a variety of complex forces. Physical and physiological factors include genetic predispositions, overall health, vertebrae alignment, age, nutritional habits, environmental factors, and so forth. The semantic and psychosocial factors may include level of stress, personality style, self-image, body posture at work, lifestyle, beliefs about health and illness, friend and family influences, intentions and objectives, values, and worldviews.

All these forces contribute, to different degrees, to the event-in-making; each points toward a certain outcome—a possible end-state—within a given time frame (e.g., lumbago occurring in three months). We can therefore assign a strength or weight to each force, representing its specific impact upon the future event.

Whenever a plurality of probable outcomes seems to converge within the same region of the state space—leading to a similar event, in a delimited time range—this suggests the existence of an attractor. We may thus end up with one or several attractive regions. In our example, three attractors are shown, representing the probable outcomes at the end of a three-month period (see Figure 10.1).

If the event-in-making under consideration has, for example, only two possible outcomes (e.g., passing an exam or not), then each force points to one of the two competitive attractors. The most probable outcome will then be represented by the attractor with the greatest strength, that is the one displaying the densest, most weighted attractive region.

Prior to the actual occurrence of the event, each time we take a "snapshot" of the event-in-making-SeCo, it will point to a somewhat different probable configuration of the future event. Over time, given the multiple forces feeding into a specific event and all the possibilities for change in any of these forces, the event-in-making appears as an *evolving semantico-physical system.*

The various forces, of course, interact with each other, reinforcing or decreasing their strengths and the probability of certain outcomes. The strength and direction of the forces at play may also be modified, drastically or subtly, with the introduction of a new contextual force, or by virtue of a person's sudden decision or action.

All along the development of the event-in-making, these diverse interacting forces give birth to micro-events that will produce shifts in the probable outcomes. In our illness example, P may experience, in rapid succession, two apparently unrelated micro-events: an instance of great fatigue and serendipitously tuning into a talk show concerning sports and health. The interaction of these two micro-events may set the stage for a major resolution—to start an intense regime of daily exercise—that then leads to a significant reorganization of the event-in-making-SeCo (see Figure 10.1).

At any moment, in other words, the event-in-making-SeCo may be subject to minor changes, major fluctuations, or radical shifts in its organization. We are dealing here with complex nonlinear systems in which subtle contextual influences may suddenly bring about a dramatic change or bifurcation in the SeCo's organization. Thus the event-in-making-SeCo is a dynamical system binding together all probable states of the future event, and displaying their respective weights at each instant in time.

Figure 10.1
Lumbago Event-in-making

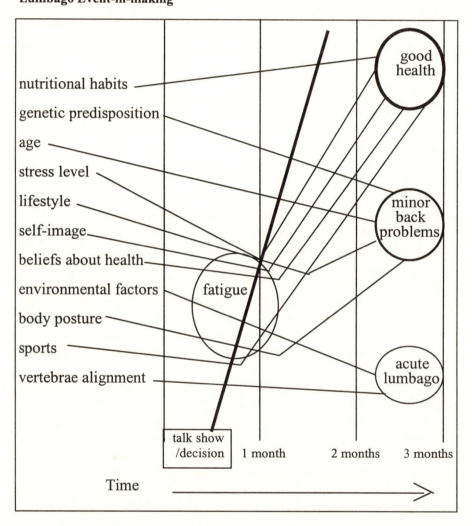

In the present framework, then, the forces informing the event-in-making-SeCo are not just external forces, linearly causing an objective event, but rather a system of forces interacting nonlinearly to shape probable outcomes. While physical forces clearly play a role, these are certainly not the *only* factors contributing to an event; their effect is, in fact, modulated and specified by the whole ensemble of semantic and psychosocial forces at work in the system. Other factors may also contribute to an event-in-making: a certain degree of randomness in the system,[2] haphazard interactions with unrelated systems, and, as we will see in the following chapter, synchronistic occurrences.

Synergy between Individuals and the Event-in-making

Because of its semantic dimension, the event-in-making is in synergy with the noo-fields of all people strongly connected to it. This is a little tricky, as we have to distinguish between the event-in-making-SeCo (often involving a collective construct), and the internal event-SeCo; the latter is within the person's noo-field and expresses this person's particular view of the event. The distinction here is analogous to that between the eco-field of an object (typically a collective projection, attached to the object itself) and its internalized counterpart in each subject's noo-field (the internal object-SeCo).

The internal event-SeCo is quite different from the event-in-making-SeCo, because it reflects the specific dispositions of a person vis-à-vis the future event, that is, his or her own meanings about the event to be. Of course, the more an event-in-making is one's private affair, the greater the similarities between the internal-SeCo and the event-in-making-SeCo. Conversely, the greater the number of people involved in the future event (for example, the Academy Awards), the weaker the relationship between each person's internal-SeCo and the event-in-making.

So, let us examine the synergistic processes between an individual and an event-in-making. A person's internal event-SeCo links semantic elements that situate that person vis-à-vis the future event. This internal event-SeCo is coupled with the event-in-making-SeCo itself—just as, in the case of objects, the internal object-SeCo is coupled with the eco-field of the object, in an injection/retrojection process.

As long as the subject nurtures thoughts and emotions about the future event, he or she keeps interacting with the event-in-making-SeCo, injecting meanings unto it and thus modifying—subtly or dramatically—the event-in-making. The meaning clusters are then retrojected from the event-in-making-SeCo back to the subject, modifying the internal-SeCo. In other words, the synergy instantiates an ongoing dynamical process of injection of meanings into the event-in-making, and a retrojection of meanings back to the psyche (see Figure 10.2).

Figure 10.2
Person/Event-in-making Synergy

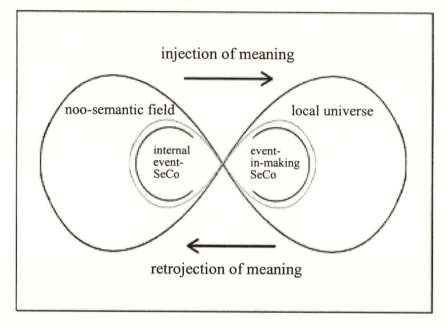

injection of meaning

noo-semantic field

local universe

internal
event-
SeCo

event-
in-making
SeCo

retrojection of meaning

Thus, unlike observational theories in quantum physics (see chapter 8), it is here held that individuals' influence on an event starts well before its observation—even before the actual unfolding of the event itself. The mere fact of nurturing feelings or thinking about a possible event creates an event-in-making-SeCo, or influences it, if it already exists.

Anyone participating in the implementation of a given event (e.g., performers, people analyzing the feasibility of a project, a futurist entertaining alternative scenarios) co-shapes the final configuration of that event. Each participant can thus be viewed as a force (or a set of forces) feeding the event-in-making-SeCo and moving the event-to-be toward a certain configuration.

Let me outline the main parameters that are relevant to this imprinting of an event-in-making.

Semantic Intensity. While many persons may contribute to an event, not all individuals relate to it in the same manner. Of crucial importance, then, is the parameter of semantic intensity—the degree of involvement or implication of an individual in the event-in-making. The way somebody thinks and feels about the event before its advent and the way he or she perceives and starts reacting to it when it unfolds are immediately input into the system of forces informing the emerging event.

Ownership. Another relevant parameter here is ownership—the number of people contributing to the event-in-making. In the simplest case of a person intending to do something that concerns her alone (e.g., her solo holiday), she is the main person informing the event. If she changes her mind-set or her behavior, one of the major forces feeding the event-in-making-SeCo is modified, and the event itself will be drastically changed or even suppressed. On the other hand, all things being equal, the more people are involved in a future event, the more each participant's semantic influence on the collective event will tend to be diluted.

Coherence. This is also a relevant parameter. The extent to which diverse individuals' inputs are coherent or consistent with each other will clearly affect the event-in-making. The more conflicting or desynchronized the various inputs, the less influence they will collectively have on the event-in-making-SeCo. Inversely, whenever beliefs, intuitions, or predictions about a future event are shared by several people (thus pointing to the same outcome), this reinforces their influence on the event and increases the strength of the attractor representing this outcome.

This semantic synergy between individuals and events leads to some very interesting consequences. When a participant believes or stipulates that two factors are linked in a certain way—and should therefore bring about such and such a consequence—this specific semantic linkage gets to be injected into the events-in-making-SeCo. Thus the process of imagining and attributing relations between factors or events can contribute to the creation or amplification of these relations in reality. Perhaps one of the most dramatic illustrations of this can be found in the extensive research upon expectancy effects. Whether in experimental, medical, educational, or work settings, these expectancy effects show that our values, assumptions, hypotheses, beliefs, and convictions constitute powerful parameters in the shaping of reality.[3]

NOTES

1. Guastello (1995).

2. E. Lorenz (1993), *The essence of chaos,* Seattle: University of Washington Press. See also D. Ruelle (1993), *Chance and chaos*, Princeton, NJ: Princeton University Press.

3. Expectancy effects have been studied in several domains, including experimental psychology, industrial and organizational psychology, education, and psychosomatic medicine. For a complete review of interpersonal expectancy effects up through the 1970s, see R. Rosenthal & D. Rubin (1978), Interpersonal expectancy effects: the first 345 studies, *Behavioral and Brain Sciences*, 3, 377-415.

Important insights on experimenter effects in laboratory research can also be found in the parapsychological literature; for a review, see M. Varvoglis (1992), *La Rationalité de l'Irrationnel,* Paris: InterEditions.

II

COMMUNICATION AND
COLLECTIVE CONSCIOUSNESS

Transpersonal and collective modes of thinking and feeling are beginning to be highlighted in a wide range of scientific domains. For sociologist Pierre Lévy, the thinking process reaches beyond the individual; it is collective and transpersonal, being shaped not only by language, but also by cultural objects such as computers, information storage devices, simulation systems, and so forth.[1] Lévy talks about a "collective cognitive network" that comprises both society at large, and the products and objects of a culture—especially technological and informational objects.[2]

Of great interest, also, is the position of philosopher of science Isabelle Stengers.[3] She stated that "technological innovation . . . constitutes a creation of meanings" that can only impose itself only if and when "it succeeds in taking on meaning" in the collectivity at large.[4] This means an innovation not only has to be accepted by the scientific community, but also within a plurality of platforms—social, cultural, economic, and political. Stengers thus concurs with a growing number of thinkers who view scientific "facts" as neither purely objective nor purely abstract representations, but rather as constructions based on extremely complex interactions between social, cultural, political, and economic factors.[5]

Based on the study of insect societies like ants, William Sulis introduces some interesting insights about the workings of collective intelligence.[6] Insect collective intelligence demonstrates dynamics based on stochasticity, contextual dependency, and interacting subprocesses, while it is devoid of hierarchical controls. This collective intelligence, constantly and intensely interacting with the environment, is highly adaptive. Similar "irrational" cognitive processes are, in his view, instantiated within the human brain and within human groups, such as organizations. Indeed, Sulis suggests that these were the cognitive processes humans used before the advent of rational thought, and that they are still used by individuals, in parallel with rational thought.

Carl Jung highlighted collective aspects of the unconscious, posing that archetypes were psychic roots shared by all of humanity, and emerging in the psyche through dreams, art, and myths.[7] Following his pioneering work, a growing number of thinkers are underscoring the collective aspects of consciousness.[8]

The present chapter outlines ways in which semantic fields theory may break new ground in this domain. The parameters specific to the semantic dimension pose the premises for nonlocal interactions and interconnectedness. These, in turn, are the foundation for interpersonal and collective forms of consciousness, in the sense that individuals co-create collective constellations. Whether on an interpersonal or collective level, individuals remain connected through the semantic networks they weave between them.

A BRIDGE BETWEEN MINDS

The Many Levels of Communication

Communication is among the most important facets of human nature. It is largely through the many forms of communication that culture—as a shared set of significations—is constructed. It is through communication that each and every individual develops meaning-generative methodologies and partakes of human society. A baby could not become fully human without communicating with others, that is, without familiarizing himself or herself with, and actively participating in, the human semantic dimension—language, beliefs, value-system, cultural objects, social organization, collective know-how, and so forth.

The sharing of meaning is what keeps us mentally alive. For as long as we interact with other people and with things that mean something to us, we remain in an integrative and evolving process. Meaning that is shared is meaning that is created and re-created with each moment, with each new situation.

Of course, as discussed here, meaning has to be distinguished from information in the sense of Shannon, which is an encoded message, quantified in terms of bits, and transmitted from a sender to a receiver.[9] It seems more and more obvious that Shannon's theory of information—a misnomer, at that—is strictly a theory of message transmission; it does not, in any way, account for the semantic aspect of the message, that is, its interpretation by a given person, in a given endo- and exo-semantic context.

While communicating, we perceive others through our own semantic lattice: we "understand" them through the SeCos of our past experiences and through our own particular connections to collective constellations (e.g., cultural frameworks or theoretical paradigms, values, social, political, or religious groups, etc.). Thus, a person's interpretation of another's words is a complex emergent, deriving from her or his own, highly idiosyncratic noo-field. The words and concepts we exchange cannot be viewed as stable, fixed entities that are passed on from one person to the other as if we were tossing objects between us.[10] Although a consensual platform allows for basic, practical understanding, we never grasp exactly what the other person intends to communicate. Despite the existence of norms and conventions, even a single concept can never have the exact same meaning for any two persons.

Indeed, it could even be argued that what we ourselves express is never exactly what we mean to communicate. Freudian slips may be just flagrant examples of something far more general: the multiple—and possibly conflicting—levels of meaning that exist in each of us, and the complexity of the processes involved in recognizing and expressing these different levels of meaning.

Recent research on communication is beginning to integrate certain psychoanalytic concepts, exploring the interplay of conscious and subconscious dynamics during interpersonal exchange.[11] This approach takes into account the interweaving of two distinct levels of meaning during communication. I believe however, that the concept of semantic constellations permits a more complex perspective on communication dynamics.

Let us examine an exchange between two persons, Annie and Ken. They have both seen a particular film and are discussing their respective perceptions of it. A rather common situation—but the mental processes involved in such an exchange can be very complex. While describing a particular scene, Annie may simultaneously be silently analyzing a certain event in that scene, preparing her argument and the appropriate words and expressions to present it, adapting her style to the theme or to Ken's communication style, pondering whether it would be appropriate to share a certain joke triggered by her reflection, and so forth.

Beyond all these conscious-intentional processes much more is also going on. While Annie hears Ken speak, new chain-linkages are continuously activated in her lattice. For example, a particular phrase by Ken activates the sub-SeCo of a childhood souvenir in Annie, instantiating, in turn, numerous auxiliary processes. Furthermore, chain-linkages within Annie's semantic lattice will be triggered not only by Ken's explicit verbal message, but also by other sources—for example, by Annie's interpretation of Ken's body-language and facial expressions, or by Annie's processing of other sensory inputs from the surroundings (shapes and colors, smells, background noises, etc.). All these semantic activations will, of course, branch into neurophysiological processes that, in turn, could activate other SeCos, or simply contribute to the overall endo-context through which Annie interprets Ken's message.

Out of the dense connective processes taking place within the network of activated SeCos, the more intense or reiterated meanings may emerge into the flow of consciousness. For example, Annie's childhood memory, triggered by Ken's description of a scene in the film, may have popped into consciousness because the affective charge associated with it exceeded a certain threshold of intensity, or because several chain-linkages converged upon that memory.[12] Many other activated Links, however, will remain below the threshold of awareness.

Communication then, engages several physiological and cognitive levels simultaneously. Insofar as similarly layered activation processes are being triggered in both interlocutors, we must suppose that semantic intersubject linkages occur on several levels as well. Thus, in parallel to their explicit, verbal dialogue, Ken and Annie will unconsciously be engaged in other forms of exchange, such as body language, mirrored sensations or emotions, and so forth. For example, they may both be subliminally registering identical kinds of information from the environment, or experiencing and interpreting subtle emotions evoked by their discussion. This implicit type of communication may go unnoticed or it may briefly break through into the flow of awareness—for example, as an insight about the other's health, personality, or emotional life, or as an apparently innocuous question (that just so happens to be the topic that the other person had been trying to avoid!).

Interface-SeCo

Let us take a closer look at our example. At the moment Ken evokes the film, the SeCo associated to that film—call it F_k—is activated in his lattice, while the corresponding F_a SeCo is also activated in Annie's lattice. Obviously, since each individual's endo-context is unique, the two "Film" SeCos will be different and the array of activated Links will be specific to each person. It is hardly surprising that Ken and Annie will experience the film somewhat differently.

However, there is sufficient common ground between Ken and Annie for the discussion about the film to create semantic bridges between the F_k and F_a SeCos. Indeed, the discussion about the film will induce a number of new inferences, insights, and shared or divergent interpretations in both individuals. As the F_k and F_a SeCos evolve, the exchange will give birth to a new SeCo that includes elements from both persons' experience, as well as elements from their current dialogue. Essentially, through their discussion, Annie and Ken are generating a shared semantic constellation that acts as an *interface-SeCo* between them. It organizes itself according to the ongoing dynamics of the exchange: agreement, disagreement, distinctions, associations, and so forth. This interface-SeCo will thus link all semantic elements brought into the discussion— although the input and position of each interlocutor in the discussion will be preserved through specific relators attached to the Links.

The interface-SeCo is a semantic network of shared meaning, generated by an interaction between individuals who are focused on a common attentional object. It includes both shared and divergent meanings, as well as emergent significations that spring forth from the exchange and that were not previously contained in the individual SeCos of the interlocutors.

Each person will, of course, evolve unique connective links between the interface-SeCo and her or his own internal SeCo (F_k or F_a); so each will relate to the interface-SeCo in his or her unique way. On the other hand, the interface-SeCo may produce chain-linkages that move beyond the F_k and F_a SeCos, reaching into broader regions of the two persons' noo-fields. In this manner, the interface-SeCo may allow each of the two individuals to "penetrate" deeper into the other's noo-field, while following the activated links. As a striking side effect of their exchange— and depending upon the level of empathy between the two individuals—a "fusional" dynamic may emerge, whereby one person is practically capable of perceiving things through the other person's mind.

The interface-SeCo thus constitutes a shared platform; potentially, it may become a semantic bridge for subsequent exchanges, intertwining the noo-fields of people and strengthening their relationship on the semantic level.

Of course, depending on several factors (e.g., depth of communication, degree of empathy between individuals) the interface-SeCo could either subsist as a complex semantic network, or quickly dissipate. On the one hand, it might turn out to be little more than a transient structure, lasting no more than the period of the discussion. Following a quick and superficial exchange the interface-SeCo will then rapidly break down, leaving but minor modifications of the activated internal SeCos. For example, after the two friends go their separate ways, many of the Links pertaining to the interface-SeCo will then weaken and dissolve, while other Links will be reorganized, their elements recombining or creating new Links within the noo-field of each person.

On the other hand, some facets of the interface-SeCo might remain intact and then will be reactivated, modified, or enlarged upon whenever the friends meet and exchange anew. To the extent to which they continue to see each other and nurture their relationship, the interface-SeCo will be reinforced and grow with each new exchange, housing clusters of topics that are of shared interest, integrating more sub-SeCos, and linking to more and more associated SeCos.

A striking consequence of this dynamic is that interface-SeCos can serve as a nonlocal link between two individuals' minds, allowing for exchanges at a distance. As we have seen, the parameters relevant to the semantic dimension are quite distinct from those used to describe classical space-time. For example, on the basis of *semantic proximity*, two spatially distant individuals can be quite close in the semantic dimension. It follows that if, at some point, Ken recollects his conversation with Annie, the reactivation of the interface-SeCo will also activate associated SeCos in Annie—independently of where she is situated. A sufficiently elaborate and extensive interface-SeCo could thus constitute a bridge for many low-level semantic interactions that mostly pass unnoticed, or remain entirely nonconscious. However, situations of intense activation of certain SeCos in one person—and, consequently, of the interface-SeCo—could lead to intense semantic activation of corresponding SeCos in the other person, and to a breakthrough of specific information into the flow of consciousness.

The interpenetration of the interface-SeCo into two individuals' noo-fields could thus be the basis of synchronistic experiences between people, of "intuitions" we have about people, or of telepathy (empathically experiencing the thoughts or sensations of another person at a distance).[13] Beyond this coupling between individuals, however, the concept of interface-SeCo can be extended to shed light on broader, collective forms of meaning-generation.

WEAVING THE TRANSPERSONAL NETWORK

Synchronicity

While allowing for chance (or fortuitous coincidences) in the formation of events, we nevertheless must also consider another kind of factor that, all too often, is confused with chance events: meaningful coincidences, or synchronicities.

The psychiatrist Carl Jung introduced the concept of synchronicity to denote striking meaningful coincidences between an external, objective event and a person's internal, mental processes. According to Jung, synchronicities are instantiated between the psyche and a distant event, or between the psyche and a future event; they are identified by the meaning a certain event (or name, or object) takes on for a person, given her or his mind-state at the moment. One of the most oft-cited examples involved a golden scarab. Jung had a patient who was "stuck" in her treatment—a woman who seemed to resist all attempts to initiate a constructive therapeutic process. One day, she came to Jung with a dream about a golden scarab. Just as she was relating it, a scarab with golden hues popped into the room through the half-open window. Both she and Jung were so startled by this meaningful coincidence that the communication barriers suddenly collapsed with an in-depth exchange, centered on this event. As Jung commented, the synchronicity triggered the transference process and was clearly the turning point in this woman's therapy.

Synchronistic events such as these are particularly impressive, for they act as a catalyst—they bring about a totally new mind-set or situation in the persons who experience them. In the above case, the synchronicity not only reinforces the meaningfulness of the scarab symbol in the patient's dream; it also helps bring about insight and a whole new attitude in her relationship with her therapist. In other words, it launches a semantic process of meaning-generation.

In his book on synchronicity, Carl Jung argued that such occurrences are "acausal processes," revealing a completely different order of interactions than those implied by classical notions of causality. This perspective was amplified in Jung's work with the physicist and Nobel laureate Wolfgang Pauli, in which they elaborated upon the idea of synchronicity as a particular class of phenomena, involving an acausal principle.[14] Coupled with the Jungian concept of the collective unconscious, these views suggest that Jung considered the psyche as somewhat independent of the space-time constraints of classical physics—an idea which is certainly endorsed by the present model as well, when it refers to the semantic dimension.

The discovery of synchronicity and the description of its essential characteristics were certainly an act of genius. The concept is rich and fertile; one gets the impression that we have hardly scratched the surface, as it keeps stimulating new insightful studies.[15] Nevertheless, we are still confronted with the basic question: How do synchronicities work? The semantic linkage process could, I believe, explicate the dynamics underlying synchronicities, and help explain how they are instantiated.

As with Jung and Pauli's "acausal processes," the semantic model is based on an understanding that in synchronistic events we are not dealing with a sequential, linear form of causality, but rather with a completely different type of process—one that displays nonlocal connective influences.

Nonlocality here refers to the fact that semantic linkages are independent of distance between two semantic fields and are governed by semantic parameters (such as semantic proximity), as opposed to space-time parameters. Also, in referring to connective "influences" rather than "causes" (see chapter 5), I am emphasizing the idea that the processes involved do not strictly determine the semantic system's state; rather, they contribute to the manner in which the semantic system evolves and self-organizes.

In synchronicity, connective influences arise from contextual events that are semantically related to the main event. What makes these contextual events take on a particular meaning (while scores of other background events do not) is that their signification is strongly linked to that of the main event itself. Once endowed with meaning, they become an integral part of the event-SeCo.

"Relationship" dual SeCo. Let us consider a fictitious example of synchronicity, so as to illustrate the role of connective influences, their relation to a core event, and the way in which they may influence a person's creation of meaning and decision making.

After three days of hesitation and anxiety, Ted decides to go see his longtime girlfriend Anita, and put an end to their love affair. He leaves his place at 4:30 pm, and, unexpectedly, just a few blocks from Anita's home, he runs into his friend Dan, whom he had not seen for months. He tells him he is on his way to Anita's to end their relationship. Dan suggests that he buy Ted a drink, and they go to a cafe to discuss the matter further. By the end of the drink, Dan has dissuaded Ted from his plan; Ted turns back and heads home.

The event-in-making here is "Breakup." During his three-day torment, Ted was struggling with the dilemma—should he break up with Anita or not? We can use the semantic fields model to trace the evolution of his relationship and understand something of the underlying semantic dynamics. At some point in the relationship, following a particular problem, a tiny cluster of frustration and rejection may have formed within Ted's "Relationship" (R) SeCo. Having gradually grown in density and intensity, this cluster ended up becoming a sub-SeCo itself, thus depleting the original R SeCo. Later on, with added aggravations or frustrations, the original R SeCo transformed into a dual configuration consisting of two sub-SeCos. The *"Breakup" sub-SeCo (B)* groups and interlinks all the semantic elements reinforcing this outcome: memories of arguments, topics of discord, complex dynamics of rejection and fear, negative referential concepts, rationalizations ("reasons" for breaking up), and so forth. The *"Continuation" sub-SeCo (C)* groups diverse semantic elements in support of sustaining the relationship (or the event non-B): recollections of special moments, vacations together, topics of mutual interest, shared hobbies, and so forth.

Note that the B constellation is not just a negative (or mirror) image of the C SeCo; its organization might be quite different, with the densest clusters concentrating around a different set of qualities. For example Ted's rationale for breaking up may be tied to a frustration in the affective/emotive cluster, while his rationale for sustaining the relationship may be more concerned with gratification in the artistic/intellectual clusters.

The dual SeCo, then, involves two attractors: Attractor B organizes the forces that tend toward the event "Breakup," while Attractor C organizes those leading to the alternative event "Continuation." At some point, the two sub-SeCos attained equal intensity, thus triggering Ted's three-day crisis and the acute phase of his dilemma. His depressive state during this period feeds negative thoughts and memories about the relationship and encourages pessimism, thus increasing the intensity and density of the B sub-SeCo. Allan Combs said such self-reinforcing psychological dynamics as autopoietic in nature: a network of processes (like recalling past experiences), all generated by a specific mood, concur to deepen the mood itself.[16] In the "Breakup" case, besides the constant reflection about the past, Ted is also anticipating and imagining the future—in particular, the "Breakup" event.

This period of reflection leads to an inhibition of forces coherent with "Continuation," weakening the C attractor; simultaneously, forces contributing to the "Breakup" outcome are reinforced, strengthening the B attractor. By the end of the third day, the B sub-SeCo has become so dense and charged with semantic energy that it overrides the C sub-

SeCo—at which point, Ted "makes up his mind" and sets out to break up with Anita.[17]

It is at this crucial point that a seemingly "chance" event interferes. Unexpectedly, Ted runs into Dan, and the whole course of action—"Breakup"—shifts. In ordinary language, we would say that the "chance" meeting with Dan "caused" the reversal of the situation. However, the question is whether the interfering event should be seen as purely fortuitous, or as a significant coincidence, a synchronicity.

We can reasonably posit that an apparently random external event is synchronistic if (1) there is a low probability that the event would occur by chance alone; (2) there are numerous significant links between the interfering event and the subject's activated SeCo; and (3) the meaning of the external event clearly influences the person, to the point of drastically modifying the SeCo.

In this case, Ted and Anita had a long-lasting relationship—more like that of a married couple than just of lovers. Dan, on the other hand, was Ted's only divorced friend; and it so happened that he truly missed his relationship with his ex-wife. He definitely could relate to Ted's turmoil and intent to break up with Anita, and it was he who proposed they go to a bar and discuss things. During their exchange, Dan compared his own divorce experience to Ted's current situation—specifically focusing on the dilemma phase that had preceded his own decision. Dan's position, from the outset, was that Ted was on the verge of making the same mistake he felt he had himself committed: breaking up while in a depressed, low phase.

We can see, then, that we have the kind of suggestive evidence that points to a synchronicity. The encounter between Ted and Dan, moments before the "Breakup" would have occurred, was a highly improbable event; the numerous significant links between Dan's past and Ted's planned action rendered Dan a most appropriate person to run into "by chance"; and, finally, Ted did change his mind, following his exchange with Dan, suggesting that this was indeed a significant encounter.

Now let us examine the processes that might have been responsible for the occurrence of the synchronicity. As we have seen, semantic Links are independent of the distance between two persons, depending instead upon semantic proximity and other descriptors of semantic space. In the dense interrelational network existing between Ted and his numerous friends,[18] his connection to Dan suddenly is "primed" by certain especially intense parallels. Ted's turmoil over the course of three days reactivates an analogous SeCo in Dan's semantic lattice—namely, the SeCo of his divorce. Insofar as Dan had gone through a similar dilemma just before deciding to divorce, strong semantic Links are generated between his "Divorce" SeCo and Ted's dual R SeCo.

Dan's semantic lattice interprets Ted's dilemma according to its own organization: if splitting leads to regrets, then dissuading Ted amounts to helping him avoid the same mistake. Dan's lattice thus prompts him to action when it senses Ted is heading out toward Anita's place with his "Breakup" plan. Insofar as their respective lattices are linked, a "fortuitous coincidence" in time and space occurs: Dan strolls toward the park just as Ted is turning around the corner.

All these processes are opaque to the conscious mind, of course. For example, at a conscious level, Dan decided to walk in the vicinity of Anita's place simply because he felt like taking a nice, long stroll in the park. So from the perspective of the conscious mind, and in the absence of any explicitly formulated intentions or plans to meet Ted, the meeting appears as a coincidence. In fact, however, the synchronicity reflects the links between the two friends' lattices, and the ways in which Dan's semantic lattice uses auxiliary information to work out a seemingly fortuitous encounter with Ted. In short, the meeting between the two friends, at a critical moment, points to nonconscious semantic exchanges between their empathically linked lattices.

While the analysis of this example is meant to describe synchronicities between human agents, the semantic model can also deal with synchronicities that involve objects—for example, a coincidence in which a written name or symbol appears in the environment at the very moment the person is intensely thinking about just such a concept.

The core of the present theory is that meaning is created by consciousness within and through the semantic lattices that link individuals to their environment at large. As we saw earlier, connective logic works at a finer grain than rational logic, being more basic to the workings of the mind. The semantic linkage process is the foundation not only of our mental and affective lives, but also of our being-in-the-world, our interactions with the environment. While connecting us to surrounding semantic fields, it connects us to objects as well as to sentient beings.

These connective processes actively influence and organize the environment through the modification of surrounding eco-fields. Usually, in the injection-retrojection process a semantic cluster is retrojected back to the individual. However, in some situations an initial meaning projected outward will be retrojected to the person not as a purely semantic energy, but in the form of a concrete event or object—as in the case of the golden scarab. In other words, while interacting with the semantic fields of life-forms or objects, we may sometimes influence the entities themselves—insofar as the semantic field is an important dimension of the entity.

From the perspective of the current model, synchronicities are the tip of the iceberg, pointing to a far more general phenomenon—the *process of reification*, that is, the way semantic energies become embodied or incorporated in matter and objects.[19] Such reification of semantic energies is occurring all the time—as for example in the creation of new art objects out of ideas and intentions, or in the slow imprinting of our local universe; but the process is generally so gradual that it tends to slip by, unnoticed. Synchronicities are the not-so-rare exceptions to this rule, bringing the internal SeCo and external event into an instantaneous—and hence noticeable—relation.

Simultaneous Discoveries

In chapter 7 we saw how a group of individuals co-create and nurture a collective SeCo—for example, when focused upon similar activities, such as research in a particular scientific domain. This co-creation of collective SeCos depends essentially upon semantic parameters, such as intensity, recurrence, coherency (see chapter 9). In particular, the parameter of semantic proximity generates strong linkages between individuals' minds, or between minds and objects or events, whatever the spatial or temporal distance between them. Insofar as the collective SeCo is nurtured by the minds of a great number of people, all these minds will influence—to different degrees—the way the theory, belief system, faith, or science is understood and practiced. The evolution of a collective SeCo thus depends not only upon local exchanges but also upon nonlocal forms of communication.

Historians of science have noted how, over the course of centuries, certain theoretical or technological discoveries were made simultaneously by widely separate scientists, having no knowledge of each other's work. For example, the theory of evolution was independently, and simultaneously, presented by Charles Darwin and Sir Alfred Wallace. From a semantic fields perspective, such "co-discoveries" are manifestations of collective SeCo dynamics.

"Anomaly" Collective SeCo. Consider, for example, a highly specialized domain of medical research, involving just a handful of research laboratories across the world. Let us say that, while investigating the effects of a particular molecule, a few researchers independently stumble upon an anomaly: the experimental results contradict what would be

expected, given past data and theory. Three investigators, geographically isolated from one another, begin to focus upon this puzzling finding; but none of them suspects that two other individuals are working on the same problem.

The anomaly is the attentional object for all three investigators' mental efforts; for each of them, its basic structure and dynamics form the nucleus of a new SeCo "Anomaly." Of course, each researcher's "Anomaly" SeCo is somewhat different from the others,' as it is partly an emergent of her or his past research experience, preferred tools and methodologies, and so forth. Nevertheless the fact that all three individuals are focused on the same object introduces sufficient identical elements as to trigger spontaneous linkages between the three SeCos. Unknowingly, then, the researchers are creating an emergent collective SeCo "Anomaly." Even in the absence of any direct, physical contact between them, or knowledge of each other's work, their mental activities create and feed into the collective SeCo, the nucleus of which is the anomaly cluster, and which attracts and organizes all the elements already linked in each individual SeCo.

Now, let us say that one of the researchers discovers a possible solution to the puzzle and begins to pursue a very promising line of investigation. Following the logic developed above, this means that, on the basis of the collective SeCo, the other two scientists potentially have access to the insight of the first researcher. Of course, this does not mean that they will automatically reach the same solution. Each person's semantic organization will determine whether or not the information will actually emerge into consciousness. Depending on each researcher's own lattice—and its unique network of Links and cognitive processes—one of them may come up with a nearly identical solution, while another may have only a vague sense of a promising research direction. Such a dynamic, then, could account for simultaneous scientific discoveries, as well as synchronicities on a collective scale.

Experiments on Collective Consciousness

In recent years, the concepts of collective or transpersonal consciousness have begun to be addressed experimentally. Perhaps the best known investigations are several large-scale experiments assessing Rupert Sheldrake's "morphic resonance" hypothesis, that is, the hypothesis of species-based memory fields.[20] A review by Suitbert Ertel shows that results are globally encouraging[21]; however, there are too many uncontrolled factors to unambiguously interpret the data in terms of an intra-species or collective memory.

Other researchers aim at detecting possible "consciousness fields," by determining whether group or cultural events, involving the coherent attention of large numbers of individuals, affect elementary physical processes. This is a new research domain and the data are still too limited to permit any definitive conclusions; nevertheless, the experiments conducted so far in three different laboratories[22] have provided evidence for an organizing influence of collective consciousness upon probabilistic physical systems.

This research is conducted using electronic Random Number Genera-tors or RNGs—also called Random Event Generators or REGs—which, as we have seen earlier, are commonly used in parapsychological research to detect subtle informational or psychokinetic perturbations in random distributions (see chapter 8, note 6). Most RNG experiments involve the focused attention of a subject and his or her conscious intention to affect the random source (via feedback shown on a computer screen). However, in a number of experiments[23] perturbations in the RNG were demonstrated even when the subjects were not aware of its presence, i.e., when there was no feedback and it was a "silent" RNG. These results showed that the psi effect did not depend on conscious intention, and could be triggered unconsciously; they also pointed to the possible existence of psi field effects—that is, that psychokinetic effects would imply a certain region of space, rather than just the system which the subject consciously "aims" for.

While these investigations of fieldlike psi effects, dating back to the late 1970s, were focused on the mental activities of a single subject, the more recent work explores fieldlike effects which seem to be associated with large numbers of individuals.

An example is one of a series of studies by Dean Radin and his colla-borators at the University of Nevada. The study focused upon the live broadcast of the 67th Annual Academy Awards ceremony. As Radin put it, "This study examined whether a common focus of attention in a very large group of people, estimated at one billion worldwide, might cause negentropic 'ripples' worldwide."[24] Two RNGs were placed 12 miles apart, and were each set to be continuously sampled by a computer during the broadcasting of the award ceremony. It was hypothesized that the RNGs would show less randomness (i.e., more organization or structure) during the emotionally stronger moments of the show (as opposed to the more boring moments). Radin independently rated the meaningfulness and emotional force of each event in the show. He then proceeded to correlate these ratings with the collected RNG data. The significant positive correlation suggested that "peak" moments of the Academy Awards somehow induced an organizing (or negentropic) effect in the remote RNGs. This suggests that the common focus of large numbers of persons on a common event may somehow induce increased coherence between peoples' minds—negentropic "ripples" that then affect surrounding physical systems. In other words, the experiment shows that semantically linked minds have an organizing influence on ambient eco-fields—a result coherent with the present theory.

Another series of experiments were conducted by Roger Nelson of the PEAR laboratories at Princeton University. Nelson started a pilot study in 1993 to test what he called "fieldREG anomalies." His assumption was that a strong mental cohesiveness achieved in a group situation would affect a REG set up in the gathering room, whether people knew about it or not. Positive results lead him to perform ten experiments in different settings, mostly professional, scientific, or religious gatherings.[25]

Typically, the REG shows peaks of deviation from the baseline during particularly intense and interesting moments. For example, at a 1993 meeting of a research group on healing (called DMHI session) the REG was sampled during the whole 35 hours of the meeting. During one presentation, which was especially appreciated by the audience, the REG showed a highly significant deviation from chance (Z-score of 3.05, p = 0.002). Says Nelson, "One conceptual hypothesis for the group-related anomalies indicated by FieldREG is that the emotional/intellectual dynamics of the interacting participants somehow generate a coherent 'consciousness field,' to which the REG respond via an anomalous decrease in the entropy of its nominally random output."[26] However, drawing on previous experiments showing no dependence of psi effects on either distance or time, he concludes that if the FieldREG phenomena are of the same kind as the previous operator/machine REG phenomena, "no conceptual models based on currently known physical fields . . . are likely to suffice. . . . Generalization of the inherent human concepts of 'distance' and 'time' to encompass subjective as well as objective aspects can be a profitable, indeed powerful, strategy for representation of many forms of conscious experience, both normal and anomalous (Jahn and Dunne, 1986)."[27] Indeed, I was astonished that Roger Nelson emphasizes, instead of distance, the concept of "attentional or emotional proximity," and instead of time the concept of "intensity of subjective investment"; he thus is independently proposing two of the three parameters I myself pose for studying the semantic dimension (semantic proximity, intensity, and coherency).

The need for both classical and nonlocal forms of exchange has been recognized in the physical sciences. For example, quantum mechanics accepts both the wave function with abstract wavelike properties and the particle, defined through space-time coordinates; similarly, "Fourier transforms" integrates both wave and particle descriptions as well as the transduction from one to the other. It is time to accept analogous dual descriptions in the cognitive sciences as well: any formalization of communication would need to account both for the habitual, *local* dimensions of communication processes (embodied in different support structures) and for the semantic, *nonlocal* dimension, revealed in subtler forms of exchange.[28]

NOTES

1. Lévy (1990).

2. Ibid., p.197.

3. I. Stengers (1988), Le pouvoir des concepts, in I. Stengers & J. Schlanger, *Les concepts scientifiques,* Paris: La découverte.

4. Ibid., p. 43.

5. P. Latour (Ed.), (1989), *La science en action,* Paris: La découverte. see also M. Callon (1988), *La science et ses réseaux,* Paris: La découverte.

6. W. H. Sulis (1997), Fundamental concepts of collective intelligence, *Nonlinear Dynamics, Psychology and Life Sciences, I* (1), 35–54. See also W. H. Sulis (1998), Collective intelligence and irrational decision making, Presentation at the conference "Managing the Complex," Toronto, Canada, April 2-5, 1998. (To be published in the proceedings.)

7. Jung (1967), Jung (1968). See also R. Robertson (1995), *Jungian archetypes. Jung, Gödel and the history of archetypes,* York Beach, ME: Nicolas-Hays.

8. Laszlo (1995). See also A. Combs (1996), *The radiance of being. Complexity, chaos and the evolution of consciousness,* St Paul, MN: Paragon House.

9. L. Brillouin (1988), *La science et la théorie de l'information,* Paris: J. Gabay.

10. J. Stewart, E. Andreewsky, & V. Rosenthal (1988), Du culte de l'information en biologie et en sciences du langage, *Revue Internationale de systémique, 2* (1), 15–28. See also H. Trocmé-Fabre (1987), *J'apprends donc je suis,* Paris: L'organisation.

11. J. Kihlstrom (1996), Unconscious processes in social interaction, in S. R. Hameroff, A. W. Kaszniak, & A. C. Scott (Eds.), *Toward a science of consciousness,* Cambridge, MA: MIT Press/Bradford Books.

12. Following Libet's pioneering research, some scientists have invoked processing time as a major factor for awareness of sensory inputs. See B. Libet, E. W Wright Jr., B. Feinstein, D. K. Pearl (1979), Subjective referral of the timing for a conscious sensory experience, *Brain 102,* 193–224.

13. For a review of contemporary parapsychological research, see D. Radin (1997), *The conscious universe,* San Francisco: Harper-Edge; M. Varvoglis (1997b), *Psi Explorer CD-ROM,* San Antonio, TX: Innovative Product Marketing.

14. C. G. Jung (1960), Synchronicity: An acausal connecting principle, in *The collected works of C. G. Jung: Vol. 8. The structure and dynamics of the Psyche,* (Bollingen Series, XX), Adler, G. & Hull, R. F. (Eds.), Princeton, NJ: Princeton University Press.

C. G. Jung & W. Pauli (1955), *The interpretation of nature and the psyche,* New York: Pantheon Books. This book contains both Jung's essay on synchronicity and Pauli's "The influence of archetypal ideas on the scientific theories of Kepler. On Pauli, see also H. Atmanspacher & H. Primas (1996), The hidden side of Wolfgang Pauli, *Journal of Consciousness Studies, 3* (2).

15. F. D. Peat (1987), *Synchronicity: the bridge between matter and mind,* New York: Bantam Books. See also A. Combs & M. Holland (1995), *Synchronicity: Science, myth, and the trickster,* New York: Marlowe.

16. A. Combs (1995), Psychology, chaos, and the process nature of consciousness, in F. D. Abraham & A. R. Gilgen (Eds.), *Chaos theory in psychology,* Westport, CT: Praeger Publishers.

17. In the semantic fields framework, a mature conscious decision process involving two or more choices is often supported by an equal number of clusters or sub-SeCos. The path of least resistance will thus be the decision associated with the SeCo displaying the greatest strength. However, consciousness and thought-processes are what create the SeCos in the first place. In the "Synergy" SeCo, we saw how a person could adopt new interpersonal values and behaviors (and generate the associated SeCo) on the basis of reflection and free will.

18. We saw earlier in the chapter how our close interrelations with others create interface-SeCos, forming broad interpersonal networks with relatives, friends, or colleagues.

19. The term "reification" comes from the Latin word *res,* signifying a thing. Reification here means "thing-ification," or "objectification"—the process by which an abstract form or thought may become a thing, an objective reality.

20. R. Sheldrake (1981), *New science of life: The hypothesis of causative formation,* London : Blond and Briggs.

21. S. Ertel (1991), Testing Sheldrake's claim of morphogenetic fields, *Proceedings of the Annual Convention of the Parapsychological Association 1991,* Heidelberg, Germany.

22. PEAR laboratories at Princeton University's Department of Engineering; Parapsychology Chair, University of Amsterdam; Department of Psychology, University of Nevada.

23. C. Honorton & L. Tremmel (1979), Psi correlates of volition: A preliminary test of Eccles's neurophysiological hypothesis of mind-brain interaction. *Research in Parapsychology 1978,* Metuchen, NJ : Scarecrow Press.

M. Varvoglis & D. McCarthy (1986), Conscious-purposive focus and PK: RNG activity in relation to awareness, task-orientation and feedback, *Journal of the American Society for Psychical Research, 80,* 1–30.

24. D. Radin, J. Rebman & M. Cross (1996), Anomalous organization of random events by group consciousness. Two exploratory experiments, *Journal of Scientific Exploration, 10,* 143–68. See also D. Radin (1997), *The conscious universe,* San Francisco: Harper-Edge; M. Varvoglis (1997a), Conceptual frameworks for the study of transpersonal consciousness *World Futures, 48,* 105–13.

25. R. D. Nelson, G. J. Bradish, Y. H. Dobyns, B. J. Dunne, & R. G. Jahn (1996), FieldREG anomalies in group situations, *Journal of Scientific Exploration, 10* (1), 111–41.

26. Ibid.

27. Ibid.

28. I have presented some examples of a dual description (local-nonlocal) of the properties of SeCos. For example, the "Relationship" SeCo featured a nonlocal synchronistic interference in the more deterministic evolution of the SeCo toward the break up. In the "Anomaly" collective SeCo, semantic proximity allows for the interweaving of minds at a distance, thus building the collective SeCo (see chapter 11).

CONCLUSION

This book represented a double challenge for me. On the one hand, I sought to lay the foundations of a cognitive theory that, building on recent scientific advances, could account for some of the most complex phenomena of the mind: the generation of meaning and creativity, intention and free will, intuition and insight.

On the other hand, I consciously sought to move beyond the usual self-imposed limits of the cognitive sciences, and extend semantic fields theory to address mental phenomena that transcend the personal mind. The real challenge here, of course, was to do this in a way that follows consistently from the premises of the cognitive model.

My first objective translated to understanding the mind's architecture and dynamics: fathoming the kind of structure and mechanisms that the human mind must have in order to generate such rich and complex mental phenomena.

At the core of semantic fields theory lies the transversal SeCo architecture, based on specific networks of semantic elements and processes. Within SeCos, the idiosyncratic interlacing of concepts with sensations, images, emotions, feelings, and behaviors is the necessary ground from which stems a rich qualitative experience.

The mind, I have proposed, operates through a low-level connective dynamic, the spontaneous linkage process. Shaped both by the endo-context (the SeCos) and by different exo-contexts (eco-fields), it is the highly generative process by which our mind-psyche thinks.

The fact that Secos are dynamical systems organized by attractors means that the organizations achieved will shape the organization of similar, subsequent experiences. This, then, amounts to a convergent force; were it not for the existence of a complementary force of divergence, the mind would show little flexibility. As I have suggested, divergence comes through the spontaneous linkage dynamic. A sufficiently dissimilar cluster of semantic elements will trigger new chain-linkages, and new trajectories through the SeCo (or across SeCos); this may bring about a bifurcation whereby a novel or modified attractor reorganizes the SeCo.

As self-organizing systems, SeCos display enormous flexibility, adaptability, and generativity, as well as structure and coherence. Healthy SeCos must have chaotic attractors and display sensitive dependence to initial conditions; they balance dynamical stability with the ability to change and evolve. On the contrary, unhealthy SeCos are either too chaotic (have too much lability) or too rigid for learning and evolution to occur.

The conjunction of the SeCos architecture and the linkage process endows us with intuitive, analogical, and truly innovative thinking—what amounts to heuristic knowledge and adaptive intelligence. It also ensures the uniqueness of individuals, as each person's life experience necessarily generates highly diversified links and semantic clusters. Finally, the proposed architecture guarantees our freedom of choice and our ability to intentionally transform ourselves. As I have suggested, it is the similarities, redundancies, and even competitiveness among diverse SeCos that affords us an exquisite flexibility in choosing among cognitive and behavioral alternatives.

The second challenge I sought to deal with in this book was to address transpersonal and collective facets of "mind-in-the-world." With some significant exceptions, the cognitive sciences have focused exclusively on internal processes, ignoring the complexity and richness of the world, and, hence, our exchanges with that world. Modern physics has introduced some radically new concepts in our understanding of mind-matter interaction, going so far as to pose the influence of the observer on what is observed. At the same time, theories focusing on quantum processes in the brain highlight the possibility that the paradoxes of quantum mechanics—such as nonlocal correlations—may be directly pertinent to consciousness. Finally, scientific parapsychology has now built a strong case for the reality of anomalous mind-matter interactions and nonlocal communication such as telepathy.

It seemed to me, then, that the time was ripe for a cognitive theory that deals directly with the nonlocal interactions of the mind with the world. In view of this, I have introduced two basic premises: (1), the semantic dimension pervades "objective" reality—for example, objects—and not just the "subjective" reality of individuals; and (2), this dimension is governed by its own parameters, such as semantic proximity, that are distinct from those of space-time.

As we have seen, the conjunction of these premises leads to a number of interesting consequences. For one, within human culture, artifacts and natural objects have a semantic history, so to speak; they reflect the imprint of individuals upon their eco-fields. The injection-retrojection of meaning clusters occurs independently of the distance from this object. Though a person's imprint on eco-semantic fields tends to be greatest in the contexts and environments most frequented by that person, the local universe has more to do with thinking and feeling, generally with semantic proximity, than with physical presence per se.

Second, understanding the different parameters of the semantic dimension helps account for various nonlocal phenomena, such as the occurrence of synchronicities or of a telepathic exchange between two individuals. For example, to the extent to which two persons entertain a meaningful relationship with each other, they are linked through interface-constellations, rooted in both lattices. An activation of particular SeCos in one person may, through the linkage dynamic, activate elements of the interface-SeCo, and thus of the other person's SeCo. Though typically remaining unconscious, these activations may occasionally pop up in the flow of consciousness, yielding precise information about the remote person's experience or state.

Finally, semantic proximity allows for dense network connections between large groups of people, independently of the spatial distance between them. The co-creation of meaning and knowledge systems in groups and cultures produces powerful collective SeCos that link together the concerned individuals. Insofar as they are largely governed by semantic parameters, these collective SeCos will show certain nonlocal properties, for example, nonlocal semantic exchanges between the individuals.

Today, with the new technologies of communication, we are growing accustomed to the idea that we live in a world of inter-dependence and mutual influence. I think it is becoming clear, now, that our interconnectedness is even more subtle and profound.

We live in a world of meaning—where meaning creates reality, where meaning *is* reality. Whether we are aware of it or not, the thoughts, beliefs, values and feelings we project shape our own destiny. The freedom to shape our life-trajectories comes with a major responsibility: collectively, we co-create our culture and civilization, we inform the future of humanity.

BIBLIOGRAPHY

Abraham, F. (1997). Nonlinear coherence in multivariate research: Invariants and the reconstruction of attractors. *Nonlinear Dynamics, Psychology and Life Sciences, 1* (1).

Abraham, F., Abraham, R., & Shaw, C. (1990). *A visual introduction to dynamical systems theory for psychology*. Santa Cruz, CA: Aerial Press.

Abraham, F. D., & Gilgen, A. R. (Eds.) (1995). *Chaos theory in psychology*. Westport, CT: Praeger Publishers.

Anderson, J. A., & Rosenfeld, E. (Eds.) (1988). *Neurocomputing: Foundations of research*. Cambridge, MA: The MIT Press.

Anderson, J. R. (1976). *Language, memory and thought*. Hillsdale, NJ: Erlbaum.

Anderson, J. R. (1983). *The architecture of cognition*. Cambridge, MA: MIT Press/Bradford Books.

Atlan, H. (1972). *L'organisation biologique et la théorie de l'information*. Paris: Hermann.

Atmanspacher, H., & Primas, H. (1996). The hidden side of Wolfgang Pauli. *Journal of Consciousness Studies, 3* (2).

Baars, B. J. (1988). *A cognitive theory of consciousness*. Cambridge, MA: Cambridge University Press.

Bateson, G. (1979). *Mind and nature*. New York: Bantam.

Bechtel, W., & Abrahamsen, A. (1990). *Connectionism and the mind: An introduction to parallel processing in networks*. New York: Blackwell.

Bohm, D. (1980). *Wholeness and the implicate order*. London: Routledge & Kegan Paul.

Bohm, D. (1986). A new theory of the relationship of mind and matter. *Journal of the American Society for Psychical Research, 80* (2),113–36.

Bohr, N. (1972). *Physique atomique et connaissance humaine*. Paris: Gauthier-Villars.

Boole, G. (1992). *Les lois de la pensée*. Paris: Vrin.

Boshier, A. (1973). African apprenticeship. In A. Angoff & D. Barth (Eds.), *Parapsychology and anthropology*. New York: Parapsychology Foundation.

Bourguignon, E. (1976). *Possession*. Corte Madera, CA: Chandler & Sharp.

Bramly, S. (1981). *Macumba, Forces noires du Brésil*. Paris: Albin Michel.

Brillouin, L. (1988). *La science et la théorie de l'information*. Paris: J. Gabay.

Callon, M. (1988). *La science et ses réseaux*. Paris: La Découverte.

Carpenter, G. A., & Grossberg, S. (1987). A massively parallel architecture for a self-organizing neural pattern recognition machine. *Computer Vision, Graphics, and Image Processing, 37,* 54–115.

Casti, J. (1989). *Lost paradigms*. New York: William Morrow.

Chalmers, D. (1996). Facing up to the problem of consciousness. In S. R. Hameroff, A. W. Kaszniak, & A. C. Scott (Eds.), *Toward a science of consciousness*. Cambridge, MA: MIT Press/Bradford Books.

Changeux, J. P. (1997). *Neuronal man: The biology of mind*. Princeton, NJ: Princeton University Press (First printed in 1983).

Chomsky, N. (1972). *Language and mind*. Hbj College & School Division.

Chomsky, N. (1975). *Questions de sémantique*. Paris: Seuil.

Combs, A. (1995). Psychology, chaos, and the process nature of consciousness. In F. D. Abraham & A. R. Gilgen (Eds.), *Chaos theory in psychology*. Westport, CT: Praeger Publishers.

Combs, A. (1996). *The radiance of being. Complexity, chaos and the evolution of consciousness*. St. Paul, MN: Paragon House.

Combs, A., & Holland, M. (1995). *Synchronicity: Science, myth, and the trickster*. New York: Marlowe.

Conrad, M. (1992). Molecular Computing: The lock-key paradigm. *Computer*, Nov 1992, 11–20.

Conrad, M. (1996). Percolation and collapse of quantum parallelism: A model of qualia and choice. In S. R. Hameroff, A. W. Kaszniak, & A. C. Scott (Eds.), *Toward a science of consciousness*. Cambridge, MA: MIT Press/Bradford Books.

Cook, E. W. (1994). The subliminal consciousness. *Journal of Parapsychology, 58* (1), 39–58.

Costa de Beauregard, O. (1963). *Le second principe de la science du temps*. Paris: Seuil.

Crick, F., & Koch, C. (1990). Toward a neurobiological theory of consciousness. *Seminars in the neurosciences, 2,* 263–75.

de Bono, E. (1970). *Lateral thinking*. New York: Harper & Row.

de Broglie, L. (1947). *Physique et microphysique*. Paris: Albin Michel.

Dennard, L. (1996). The new paradigm in science and public administration. *Public Administration Review, 56* (15), 495–99.

Dixon, N. (1981). *Preconscious processing*. Chichester: John Wiley & Sons.

Eccles, J. C. (1989). *Evolution of the brain: Creation of the self*. New York: Routledge.

Edelman, G. M. (1992). *Bright air, brilliant fire: On the matter of mind*. New York: Basic Books.

Ertel, S. (1991). Testing Sheldrake's claim of morphogenetic fields. *Proceedings of the Annual Convention of the Parapsychological Association 1991*. Heidelberg, Germany.

Feinstein, D., & Krippner, S. (1997). *The mythic path*. New York: Tarcher/Putnam.

Fodor, J. A. (1981). Methodological solipsism considered as a research strategy in cognitive psychology. In J. Haugeland (Ed.), *Mind design*. Cambridge, MA: MIT Press.

Freeman, W. J. (1995a). The kiss of beauty and the sleeping beauty of psychology. In F. D. Abraham & A. R. Gilgen (Eds.), *Chaos theory in psychology*. Westport, CT: Praeger Publishers.

Freeman, W. J. (1995b). *Societies of brains: A study in the neurosciences of love and hate*. Hillsdale, NJ: Lawrence Erlbaum.

Freud, S. (1988). *The essentials of psychoanalysis*. New York: Penguin.

Gardner, H. (1983). *Frames of mind. The theory of multiple intelligences*. New York: Harper Collins/Basic Books.

Gardner, H. (1985). *The mind's new science. A history of the cognitive revolution*. New York: Harper Collins/Basic Books.

Gauld, A. (1989). Cognitive psychology, entrapment and the philosophy of the mind. In J. R. Smithies & J. Beloff (Eds.), *The case for dualism*. Charlottesville: University Press of Virginia.

Gazzaniga, M. (1985). *The social brain: Discovering the networks of the mind*. New York: Basic Books.

Gibson, J. J. (1986). *An ecological approach to visual perception*. Hillsdale, NJ: Lawrence Erlbaum. (First printed in 1979).

Goerner, S. (1995). Chaos, evolution and deep ecology. In R. Robertson & A. Combs (Eds.), *Chaos theory in psychology and the life sciences*. Mahwah, NJ: Lawrence Erlbaum.

Goertzel, B. (1994). *Chaotic logic. Language, thought and reality from the perspective of complex systems science*. New York: Plenum Press.

Goleman, D. (1995). *Emotional intelligence*. New York: Bantam.

Guastello, S. (1995). *Chaos, catastrophe, and human affairs*. Mahwah, NJ: Lawrence Erlbaum Associates.

Güzeldere, G. (1995). Problems of consciousness: A perspective on contemporary issues, current debates. *Journal of Consciousness Studies, 2* (2), 112–43.

Hameroff, S. R. (1994). Quantum coherence in microtubules: A neural basis for emergent consciousness? *Journal of Consciousness Studies, 1*(1). Thorverton, UK.

Hameroff, S. R., & Penrose, R. (1996). Orchestrated reduction of quantum coherence. In S. R. Hameroff, A. W. Kaszniak, & A. C. Scott (Eds.), *Toward a science of consciousness*. Cambridge, MA: MIT Press/Bradford Books.

Hardy, C. (1988). *La science et les états frontières*. Paris: Rocher.

Hardy, C. (1991). *Le vécu de la transe*. Paris: Le Dauphin.

Hardy, C. (1996). Théorie des champs sémantiques: Dynamiques de l'interprétation et de la création de sens. *Biomath, 34* (135). Paris.

Hardy, C. (1997a). Semantic fields and meaning: A bridge between mind and matter. *World Futures, 48,* 161–70. Newark: Gordon & Breach.

Hardy, C. (1997b). Modeling transitions between states of consciousness: the concept of nested chaos. Presentated at the SCTPLS annual conference at Milwaukee, WS, July 31-August 2, 1997.

Haugeland, J. (Ed.). (1981). *Mind design*. Cambridge, MA: MIT Press.

Haugeland, J. (1985). *Artificial intelligence: The very idea*. Cambridge, MA: MIT Press.

Heim, A. (1892/1972). The experience of dying from fall. *Omega, 3,* 45–52.

Heisenberg, W. (1958). *Physics and philosophy*. New York: Harper & Brothers.

Held, R., & Hein, A. (1958). Adaptation of disarranged hand-eye coordination contingent upon re-afferent stimulation. *Perceptual-Motor Skills, 8,* 87–90.

Honorton, C. & Tremmel, L. (1979). Psi correlates of volition: A preliminary test of Eccles's neurophysiological hypothesis of mind-brain interaction. *Research in Parapsychology 1978*. Metuchen, NJ : Scarecrow Press.

Jordan, M. J. (1986). An introduction to linear algebra in parallel distributed processing. In D. E. Rumelhart & J. L. McClelland, *Explorations in the microstructure of cognition: Vol. 1. Foundations* (Chapter 9). Cambridge, MA: MIT Press/Bradford Books.

Josephson, B. D., & Pallikari-Viras, F. (1991). Biological utilisation of quantum nonlocality. *Foundations of Physics, 21,* 197–207.

Jung, C. G. (1960). Synchronicity: An acausal connecting principle. In *The collected works of C. G. Jung: Vol. 8. The structure and dynamics of the psyche* (Bollingen Series, XX), Adler, G., & Hull, R. F. (Eds.). Princeton, NJ: Princeton University Press.

Jung, C. G. (1964). *Man and his symbols*. Garden City, NY: Windfall Books/DoubleDay.

Jung, C. G. (1965). *Memories, dreams, reflections*. New York: Vintage Books/Random House.

Jung, C. G. (1966). *The collected works of C. G. Jung: Vol. 7. Two essays on analytical psychology* (Bollingen Series, XX), Adler, G., & Hull, R. F. (Eds.). Princeton, NJ: Princeton University Press.

Jung, C. G. (1967). *The collected works of C. G. Jung: Vol. 13. Alchemical studies* (Bollingen Series, XX), Adler, G., & Hull, R. F. (Eds.). Princeton, NJ: Princeton University Press.

Jung, C. G. (1968). *The collected works of C. G. Jung: Vol. 12. Psychology and alchemy*. (2d ed., Bollingen Series, XX), Adler, G., & Hull, R. F. (Eds.). Princeton, NJ: Princeton University Press.

Jung, C. G. (1970). On the psychology and pathology of so-called occult phenomena. In Jung, C. G., *The collected works of C. G. Jung: Vol. 1. Psy-*

chiatric studies (2d ed., Bollingen Series, XX), Adler, G., & Hull, R. F. (Eds.). Princeton, NJ: Princeton University Press.

Jung, C. G., & Pauli, W. (1955). *The interpretation of nature and the psyche.* New York: Pantheon Books.

Kihlstrom, J. (1996). Unconscious processes in social interaction. In S. R. Hameroff, A. W. Kaszniak, & A. C. Scott (Eds.), *Toward a science of consciousness.* Cambridge, MA: MIT Press/Bradford Books.

Koch, C. (1996). Toward the neuronal substrate of visual consciousness. In S. R. Hameroff, A. W. Kaszniak, & A. C. Scott (Eds.), *Toward a science of consciousness.* Cambridge, MA: MIT Press/Bradford Books.

Koestler, A. (1989). *The act of creation.* New York: Penguin.

Krippner, S., & Welch, P. (1992). *Spiritual dimensions of healing.* New York: Irvington.

Kuhn, T. (1970). *The structure of scientific revolutions.* Chicago: University of Chicago Press.

LaBerge, S. (1980). Lucid dreaming as a learnable skill: A case study. *Journal of Perceptual and Motor Skills, 51,* 1039–42.

Lashley, K. S. (1988). In search of the engram. In J. A. Anderson & E. Rosenfeld (Eds.), *Neurocomputing: Foundations of research.* Cambridge, MA: The MIT Press (First printed in 1950).

Laszlo, E. (1995). *The interconnected universe.* River Edge, NJ: World Scientific.

Latour, P. (Ed.). (1989). *La science en action.* Paris: La Découverte.

Levine, D. S., & Leven, S. J. (1995). Of mice and networks: Connectionist dynamics of intention versus action. In F. D. Abraham & A. R. Gilgen (Eds.), *Chaos theory in psychology.* Westport, CT: Praeger Publishers.

Levine, J. (1983). Materialism and qualia: The explanatory gap. *Pacific Philosophical Quarterly, 64,* 354–61.

Lévy, P. (1990). *Les technologies de l'intelligence.* Paris: La Découverte.

Libet, B., Wright, E.W., Jr., Feinstein, B., & Pearl, D. K. (1979). Subjective referral of the timing for a conscious sensory experience. *Brain, 102,* 193–224.

Lorenz, E. (1993). *The essence of chaos.* Seattle: University of Washington Press.

Lorimer, D. (1990). *Whole in one.* London, UK: Arkana.

Ludwig, A. (1969). Altered states of consciousness. In C. Tart (Ed.), *Altered states of consciousness.* New York: John Wiley & Sons.

Mandelbrot, B. (1977). *The fractal geometry of nature.* New York: Freeman.

Maturana, H., & Varela, F. (1980). *Autopoiesis and cognition.* Boston: D. Reidel.

May, E. C., Utts, J. M., & Spottiswoode, S. J. P. (1995). Decision augmentation theory: Toward a model of anomalous mental phenomena. *Journal of Parapsychology, 59* (3), 195–220.

McClelland, J. L., & Rumelhart, D. E. (1988). *Explorations in parallel distributed processing: A handbook of models*. Cambridge, MA: MIT Press/Bradford Books.

McClelland, J. L., Rumelhart, D. E., & the PDP Research Group. (1986). *Explorations in the microstructure of cognition: Vol. 2. Psychological and biological models*. Cambridge, MA: MIT Press/Bradford Books.

Métraux, A. (1958). *Le vaudou haïtien*. Paris: Gallimard.

Minsky, M. (1985). *The society of mind*. New York: Simon & Schuster.

Morin, E. (1982). *Science avec conscience*. Paris: Arthème Fayard.

Morin, E. (1992). *Method: Toward a study of humankind; The nature of nature*. American University Studies (Series V, Philosophy, Vol. 1.).

Morin, E. (1998). *Homeland Earth*. Cresskill, NJ: Hampton Press.

Myers, F. W. H. (1886). On telepathic hypnotism, and its relation to other forms of hypnotic suggestion. *Proceedings of the Society for Psychical Research, 4,* 127–88.

Myers, F., Lodge, O., Leaf, W., & James, W. (1890). A record of observation of certain phenomena of trance. *Proceedings of the Society for Psychical Research, 6,* 436–695.

Nelson, R. D., Bradish, G. J., Dobyns, Y. H., Dunne, B. J., & Jahn, R. G. (1996). FieldREG anomalies in group situations. *Journal of Scientific Exploration, 10* (1), 111–41.

Newell, A. (1973). Productions systems. Models of control structures. In W. Chase (Ed.), *Visual information processing*. New York: Academic Press.

Nunn, C. H. M., Clarke, C. J. S., & Blott, B. H. (1994). Collapse of a quantum field may affect brain function. *Journal of Consciousness Studies, 1* (1). Thorverton, UK.

Parnes, S. (1988). *Visionizing*. New York: DOK Publishers.

Peat, F. D. (1987). *Synchronicity: The bridge between matter and mind*. New York: Bantam Books.

Penrose, R. (1989). *The emperor's new mind*. Oxford, UK: Oxford University Press.

Peschl, M. (1997). The representational relation between environmental structures and neural systems. *Nonlinear Dynamics, Psychology and Life Sciences, 1* (2).

Poincaré, H. (1952). *Science and method*. New York: Dover Publications.

Popper, K. R., & Eccles, J. C. (1977). *The self and its brain: An argument for interactionism*. Berlin: Springer-Verlag.

Pribram, K. H. (1971). *Languages of the brain: Experimental paradoxes and principles in neuropsychology*. Englewood Cliffs, NJ: Prentice-Hall.

Pribram, K. H. (1979). A progress report on the scientific understanding of paranormal phenomena. In B. Shapin & L. Coly (Eds.), *Brain/mind and parapsychology*. New York: Parapsychology Foundation.

Pribram, K. H. (1991). *Brain and perception: Holonomy and structure in figural processing*. Hillsdale, NJ: Lawrence Erlbaum.

Pribram, K. H. (1997) The deep and surface structure of memory and conscious learning: Toward a 21st-century model. In R. L. Solso (Ed.) *Mind and brain sciences in the 21st century*. Cambridge, MA: The MIT Press (pp. 127–56).

Prigogine, I., & Stengers, I. (1984). *Order out of chaos*. New York: Bantam Books.

Prueitt, P., Levine, D., Leven, S., Tryon, W., & Abraham, F. (1995). Introduction to artificial neural networks. In F. D. Abraham & A. R. Gilgen (Eds.), *Chaos theory in psychology*. Westport, CT: Praeger Publishers.

Pylyshyn, Z. (1981). Complexity and the study of artificial and human intelligence. In J. Haugeland (Ed.), *Mind design*. Cambridge, MA: The MIT Press.

Radin, D. (1997). *The conscious universe*. San Francisco, CA: Harper-Edge.

Radin, D., & Nelson, R. (1989). Evidence for consciousness-related anomalies in random physical systems. *Foundations of Physics, 19* (12), 1499–514.

Radin, D., Rebman, J., & Cross, M. (1996). Anomalous organization of random events by group consciousness. Two exploratory experiments. *Journal of Scientific Exploration, 10,* 143–68.

Reber, A. S. (1993). *Implicit learning and tacit knowledge*. New York: Oxford University Press.

Robertson, R. (1995). *Jungian archetypes. Jung, Gödel and the history of archetypes*. York Beach, ME: Nicolas-Hays.

Roll, W. (1967). Pagenstecher's contribution to parapsychology. *Journal of the American Society for Psychical Research, 61,* 219–40.

Rosen, S. (1994). *Science, paradox and the Moebius principle*. Albany: State University of New York Press.

Rosenthal, R., & Rubin, D. (1978). Interpersonal expectancy effects: The first 345 studies. *Behavioral and Brain Sciences, 3,* 377–415.

Rouch, J. (1989). *La religion et la magie Songhaï*. Brussels: Ed. de l'Université de Bruxelles (First printed in 1960).

Ruelle, D. (1993). *Chance and chaos*. Princeton, NJ: Princeton University Press.

Rumelhart, D. E., & McClelland, J. L. (1986). On learning the past tense of English verbs. In J. L. McClelland, D. E. Rumelhart, & the PDP Research Group, *Explorations in the microstructure of cognition: Vol. 2. Psychological and biological models* (Chapter 18). Cambridge, MA: MIT Press/Bradford Books.

Rumelhart, D. E., McClelland, J. L., & the PDP Research Group. (1986). *Explorations in the microstructure of cognition: Vol. 1. Foundations*. Cambridge, MA: MIT Press/Bradford Books.

Russell, P. (1991). *The awakening Earth*. New York, London: Penguin Group/Arkana.

Schacter, D. L. (1987). Implicit memory: History and current status. *Journal of Experimental Psychology: Learning, Memory, and Cognition, 13,* 501–18.

Schrödinger, E. (1958). *Mind and matter*. Cambridge, MA: University Press.

Searle, J. R. (1992). *The rediscovery of the mind.* Cambridge, MA: Bradford Books, MIT Press.

Sejnowski, T. J., & Rosenberg, C. R. (1988). NETtalk: A parallel network that learns to read aloud (First printed in 1986). In J. A. Anderson & E. Rosenfeld (Eds.), *Neurocomputing: Foundations of research* (pp. 663–72). Cambridge, MA: The MIT Press.

Sheldrake, R. (1981). *A new science of life: The hypothesis of causative formation.* London: Blond and Briggs.

Si Ahmed, D. (1990). *Parapsychologie et psychanalyse.* Paris: Dunod.

Skarda, C. A., & Freeman, W. J. (1987). How brains make chaos in order to make sense of the world. *Behavioral and Brain Sciences, 10,* 161–95.

Smith, L. (1995). Stability and variability: The geometry of children's novel-word interpretations. In F. D. Abraham & A. R. Gilgen (Eds.), *Chaos theory in psychology.* Westport, CT: Praeger Publishers.

Sperry, W. (1976). Mental phenomena as causal determinants in brain functions. In G. Globus, G. Maxwell, & I. Savodnic (Eds.), *Consciousness and the brain.* New York: Plenum.

Stapp, H. (1993). *Mind, matter and quantum mechanics.* Berlin: Springer-Verlag.

Stengers, I. (Ed.). (1987). *D'une science à l'autre; des concepts nomades.* Paris: Seuil.

Stengers, I. (1988). Le pouvoir des concepts. In I. Stengers & J. Schlanger, *Les concepts scientifiques.* Paris: La Découverte.

Stengers, I., & Schlanger, J. (1988). *Les concepts scientifiques.* Paris: La Découverte.

Stewart, J., Andreewsky, E., & Rosenthal, V. (1988). Du culte de l'information en biologie et en sciences du langage. *Revue Internationale de Systémique, 2* (1), 15–28.

Stillings, N. A., Feinstein, M. H., Garfield, J. L., Rissland, E. L., Rosenbaum, D. A., Weisler, S. E., & Baker-Ward, L. (1987). *Cognitive science: An introduction.* Cambridge, MA: Bradford Books, MIT Press.

Sulis, W. H. (1997). Fundamental concepts of collective intelligence. *Nonlinear Dynamics, Psychology and Life Sciences, I* (1), 35–54.

Tart, C. (Ed.). (1969). *Altered states of consciousness.* New York: John Wiley & Sons.

Tart, C. (1975). *States of consciousness.* New York: Dutton.

Trocmé-Fabre, H. (1987). *J'apprends donc je suis.* Paris: L'Organisation.

Vandervert, L. (Ed.). (1997). Understanding tomorow's mind: Advances in chaos theory, quantum theory and consciousness in psychology. *The Journal of Mind and Behavior, 18* (2, 3).

Varela, F. (1989). *Autonomie et connaissance.* Paris: Seuil.

Varela, F., Thompson, E., & Rosch, E. (1991). *The embodied mind.* Cambridge, MA: The MIT Press.

Varvoglis, M. (1992). *La Rationalité de l'Irrationnel.* Paris: InterEditions.

Varvoglis, M. (1997a). Conceptual frameworks for the study of transpersonal consciousness. *World Futures, 48*, 105–13.

Varvoglis, M. (1997b). *Psi Explorer CD-ROM*. San Antonio, TX: Innovative Product Marketing.

Varvoglis, M. & McCarthy, D. (1986). Conscious-purposive focus and PK: RNG activity in relation to awareness, task-orientation and feedback. *Journal of the American Society for Psychical Research, 80*, 1–30.

von Lucadou, W. (1983). On the limitations of psi: A system-theoretic approach. In W. Roll, J. Beloff, & R. White (Eds.), *Research in parapsychology 1982*. Metuchen, NJ: Scarecrow Press.

von Lucadou, W. (1987). The model of pragmatic information (MPI). *Proceedings of the 30th Annual Convention of the Parapsychological Association*. Edinburgh, Scotland: Edinburgh University.

von Lucadou, W. (1994). The endo- exo-perspective—heaven and hell of parapsychology. *Proceedings of the 37th Annual Convention of the Parapsychological Association*. Amsterdam, Netherlands: University of Amsterdam.

von Lucadou, W., & Kornwachs, K. (1980). Development of the systemtheoretic approach to psychokinesis. *European Journal of Parapsychology, 3* (3), 297–314.

von Neumann, J. (1958). *The computer and the brain*. New Haven: Yale University Press.

Walker, E. H. (1975). Foundations of paraphysical and parapsychological phenomena. In L. Oteri (Ed.), *Quantum physics and parapsychology*. New York: Parapsychology Foundation.

Walker, E. H. (1984). A review of criticisms of the quantum mechanical theory of psi phenomena. *Journal of Parapsychology, 48*, 277–332.

Wilson, M. A., & McNaughton, B. L. (1994). Reactivation of hippocampal ensemble memory during sleep. *Science, 265*, 676–79.

Zohar, D. (1990). *The quantum self*. New York: Quill/William Morrow.

Zohar, D., & Marshall, I. (1994). *The quantum society*. New York: William Morrow.

INDEX